The New You

Emerging into the Brilliance of Humanity's Heart Consciousness

Linda Dillon

The New You

Emerging into the Brilliance of Humanity's Heart Consciousness

© 2013 by Linda Dillon

All rights reserved

Book cover credit: A special thanks to Anthony Morrison and Stephen Cook at GoodWords (goodwords.com.au) for the design, artwork, and content of the front and back covers.

From Archangel Gabrielle

"The New You is the fully heart-conscious being who accepts that you are in the infinite process of becoming. You welcome that unfoldment within and without. You do not limit who you are by maintaining false beliefs which hold that you are contained within the vessel you call a body. You claim the universe as your birthright and you play within the expanded realm of knowingness that all is possible.

"Why do you awaken and choose this mantel of the New You at this time in the unfoldment? Because, dear hearts, you are not only the wayshowers you are the patternmakers, you are the ones who are laying down the new patterning of the Universe. You chose eons ago to be among the first awakened; to be the awakeners. Not formulate, but to remember the patterning of humanity and of the universe laid down long ago by the Divine Mother. It is your chosen task to be the spinners of the Divine threads of connection to ensure the warp and weave of the tapestry is in accordance with not only the Mother's plan but that which is for the highest good of the collective of Gaia. That highest good dear ones is the ascension of the planet, the kingdoms and humanity at this time – right now – not in some distant future, but right now."

Dedication

This book is dedicated to the Council of Love, the brave New You Warriors, and every Lightworker on the planet.

We are One – Hope reigns and Love wins.

Table of Contents

About the Audio Files

There are audio meditations with this book. The files are accessible depending on which format you are reading this book.

E-Junkie
If you purchased the book through e-Junkie, the files are attached as separate MP3 files.

Kindle
If you purchased this book through Amazon.com as a Kindle book, go to **http://www.screencast.com/t/BHqDYvA0**. Use the password: **13Love** to access the downloadable files.

Other E-Readers
If you purchased this book for a different e-reader, go to **http://www.screencast.com/t/BHqDYvA0**. Use the password: **13Love** to access the downloadable files.

Hard copy/Amazon
If you purchased this book as a physical copy, go to **http://www.screencast.com/t/BHqDYvA0**. Use the password: **13Love** to access the downloadable files.

For those wanting to load the files to an iPhone, iPad or iPod, you must first transfer the files to your iTunes account, then sync your device to iTunes.

If there's a problem, contact admin@counciloflove.com.

Acknowledgements
Blessings and Gratitude

Where do I begin with my acknowledgements and heartfelt thank yous? The danger in creating acknowledgements is forgetting someone or making them feel that somehow their contribution was underrated. That is simply not possible here. I have so much to be grateful for. The support I have received for many years has been phenomenal. This is the abbreviated version so if you don't see your name listed, please look up and see it written in the heavens. Each of you has graced my journey in loving insightful ways.

I begin my acknowledgements with my family – the technical, editing, inspirational, mind-provoking, soul-searching and late-night conversations that have supported me in throughout the growth and expansion, as well as the challenges of the past year. I thank Isaac for his unwavering faith in his "angel talker." I thank him for anchoring me and for letting me fly as high and as often as need be. There is a special place in my heart for my siblings who have seen me through this incredible and sometimes incomprehensible journey of spirit. My sisters, Suzanne and Debay, have been my bedrock of sanity and of love. They have always been there for me through thick and thin, laughter and tears, and have always reminded me that all that really counts is love, and making time for each other no matter what. My brother, Joe, has been my touchstone, a living example of the balance between being grounded and leading the spiritual life. Joe has taught me self-worth and valuing the work I do – a huge gift! My brother, Pat, has shown me that although the path is sometimes rocky and you don't know what lies ahead that you just have to keep going, in trust and with a smile. My cousin Patricia has been my anchor, helpmate and private booster club in this and every project and my life. My nieces and nephews are my inspiration, reminding me why I do this – they are the next generation and they get it!

There has been a small legion of friends whom I know as soul family that have and do support me in becoming who I am. There have been times when the encouragement and support has been emotional, spiritual and even financial. They have never let me give up and have continued to remind me that I am here for a purpose and that means something in the bigger picture. I don't know if I would still be here without my soul sisters, Mary Valanzano, Roz Lett, Marianne Baer, Jeri Burgdorf, Suzanne Wendelken, Suzi Fischer, Christina Mahler, and Carol Bakunas. You have propped me up and reinforced me through the good and bad times. You remind me that I'm not crazy and yes, this is all worth it – we are changing the world, one person at a time. And that brings me to Taka, my soul brother and muse, my side-kick and trusted friend. He has always understands the bigger picture and what the Council has in store.

There is a special heart thank you to my sweet annas (angels of the Lord). This phenomenal group of women and men courageously stepped forward to be the first anchors of the New You energies. This undertaking was brand new to all of us, none of us could have foretold the adventure and the extent to which we have grown and bonded as one soul circle. This book would not have been written without you.

I also wish to acknowledge and embrace the love and support of my InLight Radio family: Steve Beckow, Graham Dewyea, Suzanne Maresca, Geoffrey West, Stephen Cook, Mary Valanzano, Janie Waters, Ellen McGuffie and Rosy Lecky. The support and inspiration of this team has lifted me up, challenged me to grow, and taught me a deeper meaning of prudence, fortitude and love.

The list of thanks could be endless for there are many of you that I love and who have been so generous with their energy and support. I want to say a special thank you to my Council of

Love family who has traveled with me for so long – in Sedona, Michigan, New York, Florida, Colorado, California and Arizona. A final thank you to my newest angel friend, Andreina Womutt. You are sorely missed, and your visits are greatly appreciated.

This list would not be complete if I did not say a special thank you to Anthony Morrison for the fabulous creation of the New You cover and design. I also want to thank Stephen Cook for his input on the cover, and for stepping forward to bring the New You specials to InLight Radio.

I have been graced with a team of editors who have guided me through this process gently and with incredible encouragement. Suzanne Dillon did all my first reads and spent countless hours making human sense of very esoteric material. Mary Valanzano's contribution, especially on the bringing together of the Blessings and Virtues, was nothing short of divinely inspired. Patricia Terhune and Jeri Burgdorf rounded out this team with grace to ensure continuity, accessibility and accuracy. Another thank you goes to Isaac Cubillos, whose talent, patience, persistence and technical tenacity has brought it all together. But of course, I accept full responsibility for all content.

My final thank you is to the Council of Love. Little did I know or even begin to comprehend the 360 degree turn my life would take the day I first heard "Welcome from the Council of Love." I am eternally grateful and blessed. Thank you for helping me remember who I am and why I came. I wouldn't change it for the world.

Introduction

Did someone say ascension?

What an unexpected and phenomenal journey this process of ascension is turning out to be. The unfolding of the plan of the Divine Mother, the restoration of love on Earth, has been rocky, bumpy, exciting, amazing, fulfilling and challenging.

After the ascension of Gaia into the fifth dimension in December 2012, and the attendant human collective decision to attempt to ascend as one, I thought that my ascension work was pretty much completed in terms of writing and teaching. *The Great Awakening* clearly outlined the steps to ascension and was there to assist everybody with a sure-fire process. While I have never been one who felt that ascension did or will occur on a specific date, I know in my heart and bones that this process is well underway. It is what we came for, and it is what each heart determinedly seeks.

My plan for 2013 was to write a book on creation, sharing the details of what the Council has taught us over the years – the creation formula, the creation codes, and Universal Law – a how-to book on manifesting. I felt clear and excited about this project; it has been a long time in the works. Imagine my surprise when, in early January 2013, the Council began to talk to me about the New You.

When the Council has a new assignment for me, when they want to bring my focus to a new topic, I will walk around for days with Archangel Gabrielle repeating loudly in my ear the new topic of conversation and learning. For weeks I wandered around hearing New You, New You, New You. What's a girl to do but surrender, sit down, open the channel and listen? If I have learned anything over the years it's that Gabrielle's will power and persistence is infinitely stronger than mine. Since day one, Archangel Gabrielle has been my go-to guide, the spokes-being for the Council of Love who has shepherded me through this incredible journey. I know better than to even think of turning my attention elsewhere when she beckons.

As the information began to flow, I was as high as a kite, exhausted, elated, confused and in absolute wonderment. I haven't experienced this sense of awe since the COL first began to talk to me about the 13th Octave. The information, concepts and visions were brand new. While some of the information built upon understandings they were conveyed over the years, it was add-on, add-on, add-on. Then, there were whole areas on interdimensionality, the Stranger without, expansion of Universal Law and creation that were brand new. Exciting – absolutely; terrifying – absolutely.

My question to Archangel Gabrielle and the Divine Mother was why now? Not that I am not thrilled to be the bearer of the new – it's my dream, but why now? The answer was because this information wasn't available to us before now. Prior to the Gaia's shift in dimensions, and our attendant expansion over the last few years, we were not ready to receive, integrate and apply this information – this expansion in the comprehension and embodiment of who we are. We have evolved enough to have a broader understanding and application of our potential.

The Council channeled they wanted the New You out quickly, including a webinar series. The transformative series would be five-months long, and incorporate channeling, coaching, meditation and community building. From the beginning the Council cautioned this course was not for the timid or faint of heart but for the pathfinders and wayshowers, those who were ready and determined to step forward and adopt the new energies.

Like all the work with the Council of Love, the New You is built upon the foundation of the 13th Octave. The 13th Octave is a state of being in Divine Union, wholly and completely anchored, and aware of being anchored, in the heart of One. It is being in alignment with the heart, mind and will of God. The gift of the 13th Octave is enormous. It literally changed not only my world but the lives of thousands of people who have said "yes" and stepped forward to join in this state of Union. In case you are not familiar with the 13th Octave, I have included the explanatory chapter from *The Great Awakening* is included as Appendix A in this book. However, because this is our starting point, please let's launch this joyous journey by joining together in this initiation and meditation.

(DOWNLOAD AND LISTEN TO THE "13TH OCTAVE" AUDIO MEDITATION AT THIS TIME)

Fifty courageous souls stepped forward to embrace the New You challenge. I don't think one of us knew the magnitude of what we were entering into. The starting point of coming to know our foundational being – our soul color, bodies, sacred field, guides and guardian angels, soul mission was enough to occupy five months. But that was just the starting point. The Council then moved us through the process of clearing the false grids, embracing our interdimensional selves, welcoming and beginning to work with our Stranger, and, understanding our core issues and key motivator. We hardy souls were doing this not only for our group and circle but for humanity at the same time. And still the assignments and growth kept coming!

In the midst of this incredibly elating and soul-challenging process, the most wonderful thing happened. Each of the two groups formed unshakeable bonds of trust, sharing, expansion, inner-most thoughts, dreams, fears, feelings and visions. We came not only to rely on one another but to love each other unconditionally.

The assignment and anchoring of the New You didn't and doesn't stop there. We then were led to appreciate and implement patterns that speak directly to the care and feeding of the body, heart, mind and soul of the New You. We were ready to move into creating sacred unions – with self, partner, family, friends, community and globally. Piece of cake, right? I mean isn't the fifth dimension all about unity consciousness? But we hung in together, pushing ahead because the insights, the shifts in our energy fields were so tremendous that we would never say die.

When the Council told us all this work was in preparation to step fully into our creator self, I swear I heard a collective gasp – of both delight and trepidation. At this point we were past five months and going strong. The groups were self-supporting and generating material at a level that I have never witnessed before. From this point we began to work with the creation triangle which is composed of the creation formula, the thirteen blessings and virtues, also known as the divine qualities, and the Thirteen Universal Laws. But it was also acknowledged that the groups had been creating all along – all you had to do is go the online chat room to witness that. But this, again, was upping the ante, of stepping forward into the world and into the concrete. We have stepped into that role, we are creating, and we are having enormous success. Is there further yet to go? There is always further to go. As the Council tells us, "there is always more." That's the joy of living in an infinite universe.

I share this process with you not only to outline and introduce the contents of the *New You* book, but to share with you this process of expansion has been test-driven and it works. The miracles, shift, expansion and excitement you will glean from diving deeply into this work is nothing short of phenomenal. You do not do so alone but with we who have prepared the way, and most importantly the Council of Love.

Are you ready? Of course you are. Dive in; the water's lovely – transformative, deep, mysterious and fun. You will discover a whole new world, and a whole New You eagerly waiting for you just below the surface.

Universal Mother Mary sums up the New You process: "You are a sacred circle reunited in this sacred purpose of this unfoldment, of your unfoldment, and my unfoldment. You are doing well, you are doing magnificently, and you are forging a new way. This is not a pattern that is simply made up of tissue paper and pins; this is a pattern that is forged on heaven and on earth and far beyond. This is the pattern that I forged with you and into you and that you forged within your sacred self, long ago. It is forged in light. It is forged in love. It is not erasable or replace-able, it does not fade, it is not just permanent, it is eternal and it is infinite, just like you. Finally you are coming to recognize that, to embrace that, that singular truth of who you are. It is not of pride, if anything, you do it reluctantly, but it is truth, it is stand-alone; it is fact; and it is of grace, heart and love."

Who is the New You?

There is a phenomenal opening occurring right now for humanity. It is the potential to make the quantum leap from the restrictive reality of third dimensional experience to the interdimensional/multidimensional self. It is the opportunity to reclaim the original design for human experience and to live in the fullness of the creator self. It is the potential to transition from a place of struggle, lack and limitation to the full awareness of our divinity in form and action. It is the possibility to ascend from the antiquated beliefs regarding human evolution to the place of thriving as a Nova Being on Nova Earth.

This unique opportunity is offered equally to all. It entails changing the way we have conceived and perceived ourselves. It requires that we relinquish belief systems and opinions that we have about ourselves and our capacities. It allows us to rise from the ashes of the old and fly like the phoenix into that place of freedom, wholeness and love we all so deeply yearn for. It requires embracing The New You.

Archangel Gabrielle defines the New You as a Nova Being – an evolved new species of human. The New You is the being that has cleansed, cleared, relinquished, integrated, anchored, embraced and surrendered to the totality of their being. It is not simply a matter of being interdimensional; it is about living, and being anchored in the state of heart consciousness while in physical form. Garbrielle says:

"The New You is not simply one who adheres and lives by the Blessings and Virtues; it is someone who is the embodiment of those divine qualities while in physicality. It is living, breathing, walking, talking, and being in the totality of your divinity, of accepting your divine grace and role within the unfoldment of the Universal Mother's plan. It is the embrace and surrender to your plan within that plan.

"The New You thrives in the enjoyment of every moment of existence even in the midst of change, chaos and what appears to be the destruction of the old paradigms. It is the knowing that within the destruction of the old, the new is being born. It is not only alignment with Divine Will but acceptance that you are the infinite instrument of that Will. You go forward in the creation and co-creation of Nova Earth because that is the reality within which you choose to live and operate. It is the incorporation of you, sweet angels of light.

"Finally, the New You is the fully heart-conscious being who accepts that you are in the infinite process of becoming. You welcome that unfoldment within and without. You do not limit who you are by maintaining false belief systems which hold that you are contained within the vessel that you currently think of as your body. You claim the universe as your birthright and you play within the expanded realm of knowingness that all is possible."

The New You is an intrepid soul adventurer; one who is determined and excited at the prospect of exploring unknown territory. Valor is the divine quality the New You carries; the knowingness that there is more to our soul journey than what we have witnessed to date. It is the knowingness that we are more, that our divine essence carries greater capacity and potential than we have previously been aware of. The New You welcomes the opportunity to chart the unknown universe and to be the wayshower for others who wish to venture forth in this journey of self-discovery.

The New You person is aware they are acting on behalf of the collective. They are aware they have chosen to go through the veil of interdimensional reality and blaze that trail for others. While you may not be immediately aware of all the changes you are going through, you know intuitively that a process of significant change is underway, and you have no desire to halt it or turn back.

Archangel Gabrielle further describes The New You as "The fully awakened interdimensional self, living in perfect alignment and wholeness with the Divine. Your sacred purposes are unique and beautiful, yet intricately woven and essential to the tapestry of the Divine Plan.

"You are not only the wayshowers you are the patternmakers, you are the ones who are laying down the new patterning of the Universe. You have chosen eons ago to be among the first awakened; to be the awakeners, to not formulate but to remember the patterning of humanity and of the universe laid down long ago by the Divine Mother. It is your chosen task to be the spinners of the Divine threads of connection to ensure the warp and weave of the tapestry is in accordance with not only the Mother's plan but that which is for the highest good of the collective of Gaia. That highest good dear ones is the Ascension of the planet, the kingdoms and humanity at this time – right now – not in some distant future but right now.

"Long ago your chose to create with us the pattern laid down by the Mother, a reflection of her beauty and essence. The idea of this pattern is that the very fabric of the tapestry be love, joy and nurturing. You are well under way to remembering and accepting this role, but eagerly embracing it. This is not a walk of patience, that portion of the journey is completed. This is a walk of exuberance, of laughing, skipping and flying to the finish line. My sweet angels, we thank you, we support you, and we reassure you – you are ready. Go in peace."

The transition to The New You involves work and diligent participation in your soul journey and shift. It isn't simply a matter of accepting change or allowing the energetic downloads and increased frequencies to penetrate you – that is a given. The New You carries a willingness to let go of old outmoded ideas of humanity that no longer serve. The shift necessitates expansion of all aspects of your being and body, a redefinition of who and what you are. It is an assignment you signed up for long before this incarnation, and it is an undertaking you can't wait to get on with. It is a journey and the birth of a new perspective, an expansion of definition of who we are that we take together – as brothers and sisters of the soul. It is a journey of embodying the Nova Being of Nova Earth.

WHAT IS NOVA EARTH?

To fully understand The New You it is important that we understand Nova Earth, and all that is implied in that term. Nova Earth and Nova Being are terms that have been used by the Council of Love more than a decade. Knowing this, I went through reams of channeled material to find just the perfect explanation of Nova Earth. I found incredible lovely descriptions of what Nova Earth will look and feel like, all of them also included guidance and insight into the shifts within the human condition that would be necessary to bring about and anchor Nova Earth. Humans have to reclaim their divine qualities, awe, innocence, wonder, gentleness, and step into their creator selves as stewards and co-creators of Earth. I realized that no one channel succinctly described Nova Earth since the shift in dimensions that Gaia has gone through.

Gaia came to me in in all the splendor of her sacred silence. The sacred silence that we often don't listen closely enough to hear – the long rolling waves in the middle of a majestic ocean, the silence of the forest before the birds awaken, the silence of an autumn leaf turning from gold to red to russet, the silence of the cave deep within her womb. She came to me in this way and I listened.

"I am Gaia; known long ago as Archangel GQi'anna, archangel of love, change and metamorphosis. I come to speak to your heart and the heart of humanity this day to share with you my plan and the plan for Nova Earth. The key to this understanding is also the key to understanding the essence of who I am – constant change and metamorphosis. I and all kingdoms who walk upon me and live within my soil, waters, rocks and core are always in the process of change and transition. It is simply that the nature of this change, this shift to Nova Earth, is so profound and noticeable that you are in any way aware of something unusual transpiring. But be clear my children that change and transformation have always been part of my expression of love for the Divine Mother.

"All things associated with my being are cyclical, progressing and moving back to the One. Because you are familiar you do not consider these changes as significant; the shift from winter to spring to summer to fall; the shift from stream to river to ocean; the shift from fetus to child to adolescent to adult to ancient one. You notice these changes but you do not pay adequate attention.

"It has always been part of my plan, within the Mother's plan, that I would ascend and return home at some point. Because I am in a different framework of time than humanity, you do not think of this. You have not taken into account the changes that I make with assistance of the company of heaven to continue on my soul journey. It matters not, and it is not something that I have been particularly concerned about drawing your attention to because as your mother I have tended to you and understood that you have been focused on your own evolution and dramas.

"You did not even pay due heed when I shifted out of the old third dimension into the fifth through seventh. You were so engaged in examining your own experiences that you did not notice that I allowed your collective decision to proceed in a manner that was outside the original plan. I allowed you to remain upon my surface and have continued to nurture you. But Nova Earth is being birthed dear hearts and this requires your participation, your love and the destruction of aberrant human behaviors that are no longer in alignment with me. For this reason I beckon forth The New You.

"The New You is a human/hybrid who chooses to live consciously, and by that I mean in the fullness of their divinity and being. A person who is not only willing but prepared to participate in the laying down the new patterns of heart consciousness, behaviors, actions and co-creation that are in harmony with my ascension. The New You is the person who is consciously co-operative, and realizes the necessity of living in harmony with All. The kingdoms, your star brothers and sisters, the inner and outer planets, the company of heaven are all in agreement and alignment with this shift. And now it is time, in your reference of time, for humanity to step forward in cooperation.

"It unfolds by you stepping forward and not only embracing but fully embodying the New You. Now let me explain my plan and then you will more clearly understand how it is that the New You patterning is required for our continued co-habitation as a happy family.

"Nova Earth, Nova Gaia, no longer is a place of pollution, desecration, poverty, war, hunger, lack, limitation, death, disease, humiliation, shame, inequality or pain in any form. These qualities of old earth do not exist in the fifth, sixth or seventh dimensions, and hence they cannot continue upon my planet. Think of it as a situation where there is no oxygen to support those life forms. Make no mistake, all of those false grids and beliefs, *vasanas* within and without, are life forms. They have assumed a power and rigor of their own and cannot, and will not, continue on Nova Earth. This is not said in any way child that is threatening. This is not an eviction notice but simply a statement of fact on how I intend to proceed.

"Too often you have thought of these false grids and conditions as qualities that you as humans either have participated in or been required to endure. That is myopic thinking; it is the thinking of the ego self and it is selfish and short-sighted. All of the false grids developed by humanity have been imposed upon not only my sacred self, but the kingdoms as well. All have suffered from the false grids and beliefs that the human collective came to value as truth and a reflection of reality. Now what I say to you is we are leaving those ways of being behind – all of us, and we, your Divine Mother, the kingdoms, the star beings, the company of heaven, have all invited you to join us in this voyage. You have accepted.

"So where do we voyage to? What is this process of change? What does Nova Earth look, smell and feel like? What is it that

we are creating and are inviting you, as the New You, to participate in?

"I have begun this day by speaking to you of my essence
of change, love and metamorphosis. We have left the cocoon of
the old third dimension behind and are emerging, as are each
of you, into the higher realms. I, Gaia, am returning to original intent. This means allowing my original soul design to be
restored and to blossom more brilliantly than ever before. My
rivers, oceans, lakes, and my life blood is cleansed. My soil, trees,
flowers, fields, and plants are restored with the vibrations of
light and love. All of this reflects as rich nutrients, purified soil,
vibrant, and abundant life force and forms. The kingdoms are
free and jubilant – not only what you conceive of as the animal kingdoms but the elementals, the fairies, the leprechauns,
sprites, devas – all are visible and working their alchemy to restore the beauty and splendor of their homes as well. The mountain ranges sparkle and soar towards the pristine sky. And most
of all my air, your air, your atmosphere is not only purified but
rarefied. Think of the air as filled with rainbows, angels, Healers
of Tralana and Halion Engineers – because it is.

"Cities will be welcomed and co-created as meeting and
gathering places for the human collective, but never again their
exclusive purview. Cities of Light have been emerging all over
the planet with support from myself, the higher realms, your star
brothers and sisters, and the company of heaven. Each city is a
cultural center for different purposes, each magnificent and self-
sufficient in their own right. But let me be clear these Cities of
Light are constructed in co-creation with the New You, the Nova
Beings who choose to work in harmony and love with all. The
New You is not simply a heart conscious awakened individual
but a vibrant full partner in these creations. And that is why the
re-patterning of the collective is necessary.

"I reach out to each of you, my beloved sons and daughters
of my heart. I beckon you to step forward and claim your original design and in that reclamation to set down a new grid for
humanity. You are the pattern-makers for humanity and as per
your request to come forth within this grander plan we await

you. But please hurry – do not be hasty, needy or fearful. Be timely, thoughtful, considerate; but also diligent, purposeful and fully present."

Yahweh, whom the Council of Love refers to as the voice and representative of the Divine Masculine, describes Nova Earth in much the same manner:

"I would be very happy to describe Nova Earth for you my beloved children. Seldom do people ask me of this. It is a planet, my beautiful Gaia, sparkling and radiant with oceans that are so clean and pure, where fish are verdant, where dolphins and whales are finally home, where Atlantis reemerges, and the cities of light that dance right now on the waves of the various oceans, come into substantiality, into materiality and these are gathering places. But they are not like the cities of old earth. I do not chastise your cities but so many of them are places of pollution and density, of crime and dirt. Those are not the gathering places of Nova Earth. Of course there will be some level of density simply because they are gathering places, but there will be no pollution, there will be no uncleanliness. I do not mean a lack of cleanliness, just in the terms of what you think of as pollution or garbage; but also emotional cleanliness, integrity, beautiful art, trees and grass and birds and children. Gaia and the Cities of Light are intended to be the gathering places where children can come and learn and play, and understand their planet, and, their role in the unfoldment.

"Mountain ranges will reemerge as well as rolling hills, plains, savannahs and jungles; the Amazon will be restored, much of what has been destroyed will be restored. There is a sense of ease about living on Nova Earth because when you are creating you have eliminated the stress and worry of your illusions of lack. People are not worried about whether there is food or currency or water or fresh air. The air is a delight and it is fragrant; it is the breath of Gaia. There is clean technology and your star brothers and sisters are clearly visible, as are many of the Masters who now choose to return because they thrive in the new reality. No one has desire to return to the old ways, it is not that it is cursed or dismissed, it is simply understood that it was an evolutionary process that never needs to be repeated. And when I say, never, I mean never throughout eternity. Go with my love and go with my blessings."

Within the context of understanding Gaia, the insights of the Divine Mother make more sense.

"Nova Earth is the positioning, the experience, and the beingness of this beautiful planet as was always intended in the fullness of how it was birthed from its very core, in complete consciousness and heart connection between all things, because everything upon this planet is living.

"Gaia has spoken to you about being an archangel of change, so understand the cycles of which she speaks of. There are seasons and divine timing and now is the season of golden radiance – it is the time of blue and gold upon the earth. It is the time of the melding of the blue of the sky, the oceans, and the streams with the gold of the sun to nourish and replenish the soil of the planet, and the soil of your heart, that all will remain and begin again as fertile, arable, workable areas of production and creation. The seeds have been sown, dear ones, not only in the springtime of your life but long ago. This is the time when all begins to grow.

"I have spoken to you of this period of time upon your planet, the time of cosmetic repair, the birthing of Nova Earth, of this decade that will take you through to 2012-2013, and the beginning of new times upon this planet. The purpose of my calling to you is to tell you all of the fortunes you hold within you. Long ago, we have told you that the keys to heaven are trust and forgiveness, the doorway is Love. Open this doorway with your keys and step into your new life. You have all you require, not only the fullness of your soul design but my blessings, my love and the love of your Father. The storehouse of heaven is wide open.

"Over many thousands of years, human beings fell into an illusion that somehow they were superior, the only living, true energy, even though they have been surrounded by all of creation always, and in all ways. Now sweet angels you have declared is that you are capable, willing, and able, as a collective race to assume the role of original design and step into that consciousness of being in harmony with All.

"What you have said is, as human vessels, multidimensional, human, physical vessels that we wish to give this a try and bring everyone along to this miraculous experience of Nova Earth. We are standing here with you in amazement and saying, 'All right.' That does not mean that vibrationally we are not assisting. And I do not simply mean in esoteric or spiritual ways, although I emphasize to you that in terms of importance that is most critical.

"Has there been adjustment to accommodate your collective desire? Yes. Are the galactics working with you? More so than ever. But it is you who are raising the vibration of the collective so that your systems are more reflective, completely reflective, of who you really are, The New You.

"The ascension of humanity is underway. Understand this ascension is both collective and individual, and it is the individuals who are stepping forward as the pattern-makers that are showing the way. You are in the middle of this, and part of what you are claiming as your Ascension process, the vehicle that you are using, is the participation and the anchoring in physicality where human beings can participate and live in harmony of Nova Earth.

"In many ways, this unfoldment is much bigger; this is much grander than originally envisioned. You have stepped from childhood to adulthood, to maturity, and you have said, 'Yes, Mother, I came to be part of this. But I think we can do more, and learn more and teach more, throughout the multiverse, if we do this diligent undertaking in this time and space.'

"We are embracing you more reverently than ever before, because you are saying, 'We can also create the miracle, and Mother, I acknowledge that I am the miracle.' And in that you are acknowledging not only the miraculous nature of creation, but my presence within you and your presence within me.

"Do not think, with your intellect, mental body and ego, that everything which has been discussed in terms of significant external, visible expressions of freedom upon your planet has simply been set aside. Gaia, her kingdoms and each of you are well underway. Your human form, your mental body, your emotional body, your expanded field are becoming unified.

"Allow the New You to emerge. Keep that sense of joy and love, knowing that you are at the beginning of this creation cycle, and the creation that you have claimed from Father and I is your ability to create. This has been something that we have been waiting for you to claim. Accept that you, like Gaia, are in the process of metamorphosis.

"Ever curious, you ask what exactly is taking place? We are holding the frequency; we are supporting you in the unified field of love. Part of our subtle assistance is this raising in frequency so that you can begin to acknowledge and embrace your inter-dimensional selves. For the past several years you have been penetrated enormously from the One, from our hearts to yours. Repeatedly we have said that this was not an energy that was specific to humanity, because it penetrated all beings upon the planet, as well as Gaia herself.

"These adjustments have and are being made to empower you as you go on that lift-off to creation. You are ready to experience blissful love. It is not simply a singular event. It is a series of events where you begin to look at each other and say, 'My God, it's happening! And I am in this partnership of creation! I'm going to be with Gaia!'

"You most certainly have a choice during this time of cosmetic repair. You can be part of the struggle or you can be part of the reconstruction; it is that simple. Now, I have not spoken to any one of you who have said to me, 'Please, Mother, let the struggle continue – I enjoy it so much.' You have turned to me in earnestness and tears and said, you are tired of this way. You want to begin again to fulfill your mission of joy. You were birthed by me into this magnificent vessel of physicality, and I am there with you.

"Finding your dream, for many of you, has been difficult,

either because you have forgotten that you are loved, or you have forgotten that you are worthy of personal dreams and fulfillment. It is in the creation of what your heart desires as your unique expression of love on Gaia that the reconstruction of the planet takes place. And, it is not just in dreaming or wanting one thing. It is in the planting of a flower, or a flowerbed – I would personally ask you to consider roses. It is in the planting of seeds within children. But, it is not just in the planting of the seeds; it is in the watering and tending, and watching them blossom, fertilizing them, pruning them where necessary – hovering but not interfering.

"For many of you the best form of creation is when you simply allow it to be a fleeting thought that crosses your field of vision – 'Oh, I would like that' - and letting it go. Each one of you has unique capacity and methods in how you create. But let us be clear, it begins with a dream, and it begins with the stillness, it begins in the silence of your heart.

"Sometimes you turn to me and you say, 'I am afraid – for I have wished and I have dreamed before and I have been hurt and disappointed because it did not come to pass.' I do not tell you that there are things that you will think of and ask for that will not be immediate – for, yes, it is a matter of Divine Timing, and this is an unfoldment, not a single day. But I also tell you that in many of these prior adventures, not everything was in place in the way that it is in this moment and this time. And let me be clear, my dear children, it is my time – it is the birthing of the Divine Feminine upon the earth. And Divine Feminine is the birthing of form – not ideas, but form.

"It will take time to rebuild this planet but each one of you has unique gifts – each one of you is healer and teacher. If your gift is to heal the oceans, to work with water then begin but do not cling to the one idea, to the one creation – let it flow. If your job is to teach, to write books do not stop with one class or one paragraph – let it flow. If your job is to introduce ethics into the workplace, and it does not matter whether it is government, education, healthcare or industry – do not stop when you have demonstrated integrity and ethical behavior in one situation, keep going.

"When you are tired and you are thinking I cannot do this anymore, then anchor in the heart of Gaia and come home. Come home and rest in my arms. I will wrap you in my cloak of blue, I will restore you and you will begin again. This is the sacred partnership that we have formed long ago.

"Do not take my message this day to mean that you are going to have to wait ten years to see any results. You have need to see results of your creations each and every day – to look in the mirror and say 'My goodness I truly am co-creator upon this Earth! I wonder what else I can do? I wonder what my next adventure is What would I like it to be?' So begin.

"Start by embracing your New You, by becoming the fullness of Nova Being creating and being part of Nova Earth. Like Gaia, I beckon to you right now, step forward, now is the time."

The Foundation of Spirit You

In order to understand where we are going with the expansion of our sacred beings into The New You, we have to have a grasp of who we are in this current time, space and reality. It's one of those situations that if you don't know where you are coming from, how do you know where you are going? We begin this section of our adventure together not by superficially reviewing who we are, but by having a deeper understanding of our being, but also expanded comprehension, appreciation and love of who we are, in and out of form.

We begin by looking at all the ways in which we exhibit and know ourselves. What are the ways in which we conceive of ourselves; how do we know ourselves spiritually, physically, mentally and emotionally? It's important to be aware of all the various pieces of your being – what your ray is, what your soul colors are, what chakras are your strong points, what are your bodies, your sacred fields, your aspects, past lives, future lives, what is your soul mission and purpose. Do you even know what your soul mission and purpose is? And if so, how are you living it? Or is it divorced from your current reality?

As we begin this voyage of discovery, remember to be the observer and to not fall into judgment. There are no parts of your being that are good or bad – it is simply information. We are examining the different elements of our being to establish our foundation. Who and what is the core of your magnificent self? How do you know you – and how does the outer world and higher realms know you? How do the spiritual pieces of you reflect in your life and the outer world? How are you going to bring these wondrous qualities to the forefront so that it is actually front and center in everything you do as you walk around, living, breathing, smiling, jumping, and watching TV?

How are you connecting, not just in prayer and meditation, but again as you're walking the dog, as you cook supper, as you drive to work? How are you connecting to the Divine? How are you connecting to your own Divine Self? How are you connecting with your guides? From this gathering of information on who you are we then move into the expansion of who you are choosing to become, the embrace of the New You.

We have a variety of ways in which we conceive of ourselves spiritually and in which we exhibit through the universe. We are going to discuss several of these just to lay some groundwork in terms of what we are discussing.

SOUL RAY & SOUL COLOR

Why do we start with soul ray and color and why is it so important?

As mentioned, the starting point of the emergence of the New You is understanding the core of who you are – your foundation; the essence upon which you are constructed and have chosen to incarnate. The purpose of the first phase of the New You is for you to become cognizant of the multitude of ways in which you are known and exhibit throughout the Universe. The starting point of that understanding of who you are is your soul color or your soul ray, similar to our earthly description five-foot-two, blue eyes, and brown hair. It's a starting point, a descriptor, not the entirety of your being.

Knowing, and more importantly, working with your soul color gives you access to a big piece of your core essence. Identifying your soul color is often no more complex than knowing your favorite color(s). Having knowledge of your soul color gives you a plethora of information about who you are: what your mission and purpose is; what you lineage and connections are to the company of heaven; why you are drawn to certain people, places, jobs, families, hobbies; who you've been; where you're headed – the list is extensive.

So aside from knowing your favorite color where do you begin – how do you access this information on your soul color. The Soul Color meditation is embedded with attunements to assist you in that process of discovery. Repeat the meditation several times because more information and colors, blends, and greater clarity will emerge each time. Each of us is remarkably complex. Even when we are travelling only on one ray or color, and I use these terms interchangeably, there is a rainbow of hues and variations within that one ray or color.

(LISTEN TO THE SOUL COLOR AUDIO MEDITATION, AT THIS TIME. DOWNLOAD THE COLORED CHAKRA CHART AS WELL)

CHAKRAS

One approach in determining your soul ray is also to discern which chakra center or chakra color that you resonate with. Chakras are energy centers, little spinning wheels, located throughout the body. While we have three meridians of chakras and hundreds of these energy centers within us, we are going to focus on the central meridian which runs down the center of your body. The Council of Love works with a system of thirteen chakras, six of which are bridge and activation chakras for the vibrations of the higher dimensions. A colored chakra chart can be downloaded from the same location as the audio meditations.

Another clue also related to the chakras is, what part of your body do you tend to live in. What are your strengths and Achilles heel? For example, your favorite color is blue and you feel that you resonate to the blue ray, and are anchored in the throat chakra area. The throat is the center for change and communication. Blue folks are often teachers, counselors, writers, involved in public affairs or relations. Blue ray people often tend towards illnesses involving sore throats, tonsillitis, sinus, sore necks and so on. They tend to either thrive on change or find it very difficult.

Similarly, blue ray people feel a close affiliation with the

Divine Mother, Archangel Michael and to some extent Archangel Gabrielle. They are the nurturers, caretakers, and the peaceful warriors. As you can see, knowing your soul color begins to reveal all kinds of information about who you are.

One way of relating soul color to chakra color is, if someone feels a deep attraction to brilliant, vibrant purple. That ray of purple relates to the crown chakra, and it is our connection to the Divine. People whose primary purpose and journey throughout many lifetimes is to help people to make that connection with the Divine and to teach that connection, will often really relate to the purple or to the violet.

For example, I am very blue and much of my focus tends to be in my throat chakra as I am a communicator, channel, and agent of change. That's what I do. I don't even get to work or talk with people if they're not going through radical change. Somehow they don't find their way to me. The key, however, is to be equally completely balanced in all of our chakras, all of our aspects. We want to be completely present in that eternal now, acknowledging other lifetimes, past, present, future, alternate, but fully present here in this eternal moment of right now, in this time of incredible change, anchoring the new.

We often use the expression that some people "live in their heads" and tend to work intensely with the head chakras. They tend to get headaches, sinus infections, head colds, brain tumors, or pains in the back of their neck. People who live in their hearts, and travel on the emerald green ray, tend to get heartburn, as well as have heart and lung issues. Heart people feel, sense, love and nurture very strongly. Then there are the incredible artists who are grounded and connected to the artistic flair and being on Gaia. Artists tend to be rooted in their sacral, pubic or solar plexus chakras; they've got passion and creativity going for them.

All soul colors, rays and chakras are equal. There is not a hierarchy of chakras or rays and it is critically important that we love, balance and respect each center. Many lightworkers have tended in the past to anchor in the higher (heart and above) chakras and not be grounded. That habit is changing and needs to change because we are anchoring the New You in physicality and on Nova Earth. The key is to be present, alive and full of vibrant outrageous joy.

In becoming the New You what you want to do is to be consistently balanced in all of your chakras. All of your chakras need to be wide open, spinning, and open to the energy, spinning out the energy, sharing it with the planet and with all of humanity equally. We acknowledge our primary connection. In my example of being blue, I certainly work with the green, with the gold and the yellow of my solar plexus, my will, and with my umbilical, which is the healing and the recreation of Nova Earth.

Soul color and soul ray does not change with each incarnation. You emerged from the heart of One as magenta then you are still magenta. It is your soul essence. It is important you don't confuse your soul color with your auric field color which does change depending on situations, environments, and generally how you are feeling. Each of us has a base line auric field color and a heart color, as well. It is exceptionally rare a person has all one ray in all three areas. For example, the first time the Council of Love addressed me, they said "soul of blue, aura of lavender, heart of green."

AURIC FIELD, THE SACRED SPACE OF YOU

Each person has a layering of several bodies surrounding the physical being. That is known as the auric field. One of the powerful shifts to the New You is that the very formation of the auric field is expanded.

The components of our field people are most familiar with and relate to, are the mental and emotional fields or bodies. Each body is important to know, understand and embrace. It is from that baseline we will then take the quantum leap to the expansion to the New You.

(DOWNLOAD "AURA MAN")

A diagram for what I call "Aura Man" can be found as part of your downloads, was formulated years ago for St. Germaine's and Einstein's healing modality of Interdimensional therapy for the advanced form of LaHoChi has exploded. We are taking our understanding of our sacred space to new levels. But let us examine each component of the auric field so you have a clear understanding of this part of your foundation.

The first area of discussion is the central channel. Our central channel comes through our crown chakra and runs down the center of our chakra system. Think of it as a pillar or a cylinder that comes down through our crown over our spinal column, continuing down throughout our body and into the Earth. Our central column is our transmission center where we are receiving and sending all kinds of information to our being; to and from the universe and Gaia. It is where we climb the sacred spiral to connect with the 13th Octave.

What we haven't been doing to the fullest extent of our capacities is pull in through our central channel all the other qualities, abilities, aspects, elements, subatomic particles of who we are. We also haven't moved out of the way to connect, not just in the 13th Octave and the higher dimensions, but out to the broader universe; to connect with those pieces of our self that is waiting to work with us. That concept is part of the New You.

The etheric body is also known as our energy body, the holographic template of our being. The emotional body or layer contains all experience and expression of our emotional self, including the conscious, unconscious and sub-conscious. The astral body is the anchor for desire, the seat of emotions and where most of the false illusions of the old third dimension are stored. The mental body is for the processing, manifestation and expression of concrete intellect.

The second layer of the etheric body is the template of the soul design which when anchored and activated allows us to align our will with the Divine Will. The causal body is the warehouse of all experiences from all incarnations.

The outer layer is the Seal of Solomon. The Seal of Solomon is the etheric seal or wrapper of our energy field. The seal was put in place eons ago as a protective measure so that we could have the experience of individuation. The Seal of Solomon is a sacred geometry construct akin to etheric cellophane holding all of our fields together. Many people think of the Seal of Solomon as their *merkaba*. It is rare that I work on a person that I don't see a Seal of Solomon not tattered and torn.

The Seal of Solomon, to put it simply is the bubble which contains us, all of our bodies, our etheric, our emotional, our astral, our mental, and our causal. It was put there originally to protect us, to contain us, to give us a sense of physicality because we were this massive sheer energy field. So, as we came into form, and particularly into this human form, we were given this seal so we would feel safe and secure in form.

Then comes the universal self, one of the final layers of who we are the biggest piece of us. But again, we haven't been integrated and pulled in and going out, or lived in that universal self. That is what the higher dimensional, and certainly what the seventh dimensional beings do. They live in their universal love self. With the anchoring of the New You, we're learning to anchor in that bigger universal part of ourselves, using the central channel. This does not imply that we ignore our other bodies, because they too are vital to having a physical experience.

Archangels Michael and Gabrielle, and Universal Mother Mary have repeatedly said "If it doesn't feel like love, don't do it; if it doesn't feel like joy, don't do it." That guidance is your litmus test. What the Council has said is "Are you living in your universal self? Are you living in a place of your totality?" While we were contained in the old third dimension we weren't. Because of the illusions and the quagmire we were caught in, we couldn't engage with our totality. Now the old third dimensional paradigms and false beliefs are dissolving, there going, going, gone. The illusion of that hologram is becomes apparent.

I use the word "hologram" very specifically. There are those of you that say "But everything is a hologram. Life is a hologram. My body is a hologram. My fields are a hologram." That's not true. When you follow that line of belief, then what you're saying is your essence, your universal self, the really big you; the you that is traveling throughout the universe, the multiverse, is just a hologram, and doesn't have any independent reality. You are denying the fact that Mother/Father/One birthed you. It's a basic denial of self.

Are there holograms around us? Yes. Have they been very powerful and seemingly real? Yes. However, do not make the assumption that everything is a hologram or we are holograms. We are as solid as rock, and as etheric as air.

It is important to note that each of these layers or bodies as we term them are inter-dependent, and in constant exchange and flow of energies between each of the fields. There are no barriers between the fields, and the energy exchange is fluid. A good way to grasp this is to consider how our thoughts influence our emotions, and then manifest in our bodies. Or how, from time to time, past life experiences bleed through and influence beliefs, fears or attractions we have in this current reality.

Let's return to the original query "how do you know yourself?" How aware are you of how you work with your soul rays, your sacred colors, your fields, and your archetypes? One of the things I hear from folks is "I am a starseed"; "I am a healer"; "I am a warrior"; that has become their self-definition. St. Germaine is emphatic that we are all of these things, a healer, teacher, nurturer, warrior, et al. None of us are uni-dimensional. If we are going to attempt to define ourselves, let's do so in a variety of ways.

There is no one who didn't start off as angelic, and there are very few of us who haven't lived on other planets or assumed different life forms. There are a few earth-keepers who have never gone anywhere else but Earth. This is what they like. This is what they like to do. We are either wayshowers, or pillars, or gatekeepers, or healers, or teachers. We have all these past and future lives, alternate lives, and alternate realities we are living in all the time. There are many ways to think of ourselves, and now the Council is asking you to expand your self-concept even further.

ASPECTS

The final area to discuss before we leave this topic of your foundation is aspects. In lightworker material aspects is used in several ways. For example, people refer to their angelic self or aspect, their star aspect, being a wayshower, healer, pillar or gatekeeper. All of these are simply aspects of their being. One way to look at the various aspects of yourself is to think of yourself as a five-pointed star. Each of your extremities is an aspect – warrior-destroyer with the creator on the opposite diagonal side; your star being aspect with your earthkeeper on the opposite diagonal side; and your head representing your I AM Presence, your universal self. And then your heart being the anchor and foundation, integrating these aspects into a unified whole.

However, for the purposes of this discussion, an aspect is defined as a part of you that you sent out, consciously or unconsciously, into the universe or Earth, to complete an undertaking on your behalf. Think of these aspects as a modified form of bilocation. For example, an issue you care deeply about is the children starving in Africa. You are not in a position to pick up and go to Africa to minister to those children. So you send an aspect of yourself to tend to the mission. Even at the same time, you are concerned about the victims of war in Afghanistan, or the injuries the troops are suffering. You send an aspect out there too.

Aspects are not full bi-locations. These aspects do not have a full life as it were. They are purpose-driven; tied to your core essence, soul contract and sacred purpose. They are not soul fragments of parallel lives. These aspects are integrally tied to your being. When there are too many aspects out there working on your behalf the result is, your life force is compromised; you feel drained. How you become aware that you have too many "parts" of yourself working is a low-energy sensation of not being quite home. You certainly are not anchored in the fullness of your physical being.

While you are sending your aspects to anchor the New You, it is crucial to call back all your aspects at some point. You need the entire being present to receive this upgrade in vibration and new way of being in wholeness. You require the fullness of your body, mind, spirit and extended field to be home for this massive shift and undertaking. Some of these aspects may have been away on duty for too long a time, in some cases for several lifetimes. It's time to bring them home.

How you retrieve and call back your aspects is through meditation. The starting point and method for all clearings, integrations, attunements and expansions is always the same with the Council of Love. You anchor in your heart; you anchor in the 13th Octave; you anchor in the heart of Gaia. You call in the archangels, your guides, and the ascended masters. You feel moved to invoke for assistance in this or any undertaking. Then you begin.

How you retrieve your aspects is by calling to them from your heart. Chances are they have picked up debris and detritus. So as part of your call to them to return home, you are also requesting they wipe their feet at the door, prior to re-entry into your sacred self. Under no circumstances do you wish to assume the pain, suffering and injuries they may have incurred while on a mission. The method the Council recommends is that you put these aspects through a car wash of white light before re-entry. In this way they emerge cleansed, refreshed and happy to be home and merged with you. Re-entry is always through the heart portal.

If there was a past-life aspect so important that when you died, you allowed the aspect to continue on with the mission. This was a joint decision between you, your guides, and the One. Very often these aspects are the clearest part of a regression because they were so prominent in that past life, and core to your mission and purpose. Sometimes the aspect is still working on that mission.

It is recommended you do this exercise several times to become familiar with your foundation and the base upon which you are building your New You. Don't be concerned if you don't see or feel the re-entry. The completion will occur; it is an exercise in intent. So while some may have Spielberg-style visions, others mild impressions, eventually you will feel the result. The proof is greater vitality, grounding, ease, and integration. It is not necessary for you to know and have intimate conversation with each of your aspects returning home. The purpose of the exercise is the re-entry, not the movie. This is the guidance of the COL that has been repeated throughout the process of building the New You.

Sometimes our aspects come in more slowly because they are completing the mission we sent them out to do. Allow for its completion and resolution. This gives us time to integrate and not get overwhelmed by all the new energy coming in. The average length of time for this meditation is between ten and twenty minutes. Don't forget to run them through the light car wash, before they step back into you. Make sure each chakra snaps into place. It is a heart process so welcome them home.

But now, you are ready to begin. What better way to bridge this with a wonderful channeling from the Universal Mother.

"Greetings I am Mary, Universal Mother, Mother of change, Mother of love, Mother of compassion, Mother of this universe and Mother, sweet angel, of each of you. Welcome, my sweet angels who have traveled from near and far to participate, to embrace, and to fulfill your desire for transformation. Welcome to the New You.

"What is the New You? It is the old you. It is the you that you've always been throughout time and space and creation. It is the you of original design, of original composition. It is the you expanding, welcoming, and claiming your birthright. You have traveled for eons, some of you always on Earth or in angelic form; some of you in the distant omniverse; it matters not because the core of you, the essence of you has never changed. Has it adapted to circumstance, environment, to the skin you've chosen to inhabit? Of course, and brings delightful diversity. But the core of you, the design of you, the essence of who you are has never changed or altered.

"You have spent the past years anchoring the fullness of that soul design, consciously and unconsciously. You have anchored the design but you have not brought to fulfillment, to conscious reality, the fullness of that design. That, is this adventure of the New You. It is the adventure of becoming, embracing, and being the totality of your wholeness. It is the adventure of eliminating anything that is of illusion, lack, limitation, despair, disease, all of the false paradigms plaguing your planet and the third dimension for eons.

"You are closing the circle, and you are returning to what you think of as true north, saying 'yes, we are the Creator Race, not the Master Race, none of what we do is based in ego, control. That is of the old.' The Creator Race is the ability to create for yourselves, your family, those you love and cherish, your community, for Nova Earth and Nova Gaia. It is the sweet reflection of who you are.

"Everything, throughout the multiverse, the omniverse, was birthed from my core. That means it is of love. Those molecules of love come together, they morph, they transform, they assume form. All you are an emanation of love, and within that emanation you chose to be certain rays, fragrances, colors; to be the embodiment of love. You may think of this as service but when you peel it, when you truly look at it, it is simply your expression of your molecular structure.

"Some of you have channeled, some of you have healed, some of you are teachers, but you also are much more. You have many faces and aspects of your being, and my purpose and the purpose of my Council is to assist you in coming to know, celebrate and live in the totality of that being. I am with you always. Let us begin with you knowing that I am your Mother and as your Mother, I cherish you beyond anything. You are the creation of my heart so turn to me, and let us walk together in this adventure of the New You. Go in peace. Farewell."

Embracing the Stranger

The Council began revealing information about The Stranger in late December 2012. At that time, I thought I had my agenda pretty much set for the upcoming year – little did I know or even suspect! The information on The Stranger was like removing your finger from the proverbial dam and the flow, or shall I say onslaught, of information began. You know the saying "People plan, God laughs." Well they must have been having a heck of a good time upstairs.

When I wrote *The Great Awakening* I felt that it was a culmination of the information and energies the Council of Love had downloaded through me for the past twenty years. In many ways it felt like my *pièce de résistance*. I thought I had shared all of the Council's instructions for a surefire ascension process. That still stands. It wasn't planning to stop channeling or retire, but I felt a huge chunk of my soul contract had been completed. In some ways it was a bittersweet feeling, especially given the collective's decision to ascend as one. While that incredibly spiritually mature decision thrilled me, it also at times gave way to frustration. I would ask, why the heck don't they just read the book? Archangel Gabrielle, my go-to gal, and I had some interesting conversations about the human behavior to say yes, and then drag their collective feet. I need to be really clear, but it's the middle of the night and I'm chuckling, because the angst and frustration is so human, and I'm just one of the tribe.

The information that began flowing through me was akin to a rip tide during a tsunami. What was stunning is the information was all new; concepts that had never crossed my mind. It brought together pieces on Universal Law, creation, and channeling the Council had talked and taught about for years, but expanded and connected it in ways that left me excited, spinning and eager to start a new chapter.

The first piece of information they spoke of was The Stanger. My first reaction was what an odd name – and then it began. Every now and then the Council speaks to me as a complete collective – archangels, ascended masters, Divine Mother, the whole huge group. While it is beyond exhilarating it is also like being lit up like a rocket on the fourth of July. The one thing I have come to understand when this group session begins is, there is no turning down the volume and the information being transmitted is pivotal.

The Stranger is a new concept based on the Universal Law of Within and Without/Above and Below. Think about it. We are a divine spark of love emanating from the heart of One, brought to form by the grace and movement of the Divine Mother within an infinite universe. Our purpose is to be an expression of love, and to continue our journey back to Source. Everything we do is part of that plan; a spiritual drive millions of times stronger than salmon swimming upstream to spawn.

But if we are really a spark, the essence of One, how does that fit into this body and this lifetime? We began as an unbelievably massive field of energy, floating throughout the universe. Where did it go? How did it get stepped down to such an extent? That essence of One cannot be limited or contained, so what happened?

Open your heart and ground, and read what the Universal Mother has to relate on this subject.

"Greetings, I am Mary, Universal Mother, Mother of Unity, Mother of Change, Mother of Love and Mother of all. Welcome to this time of change, this time of rebirth, this expansion. Welcome to the fulfillment of your plan. Welcome home.

"For the duration of our time together I embrace you and I enfold you. I gather you into my heart; I wrap you in my cloak of infinite blue to protect you, to hold you, so you will know beyond any shadow of doubt how deeply you are loved and cherished; how I nurture you through this process of expansion.

"I step forward this day to speak to you about the very beginning. Often I have said I have birthed you, I birthed you from my heart, from my soul, from my being. But you never truly comprehended what it is I am talking about. I did not birth you as angel, star seed, intergalactic, earthkeeper, healer, teacher, or warrior. I birthed you as sheer energy – clear, brilliant and without form. You tend to think of yourselves as beings of light when, in fact, you are beings of love.

"As human beings, you believe your soul comes into your form, your massive, expanded field, and then when you leave, your soul departs and your essence and your energy floats off to heaven or some other dimensional reality. That is not so, that is only a portion of you that leaves.

"Previously, you were not prepared to incorporate, let alone comprehend in a core sense, what I am suggesting. You are above and below, you are within and without, and it is time for you to access what is above and what is without, what is around you, and not incorporate anything that is not beneficial to you. This is what we will be focusing on."

You are far grander than the Milky Way, or the lotus with all her petals. It is time for you to understand this and, I am honored to guide you with Mother Mary's help.

The Universal Law of Within and Without, immutable and unchangeable, states that everything within our being also exists in the outer reality of the universe. Similarly, everything that exists in the outer universe and is of Source, rests within us. We refer to this law as Above and Below because we are more comfortable in our human minds of limitation to think, if we work, pray, serve and become god-like, we will be blessed with the divine qualities of God. Not so. We already came with that divine energy within ourselves. We have always had full access to the without; we merely didn't acknowledge it or think ourselves worthy of such blessings.

Have you ever been stymied about how you work on an issue, day after day, year after year, and never seem to be able to truly get to the heart of the matter; never able to completely grasp, eliminate or create something your essence is demanding of you? Enter, The Stanger.

The Stranger is that part of your eternal soul essence, existing and waiting in the without –floating in the broader universe. The Stranger is a field of sheer energy existing since you emanated from the heart of One. It is a part of you who is an ally, facilitator and best friend. It is an energy mass with the capacity to work in ways we can't because we are physically limited in many ways we have assumed. We cannot move in the same manner throughout the universe as The Stranger. The Stanger can get things done, because it has access to energies we don't.

My first question when the COL started talking about The Stranger was "why now, and where the heck has he been?" The answer was straightforward. I wasn't ready. As individuals and collectively, were not ready to embrace our Stranger, let alone the concept that there is part of us, floating in the universe. We had to break through and release the old false belief systems of the third dimension, and allow the realities of a higher state of being to emerge.

The embrace and acceptance of your Stranger is the first step in embracing your New You. It is our first step to accept that we are bigger, more powerful, more creative, and have far more potential that we were ever willing to concede. It also comes with a responsibility price tag. But boy is it worth it!

Think of it – there is a vast field of energy waiting to hook up with you and serve, help, guide and best of all, do. When I say do, I don't imply The Stranger operates in ways we assign to human form; it doesn't. The actions are bigger, grander, more rapid, more perfected than we can comprehend. The movement of energies in The Stranger is like having a guide who we never knew about and who was always waiting and hoping. This guide is intrinsically attached to you.

How do you connect and begin to work with your Stranger? What was your soul agreement from eons ago? What is The Stranger up to at this very moment, and how can it be of help?

Working with your Stranger is about learning to work with your expanded field, learning to work outside of yourself. This thought encompasses a new paradigm. It is about allowing new concepts of who you are settle in, and to become part of your operating system. The first step is to begin to connect with your Stranger.

I leave you with this guidance from Archangel Michael:

"Embrace the stranger within – not the shadow or darkness – but the stranger you don't know or acknowledge. The stranger you have shied away from; the one who makes you fearful because there is so much light and power behind their veil."

During The New You webinar series, with those hearty brave pathfinders, there were times when some had trouble connecting with the Stranger. This is not unusual and is certainly not a sign to give up. The key is to relax. This is not a test but a process and the key is allowing and showing up; being the observer.

When you are trying, reaching, perhaps a fearful of what you will and will not find, it blocks the energy flow. Lie down on your bed, listen to the meditation, allow yourself to float into the enormous night sky and simply allow your Stranger to approach. It is highly unlikely that it will present as a person but rather an energy field - all wavy and able to move rapidly and with ease throughout the universe; working for you.

One of the ways in which the Council works with us is through downloads of information and meditation. They have channeled this meditation in order for you to meet, embrace and begin to work with your Stranger. Do not wait until the end of the book to begin the meditation. The energies of each one are designed to expand and assist in this shift to the New You. So download it now, do the meditation, then come back and continue reading.

(LISTEN TO "THE STRANGER" AUDIO MEDITATION)

You have just had an amazing experience where you now realize the magnitude of your being and the assistance of what is available, and the of part of you that is in the universe.

I want to share a channeling from Archangel Gabrielle on the New You and The Stranger:

"The New You is a Nova Being, an evolved new species of human. You are taking the jump, you have moved. Consider your human journey from Atlantis, to Egypt, to cave man, to what was lost a long time ago, to the nomads, hunter-gatherer, farmer-agrarian, industrial, electronic, to the post-industrial and on into the information age. Now you are evolving not only as a collective species but as human beings. You are evolving into something new, incredible, and something that was planned from the very beginning. It was never intended that you would be stuck in the old mud of the third dimension. You are learning to move. The New You is the being that has cleansed, cleared, relinquished, integrated, anchored, embraced, and surrendered to the totality of their being."

Archangel Gabrielle is referring to the big you; the without you and the within you, the above you and the below you, the inside and the outside. This is a new way of thinking about yourself. Sit with this idea and let it sink in. It's not simply a matter of being interdimensional, it is a matter of being, anchored in the state of heart consciousness while in physical form. You are going to be in that place of love regardless of whether you're reaching back into the third, playing with the magic of the fourth, fifth, or in the Love consciousness, the Christ consciousness of the seventh.

Archangel Gabrielle continues:

"The New You is not simply one who adheres and lives by the Blessings and Virtues, the divine qualities. It is one who is the living, breathing embodiment of those qualities while in physical form. It is the walking, talking, breathing, laughing, playing, and accepting of your divine grace and role within the plan. This is the starting point, the foundation, where we will build upon to fulfill your role within the Divine Mother's Plan.

This is the embrace and then the surrender, the falling back, the falling onto the feather bed, the letting go and saying 'I surrender to my plan.' The New You thrives, not merely exists, not just making do, but thrives in the enjoyment of every moment of existence, even in the midst of change, chaos, and what appears to be the destruction of the old paradigms."

All of us experience vital and powerful while others aren't at peak performance. But each of us is committed to the journey and the becoming of the New You. The Council of Love, your Stranger, and I are committed to the completion of this journey with you. That is the sacred promise made long before we incarnated. We are committed to the destruction and elimination of the old. I am not just referring to the Illuminati or the dark forces or pollution, I'm talking about the old us. I'm talking about the narrow, little opinions, the feelings, and the destructive judgments that we've had of ourselves. As those are destroyed, as we let go of that feeling of lack, of limitation, the new is being born; we are being re-born.

It is not about just being born into alignment with Divine Will, but emerging as the New You, being an active conscious instrument of that Will. As we become a conscious instrument we create Nova Earth, because what we are doing is shifting the collective. As we are working with our big selves, that energy is communicated to every other person.

As always, Archangel Gabrielle has the final word: "The New You is the heart conscious being who accepts the infinite process of becoming."

The undertaking in embracing The Stranger and the New You is the gathering of tools and energies. Not only for the rest of this life, but for our entire journey back to Source. Our purpose is to keep becoming, and evolving, until we are sheer energy absorbed back into the heart of the Mother.

This starting point in your expansion, in accepting your Stranger, is aligning with Universal Law, and welcoming your unfoldment within and without. This introduction is the starting point of that new alignment. It is a joy and essential you begin to vigorously start exploring who is your Stranger.

Once you have been introduced and are coming to truly understand each other, the name Stranger will feel wrong. Asking for a name is a great idea; and assigning a name that touches your heart is an equally good idea if at first you don't immediately hear a name. The webinar groups had wonderful fun with both receiving names and naming their Stranger. It became likened to a dinner party where everyone was invited and the name plates were fascinating: Stranata, Sterling, Connection Guru, and my favorite, Lulubelle. Each person's Stranger presents uniquely and differently – just like you! The sensation of empowerment, intensity, expansion and hopefulness resulting from this connection however is consistent. The report of "things falling into place" was heard again and again. The feelings of inspiration, excitement and greater security were shared repeatedly, whether it was in artistic endeavors, career or relationship expansion.

Allowing and encouraging yourself to experience and perceive your Stranger is exactly what you want to pursue. Relax and engage with this magical mirror. Keep going with your new best friend.

Go back and look at earlier Aura Man diagram. You are inviting your universal self to introduce themself. For years, the COL has differentiated between the higher self and the universal self. Until now I never fully understood the distinction, but always intuitively knew the universal self was bigger and beyond what we tend to conceive of as the higher self.

The universal self is the totality of our being, including parts who are out in the universe. Our natural inclination when we view that energy is to pull it in, anchor it; that is not how it works. What you are seeking is a harmonious co-operative, unified, working, loving relationship with the outer you. It is not effective to pull that sheer energy field within because it's out there working for us and helping us. However, as the New You, you want to be fully aware and working with your Stranger.

Once you feel you have full connection with your Stranger it is important to begin actively working with them. This energy field is capable of moving and performing in ways we can't because of the limitations of physicality and the realm of human experience. Your Stranger is not revealing themselves to be your new best friend, but to actively assist in creation and fulfillment of your sacred contract and heart's desires.

Begin giving your Stranger assignments, recognizing this energy is committed to helping you. Areas of your life that have stymied you, or have presented challenges, can be turned over to your Stranger for assistance. The key is to honor your own request for help and not grabbing it back. Often, with our guides, the company of heaven and with our Stranger, we ask and plead for help then get nervous and grab back the very issue we have been begging to give away. Don't expect your Stranger to behave in a human manner. If anything, the results are bigger, faster, unexpected and glorious than we could ever imagine. Part of successfully working with your Stranger is surrender and trust. Trust in your new-found portion of your being. Trust this being is working for your ultimate highest good.

As you begin to understand how to work with your Stranger it's a good idea to keep track of your requests and interactions. While I am not suggesting journaling a few words to jog your memory on what was requested, what transpired, how you felt or heard. But the more you can recall given to you by your Stanger the more intimate and fulfilling your relationship will be. It is a simple matter of you coming to know and love the fullness of you.

Interdimensional You

Eighteen years ago when the Council of Love started talking to me about the 13th Octave and the process and meaning behind that gift, one of the key components of that description was the seventh dimension. Although pretty darn intelligent and aware, dimensional realities were not part of my everyday thinking. Of course I knew we existed in the third dimension but that awareness was more like background noise that anything I ever spent time actively considering. Having never been an avid science student, my inclination was more to the meaning of life and the universe rather than time, space and distance.

When I opened to channel I was not part of what one would think of as a spiritual awareness movement. I never read Carlos Castenada, I did not meditate, other than time at the end of yoga class, I wasn't a vegetarian, and I didn't want to go to India. In the intervening years people have asked if I always knew of my "gift"; if I always had experiences. The truth was, I never thought my experiences were unusual. My entire family was very keyed in, and it wasn't something we ever talked about; it was the norm. So when this inner expansion took place it wasn't a quantum leap. The quantum leap was declaring myself and leaving the mainstream, choosing and admitting that spirit, and pursuing my own path is the most important thing in my life.

In that first year as the Council talked to me about Gaia's shift from the third to the seventh dimension, I accepted the information readily into my heart; integrating it into my growing understanding about the changes taking place. From the very start the COL described the seventh dimension as the dimension of the Christ consciousness and love. Frankly that sounded good enough for me, because although I wasn't part of a spiritual movement, I was highly political and was exceptionally clear that love really was and is the solution to the world's problems.

The Council's primary message and purpose is to anchor love into every person's heart on the planet and far beyond. That is the guiding principle they bring time and time again. It is the most important thing. So when I realized early on that people weren't quite ready to hear about the seventh dimension, I downplayed it and focused on the love, because everyone understands that. Everyone desires love, even those reticent to admit it.

As the years rolled, by I started hearing more discussion about the fifth dimension, and how there were channels emerging talking about how we were about to transcend into the fifth. What was interesting about this was people who wanted to talk about this shift to the fifth were very adamant. I didn't quite realize at the time that I was witnessing the beginning of a strong movement, in many cases bordering obsession, around ascending to the fifth dimension. When I would gently mention was we would pass through the fifth, but the grander plan for humanity is to ascend to the seventh, I was vigorously corrected. I never took it personally – it just made me smile.

One of the qualities of the Council of Love is the information they share is always way ahead of the curve. It's an ego thing – after all the information isn't mine, it's theirs, it's yours. Over the years, the time lag has shortened from twenty to ten to five years and now is almost in alignment but not quite. Sometimes there is still a time difference of a year or two. The time lag was why the Council resonated with some people but not for others. When folks didn't want to hear about the seventh dimension, I didn't stop talking about it. The Council certainly didn't stop channeling about it, but I did downplay it. I took that stance through guidance because the COL always guided to "focus on the love, the rest will follow."

In the Council classes and gatherings, when this subject of what dimension are we going, my consistent response was I wouldn't engage in interdimensional wars. It almost became an inside joke because folks knew this was my standard answer. It diffused the energy of someone being right or wrong. It diffused the energy of duality-polarity. The Council's guidance was, as always: Focus on the love, everything else will follow.

When the strong energy of ascension to the fifth became akin to a tsunami, I sought guidance. A huge issue for me has always been to never misguide people. I know there is free will, and plans change, but my personal bugbear – hence the promise I have from the Council – is they will never misguide me or you. That is our soul agreement, part of the contract I struck in being their channel. Over the years there have been situations when things have not come to pass. What I have learned is to step back, observe and wait, because if the Council has been consistent in its unchanging message. I've learned, and continue to learn patience, in active understanding the company of heaven isn't in a rush and, they don't make mistakes. They will allow us our spiritual scenic tour if that is what we choose. Then, when the time is right, the unfoldment will occur. I have witnessed this time and again, and the gift in that is it has built a huge reservoir of trust within me.

In seeking guidance on the fifth versus the seventh dimension debate the Council's guidance once again was consistent: focus on the love, the rest will follow. What strikes me as hilarious as I am writing this is the realization that in all likelihood I was the only person on Earth having this debate. I was the only one saying, wait we're going to the seventh. No one cared – even the Council said not to worry because people needed pass through the fifth on the way. My reaction to wanting people to know we were going to the seventh was no different than all those adamant lightworkers who were saying we're going to the fifth. I hope you can share the humor of this, as well as the understand the human patterns this reflects.

Part of my sense of urgency to share the good news about ascending to the seventh also was my preconceptions about the fifth dimension. When Albert Einstein began talking to me about dimensions in 2004, it opened up a whole new world. His descriptions of each dimension, their qualities and purpose, allowed me to understand dimensional reality in ways I had never considered. But as always, there was more than the initial description. There is always more.

When Einstein first described the fifth dimension he described it as the dimension of change. The first experience I had visiting the fifth was being caught in those old-fashioned department store revolving doors. I would go through the door once and the world, reality, would look one way. I would blink and everything had changed. I would blink again and everything, the landscape, the people, the energy, had changed again. To me this was not only nerve-wracking but crazy-making; this was not a place I wanted to be, let alone anchor. My ability to shift, maneuver and change that fast was not within me; it was extremely anxiety provoking. I did not feel that this was anywhere I ever wanted to go, not even for the briefest blink of an eye. Part of that rapid change was because of the difference in the experience of time and dimensions. Regardless of the time issue, my reaction when everyone was so excited to be ascending into the fifth dimension was a modified horror. I wondered why they wanted to go there and thought: "you don't know what you are getting into."

But, as the Council has taught, there is always more. Even when we think we have the complete picture, part of the excitement of breathing is the knowing there is always more. The universe is bigger, more magnificent, more magical than we can imagine. So it is with our understanding with dimensional reality. The information on the qualities of each dimension has grown, and our comprehension of how we exist within that dimension has not only expanded, but exploded.

A key component of the New You is the discernment that we are interdimensional, multidimensional, trans-dimensional beings. We are not uni-dimensional, we never were. The restrictive belief we are only capable of existing in one dimension at a time is a third dimensional false grid. Part of the limiting nature of the human false grids, built up over millions of years, was the belief that we are not only limited to one dimension but through good works and behavior, we graduate from one dimensional reality to the next. This false belief has reinforced our sense of not being worthy, not being loved, not ever being quite good enough.

The initial descriptions of the 13th Octave define the realm of human experience as having twelve dimensions and within each of those dimensions twelve planes or levels. That is why the 13th Octave is such a gift; it is beyond what has ever been available to us while in human form. The Council has never indicated that the realm of human experience was restricted to the third, fourth or fifth dimension. While they have guided that we will anchor and live in the seventh dimension of Christ consciousness of love, they have consistently spoken of the twelve dimensions. The fullness of this information has only come into understanding with the bringing forth of the New You.

Let's begin our exploration of this incredible idea and state of being interdimensional.

We have spent time discovering and embracing the various ways in which we are known and manifest throughout the universe – your ray, soul color, chakra centers, soul mission and purpose. You've embraced your Stranger, and begun to adopt the approach of conceiving of yourself, your very being, in multiple ways rather than just within the scope of one transition or pathway. As we continue our New You journey, the purpose is not to stop, not even to slow down, but rather continue the expansion. Expanding in a myriad of miraculous ways we can't fathom at this juncture, conceiving yourself as an integral part of the Mother's infinite becoming. The New You is not limited in any way. Therefore, neither should your self-concept be limited. Don't you just feel your hackles go up when someone (and usually someone who doesn't know you well) tries to define you as this or that? You are not apples to be cored and quartered – you are the whole tree – the whole orchard – the whole farm.

Our next step together is to meet, examine and embrace our interdimensional selves. Part of the paradigm of the old third dimension was to box us up into patterns of limitation; to make us believe that we were fixed rather than fluid. This has been one of the strongest elements of that reality – we are bound to the human definition of the third dimension constructed with and under the very confines of that dimensional paradigm. Does that make any sense in any reality?

The third dimension has been beaten like the proverbial dead horse. Nevertheless, let us look at what we mean when we are talking about the old third. The Council differentiates between the old third and the new clean third dimension. The old third has been held hostage by these false grids of lack, limitation, duality, polarity, death, disease, greed, control, and so on. Because the process of embracing your interdimensional self is deeply related to the elimination of these old grids, the next chapter focuses extensively on those releases. Releasing is key to our ascension process, and if at any point you feel the need to jump ahead to the next chapter do so. This foundation process of understanding and integrating your interdimensional self will bring up many old false grids for release. Walking through that into the lightness that remains is well worth the effort – and remember, you don't do so alone, ever.

One of the misconceptions is we think (emphasis on mental body) we are in, or belong to this or that dimension. It is only very recently we have begun to think of ourselves as inter-, multi-, or trans-dimensional beings. Even within that expanded understanding, the focus has primarily been on moving from the old third to the fifth and then onward to the seventh and above. The Council's guidance is to set that aside and broaden our perspective. This is not only mind-blowing but fun. Everything you do needs to be fun, joyous and expansive. Don't worry about whether or not you can do this – if you weren't ready for this next step, the Council wouldn't be madly typing here at my computer.

While there has been a great deal written about the fourth and fifth dimensions, particularly in the last couple of years, for our purposes under the tutelage of the Council of Love, we are going to look at dimensions as defined and expanded upon by Albert Einstein. Einstein, who wishes to complete his work on Earth, points out that we have an incomplete understanding of dimensions. That's because our definitions are caught up in the linear time, space, and depth definitions of the old third dimension. What Einstein teaches is, rather than the restrictions of physical form, we should think of the dimensions as qualities and opportunities to learn or experience different things. When you consider one of the primary gifts of the New You is creation, and working with the creation triad, you will begin to sense the tie-in – the beautiful patterning of creation.

Prior to discussing the specifics of each dimension along with the highlights and qualities you can and will experience within each, it is important to reflect on the who, what, when, where, why and how of the interdimensional you.

The New You is an interdimensional being capable and consistently accessing all twelve dimensional realities with ease and grace. This expansion is possible because humanity is now anchored in a new dimensional reality with Gaia ascending and anchoring in the fifth dimension. It is not necessarily a new feature of being human but rather a return to original design and patterning. Humans were always intended, within the plan of the Divine Mother, to have access to the full realm of human experience, to be able to shift, experience and change dimensions at will. You do this to know the fullness of your being, and to bring back and anchor those qualities and capacities of other dimensions that assist you not only in completing your journey of this life but of creating Nova Earth.

Not only is traveling and anchoring in other dimensions more fun than a barrel of monkeys, it is pivotal to who you are. Your soul contract, your mission and purpose entail this expansion of being able to go and know the joy of other realities and vibrations; of being able to access exactly what you desire in terms of your unique creations. You were never intended to be stuck in one dimensional reality; that is old thinking and it is not the truth of who you are. By staying in that paradigm of limitation you are not only injuring yourself, you are denying your ability to assist a multitude of others through the portal of ascension.

Well into our New You webinar series with the courageous band of re-patterners, the question arose on how one achieves this dimensional shift. While the circle was more than willing to engage in this interdimensional hopscotch, some had difficulty with the practical how-to. As the group facilitator, I was some-what embarrassed; the how-to had never occurred to me. My limited direction to the circle had simply been "go." The how-to is an intentional exercise. As always, anchor in your heart; go to the 13th Octave; anchor in Gaia; call in your guides and the Mighty Ones (the archangels); and send yourself. From the core of your being, in a meditative state, send yourself to where you wish to go in that landscape of the twelve dimensions. This is not undertaken with a sense of being burdened, it is more akin to, jump in, the water's fine.

During the course of writing this chapter the information shared by Einstein and the Council has expanded. String theory and the existence of eleven dimensions now has popular accep-tance within the scientific community. What Einstein and the quantum physicists agree upon, is that all the dimensions exist simultaneously within what we experience as the third dimen-sion. What Einstein points out is the twelve dimensions don't exist in some far off realm that we have to physically travel to. Rather it is in a continuum that exist all around us. The twelve dimensions are part of the warp and weave of our environment, the air we breathe, and the space we occupy. When we talk about sending ourselves to the various dimensions, the guidance is not to leave your physical body or the third, so much as to shift your consciousness to allow your perception of the other dimensions to emerge. It is allowing yourself to bi-locate without physically moving, so that you have not only a spiritual experience but a physical one as well. In this way you are facilitating the anchor-ing of the qualities and experiences into you're here-and-now physical reality.

Time and space have a different form of existence and mea-surement in different dimensions. Sending yourself to the vari-ous dimensions is a form of bi-location while at the same time playing with time, expanding and contracting time in this physi-cal reality so that it accommodates you, rather than vice-versa which has been the rule of thumb in the old third. Sending your-self to an alternate dimension also relies upon you anchoring in your heart, knowing the truth of Universal Law; knowing everything that exists in the greater universe also exists within you. You fully and completely exist and actively participate in the outer reality. There is no barrier other than old forms of thought that bar you from being able to send yourself, within and without, Let go of the belief system that dictates your beingness, the molecules of your sacred self cannot travel and simultaneously be in more than one place at once. Let go of those false grids that rob you of the joy of this experience.

While many of the exercises of anchoring the New You involve guided meditations, downloads and activations, this portion of the journey does not, simply because the incredible journey you are about to embark on can't be proscribed. It is unique and individual. While there are similarities in what is experienced in each dimension, the texture, colors, location and interactions are and will be unique to you.

I don't want to leave you stranded attempting to grasp such an amorphous concept. Therefore, I include here the download of the Cities of Light meditation which guides you through an interdimensional experience, in order that you can have the incredible and joyous experience of travelling interdimensionally.

(LISTEN TO THE "CITIES OF LIGHT" AUDIO MEDITATION)

The sacred purpose of your traveling interdimensionally is not about you going and observing what is transpiring. It is about you discovering, and then becoming familiar with yourself in that dimensional reality. It is not about being the observer or voyeur. It is about grasping and accessing the fullness of you. The why of this exercise is the expansion of you, of your being able to access that which you desire and elements you require in your creation work in the dimensional reality in which you live. In some ways this is hard to get your head around; it is another brand new concept.

For example: Perhaps your mission and purpose in this life is being a keeper of the hearth; keeper of the heart. Usually this entails working with Gaia and bringing people's heart's to a place of acknowledging, accepting, giving and receiving love so Gaia becomes the planet she always intended to be. For many, the role of keeper of the hearth also involves working in the building and unfolding of the Cities of Light. In order to do that, you may choose to visit the tenth dimension of beauty. We instinctively know these new cities are remarkably beautiful, so it makes sense for you to visit yourself in the home of beauty; those beautiful Cities of Light. Travelling interdimensionally means you are moving through time and space, as well.

Once you have gathered the information, the vision and energy of what you need, you send yourself back to where you came from, to where your primary self is anchored. You bring back with you that which you deem helpful at this point in your creation process. Be clear, you bring back so much more – wisdom, vision, and expansion; but on the practical how-to level, you bring back the next building blocks for your journey.

Out of all the pieces of the New You journey, this acceptance of your interdimensional self is the most challenging; with the clearing of false grids and identifying of the core issue being a close second. On a very primal level, embracing ourselves as multidimensional is a fundamental departure from how we have defined ourselves, not only in this life but for thousands of years. It is a difficult belief system to let go of – but the reward of flying free is well worth it! We may not always like the third dimension but it has given us very clear parameters of who we are and how we operate. Because we have accepted those definitions and limitations as real, that framework has made us feel safe. Now you are being asked to throw off the shackles of limitation and send yourself out into the universe; to realize and accept what we thought were cement walls between the dimensions are as penetrable as air. We are adjusting to the new normal, realizing that we are invited to consciously flow between the dimensions with ease and grace. It's one of the most exciting qualities of the New You.

Now that we have discussed the five W's, we are going to spend time looking at the qualities and elements of each dimension, sharing insights from the Council and what myself and others have observed and experienced in this adventure of discovery. The most significant part of this journey of interdimensional discovery depends on you. It is up to you to take the time to meditate and travel, to discover who you are in the other dimensions, what are the offerings elsewhere, and, what you experience. It is not a matter of simply saying "Okay, I'm interdimensional." It's putting it into form and action. It's using this incredible gift to create.

A good idea is to jot down a few notes after you return from a dimensional journey because what you are doing is building your unique library. Do not hesitate to send yourself off to the far reaches of whatever level and dimension you select. Make no mistake about it – not only is this possible but you will have no difficulty differentiating one dimension, or even levels within a dimension from another, once you have the hang of this process.

The twelve dimensions are discussed in detail in *The Great Awakening* on pages forty-one through fifty-four, but for ease and simplicity that information will be included and expanded upon in this chapter. I recommend you read, and digest, or re-digest, this information on the various dimensions prior to beginning this exercise.

Again, the purpose of this exercise is not only to expand and explore your interdimensional self but to anchor that experience, knowing and comfort in your expanded New You. It is about anchoring and truly knowing yourself in all dimensions and realities – in each of the twelve planes of each of the twelve dimensions – a big order? You bet! Are you up to it? You bet!

For reasons of clarity, practicality, brevity and accessibility I am going to outline the suggested exploration of your interdimensional self.

Every day take a maximum of two of the dimensions, starting sequentially at the first dimension, and explore who you are in that reality. Not who you might have been – not what aspects are lurking there – but who you are – how you exhibit, how you experience, how you feel. I am going to select a couple of dimensions to use as examples so you understand what the COL is getting at.

The approach you take for finding and coming to know yourself in each of these dimensions is consistent with our other meditations and explorations. Relax, anchor in your heart followed by anchoring in the 13th Octave and the heart of Gaia. Express your intent (prayer) to experience this interdimensional journey; allow your mind to drift. Be the observer – do not attach to any one vision or experience – this is information and expansion. Stopping to analyze, agree or disagree, merely halts the process. The format I've chosen is first, we will review the definition channeled by Albert Einstein; discuss the purpose of exploring that particular dimension, and share the insights and impressions of those who have undertaken this journey before you. What we have learned through the New You webinar series is, there is a remarkable similarity of experiences in terms of the description and texture of each dimension.

It is important you keep in mind that, while the dimensions have been divided up for purposes of discussion, the flow between the dimensions is fluid and there is bleed-through between dimensions as well.

FIRST DIMENSION: NO CLASSIFIED FORM; BIRTHPLACE OF IDEAS

Qualities of humility and prudence.

Entry into the first dimension is incredible. It is akin to entering the void. Although there is no tangible form or sense of time, the concepts floating around can often be perceived as black or shadowy. The ideas, while observable, do not have any distinguishable form. The first dimension is an infinite cocoon of creation, the void of immense black or darkness, the infinite chamber of creation and expansion.

The first dimension is so underrated and misunderstood. This is the dimension that is the beginning and the end of our human experience. There is nothing in the realm of human reality or experience that does not begin with an idea, a concept. The idea is the blueprint, the design of what is to come into form. That includes the idea of each of us, the original blueprint, idea and design of our unique expression of God. When you understand that, it seems inconceivable you would not want to spend more time in the first dimension, exploring not only the idea of you, but infinite sea of ideas of what is, has been and will be.

The first and second dimension are often dismissed as being lower or less than the other dimensions. Nothing can be further than the truth. Consider it this way. The first dimension is the environment where ideas are born, prior to assuming form. It is the place the ideas of the Divine Mother are seeded onto the planet. There is an unsullied purity to the place where ideas are born, including the idea of you.

Albert Einstein defines the first dimension as "amorphous, having no defined or classified form." Believe it or not, ideas fall into this categorization. Ideas are simply a chemical electro-magnetic event. Ideas have no form until such time as they are brought into action and form. You have an experience of this dimension when you are brain-storming or free-associating, letting ideas move and circulate throughout the interdimensional field. That is why so often there are similar concepts or scientific discoveries at the same time. It is from this place that the understanding of the one-hundreth monkey emerges. Both the first and second dimensions hold the qualities of humility and prudence.

The first dimension is the perfect place to start your journey of interdimensional discovery, as it is not only your birthplace but the birthplace of everything that exists in physical form on Earth. The first dimension has no classified form, it is a dimensional reality defined only by ideas. Your journey into the first is your opportunity to discover your core self – the beginning of who you are. During your preparation phase, ask to learn, understand and fully integrate what the idea of your unique self is. What is the idea, the elements, and the uniqueness of your spark of light, of your sheer energy?

While most of us don't like being pigeonholed or classified by others, we tend to define ourselves as more than merely an idea. Yet isn't that where it all starts?

What is the core idea of who you are – not in this life but as your true expanded infinite self? While you have markers to show you hints of this – your soul color, your mission and purpose – those markers do not divulge your entire story. Aren't you curious to know your entire story? What was the idea that started you in the first place? What was the prime motivator?

It is not sufficient to say, "I came to serve the Mother or Archangel Michael," or "I am a healer." Those are expressions of the idea. You're going back further than that. What is your idea essence – and what does it feel like to float in that essence, to re-unite with that essence?

Take time to explore the beauty and reality of the dimension of ideas, of consciousness bringing forth form. There is no emotion in the first dimension. But, I guarantee there is an immense sense of wonder. Luxuriate in the black velvet cocoon of creation. Return to the first time and time again, understanding that ideas are never stagnant – they grow, morph, transform and become, just as you do.

SECOND DIMENSION: FLAT SPATIAL – NO DEPTH; ABILITY TO MUTATE AND GROW

Qualities of co-operation and surrender.

The second dimension is a bridge dimension, the place where ideas begin to mutate into form. While the first dimension is usually experienced as black, the second dimension is more gray often accompanied by flashing lights or orbs and geometric forms, especially circles. What's exciting about the second dimension is you are able to begin to see how the evolution into form is taking place – what a gift!

Einstein describes the second dimension as having "an aspect of flat spatial extent, meaning that there is no depth and therefore often not perceived by the human eyes." The quality of this dimension is the ability to mutate, grow and evolve from one amorphous mass into another and so on. These are often micro-organisms, virus or bacteria, such as a common cold. Cancer also falls into this dimension – evolving from a cell and often mutating into a tumor or growth. Usually the life form of the second dimension is only observable under a microscope – but the presence of this life form is clearly evidenced both in nature and within your physical bodies. This dimension teaches inter-dependence as life forms are dependent upon a host whether it is a human form, air, water and so on.

He says: "There are many life forms that inhabit this uni-verse who are of this nature, popping in and out depending on whether they are facing you or not. Not many of them inhabit your planet, but one example is of the Serros who feed energeti-cally upon humans. This is not a malign activity but simply an interdependence that one life form must attach to another in order to survive. The quality of this life form, similar to the first dimension, is that there is no experience of emotion. It is learn-ing to simply be in form and learn interdependence without the presence of emotion.

"What many of the scientists are defining in String Theory is the other eleven dimensions are in fact aspects of the twelve planes of this dimension. They have not yet made the quantum leap to understanding that dimensions are not defined by physi-cality but by qualities of growth."

I confess the second dimension has never been my favorite place – probably because of the "C" word. I never felt I had a full grasp of its mission and purpose. As I began working with the New You energies, information came rushing in, the explana-tion and understanding erasing my prejudice. How could one dimension possibly be better or worse than another – and yet isn't that what so many of us feel? Haven't we consciously, sub-consciously, unconsciously felt that the higher dimensions are somehow preferable, rather than simply part of the magnificent continuum of the Universe?

The Council helped me remember how viruses work, by spreading like wildfire. The energy of the second dimension is passing on information, energetic DNA as it were. When we have emanated from the heart of One we have originally come as an idea, which we often refer to as a spark of light, but really we are an idea, an essence. In the second dimension this energy is communicated out to the multiverse. In other words, long before that information of whom we are takes form in the third, our essence is out there doing its work – spreading its energy. The second dimension is an amplifier and a transmuter, assisting us to travel from idea into the form of the third. What appears to be a very quiet dimension of having no depth is in fact a very creative and busy place!

While in the second dimension it is not unusual to see strands of DNA, which appear as dark floating energy streamers. When you locate yours, take time to examine these DNA streamers because it is also the opportunity to recode some of your DNA should that be desirable. There is no emotion in the second dimension but plenty of thought patterns emerging from the ideas of the first. This situation presents an opportunity to examine some of your thought patterns without being emotionally attached and to change what is not of love, purity of grace.

One of the key elements of the second dimension is the quality of interdependence and co-creation. Viruses, even in the form of ideas, cannot exist in isolation; they will die. One of the most serious shortcomings of the current reality of human existence is we have forgotten and consciously placed aside this essential component of interdependence. We cry in the loneliness of our isolation, the illusion of separation, and yet all we really have to do is go back to the second dimension and re-connect, remember that all things, all energy are simply one – supporting and without emotion, co-operating and creating the next step, the New You.

It is commonplace in our virtual world to see an idea, a story, an idea go viral. How do you think this is different than the second dimension? It isn't. When you have an idea, concept or position that you want to share with the world, go to the second dimension, gather that energy, feel yourself offering it up to the planet and watch it fly!

THIRD DIMENSION: PHYSICALITY – LENGTH, WIDTH, DEPTH. ABILITY TO EMBRACE ALL DIMENSIONS AND REALITIES.

Quality of free choice.

The third dimension was created by the Divine Mother as a place for her sweet angels to have a place to play. It's a place to experience physicality, and to be able to jump in and out of form at will. The "clean" third dimension is an incredible place to be; think of Gaia as her pristine self. In the third dimension, we have the blessing of our five senses plus the knowing of who we are, as well as the ability to travel between dimensions and create in concert with the Divine. The unique quality of free will is the golden gift granted to this dimension. In other realities choice is either not an option or doesn't exist.

The COL refers to as the old third dimension as a hologram which is fading quickly. That is why the frustration and anxiety level of so many people who are not fully aware of the shift that is transpiring is so strong. They are yearning to grasp and hold on to an old illusion which is no longer in existence. That creates tremendous internal chaos, which in turn is catalyzing release. All of this is necessary to being able to fully enjoy the authentic third dimensional reality of such beauty and fun.

The gifts of the third dimension are plentiful. All you need do to experience these gifts is open your eyes, breathe the sweetness of Gaia's breath, sip the liquid water of light, feel the breeze of freedom on your cheeks. There was a time in Middle Earth when this essence and beauty of the physical experience of form was deeply appreciated and experienced to the fullest. That was lost as the false grids and paradigms of humanity gained power and hold over the collective's psyches. But that hold is vanishing, the old third is being seen as an illusion. So visit the new third and discover, explore and enjoy the beauty of this beautiful planet and all her wonders and inhabitants.

Einstein explains the third dimension "as defined by the quality of the perception or experience of physicality – meaning that the universe is perceived through the experience of length, width, depth. But the growth quality is the ability to embrace all dimensions, realities, emotion and spirit."

It also has the unique quality of freedom of choice. All of the numerically higher dimensions have the opportunity to exhibit in the third. The growth opportunity and quality of the third is the ability to choose to expand beyond the mere perception of physicality, and, incorporate all aspects of self.

This is what the Universal Mother talks about when she is discussing incorporating all aspects of self. The third dimension is not limited by the time-space continuum, it merely appears to be. The challenge and the opportunity in the third, is to reach beyond physical appearances. It is the realization that you are not limited to one dimension or reality. Your options and choices are unlimited. The shift is changing from a paradigm of duality and polarity of win-lose to win-win.

FOURTH DIMENSION: MAGIC AND ALCHEMY; TRANSFORMATION, TRANSMUTATION AND TRANSUBSTANTIATION

Qualities of wonder, awe, acceptance.

Magic has always been a part of Earth and the human experience. During the time of Lemuria, Atlantis, and Middle Earth, the ability to transmute energy from one form into another was a given. The quality of being one with nature, with Gaia, allowed us to move and experience Earth in miraculous ways that were thought of as completely normal. With the desire to control, manipulate and hate, that quality of participation, of interconnectedness and interdependence, was lost. We separated ourselves from the kingdoms, from the other species who live on this planet. We isolated ourselves and handcuffed our creativity with ego.

Most people yearn for magic, and when it happens in their lives it infuses excitement, a sense of special wholeness, and a deep desire for more. Our essential being knows that magic and alchemy are part of our essence and design. That is why so many of us are fascinated by magicians or what appears to be magical. It was what Jesus taught, reminding and demonstrating when he changed water into wine, created food for the multitudes, and healed the sick. Yeshua was showing us what we are capable of, and what we had forgotten. He was sharing from his heart and showing us what was completely possible.

We love magic because it reminds us of what is possible, of some piece of ourselves that we have misplaced. We dismiss it because our egos become threatened and believe it is losing control. Now it is time to reclaim that ability to transform and transmute, to play with particles of energy to create what is of wholeness and love; what is of joy and peace; what is of our original design, our idea.

Stepping into the fourth dimension feels magical. There are twinkling colors flashing, hues of rainbows color the air and assume magnificent patterns, golden sparkles light up the atmosphere. You can taste the magic; feel the alchemy and presence not only of the elements but the elementals – fairies, divas, leprechauns, sprites and those we no longer remember the names of. Through the pattern of joy and sense of endless possibility don't be surprised to see unicorns flying. The presence of the animal kingdom is strong in the fourth dimension, so remember to bring those renewed connections back into your current self.

The fourth dimension is defined by Albert Einstein as holding "the quality of magic, what many of you think of as alchemy. It is the growth into the realization and action of being an agent for transformation, transmutation and transubstantiation. This dimension is very easily accessible from your third, and is witnessed continually by living masters, divas, fairies, elementals and so on. It is important for you to realize that once you have anchored this growth component within yourself, i.e., once you have anchored the fourth dimension lessons and growth within your being, these beings and abilities will be not only visible, but commonplace. An everyday human example of this dimension, and one which bothered me throughout my human life, was the splitting of the atom. What you think of as science is often simply operating within this dimension."

Throughout our interdimensional journey, it is important for you to explore who you are in the fourth dimension. Who is your alchemist, and your magician? What are the qualities that you can access and activate? Many of have been magicians (a widely misunderstood term) in past lives. In this life we often avoid or deny our alchemist or magician because we have been tortured, ostracized or murdered for our practices in other lifetimes.

Whether you have chosen to acknowledge your ability to create alchemy or magic in this lifetime is not relevant. Whether you are attracted to fairies, elementals, devas is not relevant. If you have strong memories of lifetimes as a shaman, healer or magician, it is not relevant. The only thing that counts is there is a "you" existing in the fourth dimension to show you how to work with the elements and create your life and Nova Earth. So access, explore and integrate. And take notes; accept, celebrate and share the magic.

One way you will know that you have integrated and brought back the fourth dimensional energy to the renewed third is that you will experience the physicality of the third differently. Do not be surprised when you hear the animals chatting with you; the birds bringing news, the trees embracing you, and the grass singing beneath your feet. Welcome the fairies and your star brothers and sisters. Don't dismiss this as your imagination, it is part of the New You reality, and it is fabulous.

FIFTH DIMENSION: ABILITY TO MANAGE AND MANIPULATE CHANGE, INTERNALLY AND EXTERNALLY. NECESSARY FOR INTEGRATING THE QUALITIES OF THE HIGHER DIMENSIONS

Qualities of patience, stamina, humor and wisdom.

Going to the fifth dimension is a literal quantum leap in consciousness. Perceptually, the first thing you notice is the clarity of physicality, of Gaia and of everything on her. It is like looking in a perfectly crystal clear stream; everything is immaculate and pure, clear and revealing of each grain of sand, each tadpole or minnow, each rock. The water does not blur the vision of what's on the bottom of the stream – if anything it magnifies and clarifies. It is pristine and beautiful. Each element is clear and clean and yet the inter-connectedness to every other element is a given, beyond thought or emotion.

When you enter the fifth dimension you notice a distinct shift in your consciousness. You immediately feel more present. You are able to perceive not only your sweet self but others, environments and situations with unblemished clarity. There is no residue of the patterns of fault, blame, guilt or shame from the old third dimension. You know your own uniqueness while simultaneously knowing your connectedness to all. Many lightworkers refer to the energy of the fifth as unity consciousness. While unity, if allowed and recognized, flows through all of the dimensions, it is in the fifth that you become consciously aware of it and adopt it as an operating precept.

Einstein tells us that the fifth dimension is "a growth opportunity insofar as it is the ability to cope, create, manage and manipulate change. In the fifth dimension change is constant. The rationale behind this is that the being is learning how to deal with and create change. It is the precursor to creation. You live in an infinite universe, one that is constantly in the process of change and growth. If you are not able to manage change internally and externally then you cannot incorporate the qualities of the higher dimensions with grace. Therefore the growth aspect of the fifth is the ability to move through change, manipulating it in ways that are loving, kind, considerate of self and the collective, and respectful of the grander plan of unfoldment.

"There has been a great deal of discussion about the Earth, Terra Gaia, moving into the fifth dimension. This speaks to a fundamental misunderstanding of the quality of dimensions. The dimensions are not fixed points on a compass. They are a circle dancing, moving and expanding constantly. There is constant movement within and between all dimensions – they are fluid. The planet, animal and human kingdoms collectively have been intensely learning the lessons of constant change. What do you think the explosion in technology, human advances and thinking has been about? The human community has managed enormous change in the past few hundred years. No, not always well or wisely but that is the nature of the dimension – it offers the opportunity to learn the growth lessons of that dimension. Gaia which operates at a very different frequency and time/space continuum from humans has conquered the lessons of change eons ago. So have most of the other kingdoms.

"So when there is discussion about moving from one dimension to another, simply think of it as moving from one classroom to another, passing from one grade to another, while understanding that sometimes you have to go back and review basic principles in order to remind yourself what you learned and forgot. You do not eliminate the spatial and time continuum because you are moving interdimensionally. You are expanding yourself while remaining in the form and expression of the third dimension.

"The qualities of growth that occur as part of the shifting in and through the fifth dimension are patience, stamina, humor, and wisdom that the more things change the more they are constant. Love and joy are constants. Why would you think these blessings and qualities are the exclusive purview of the third dimension? That is truly of human ego."

The fifth dimension is now the heart-anchoring portal for Gaia, and therefore for everything upon her, including the human collective. It is not physically possible for us to be anchored on Gaia and not have our feet firmly planted in the fifth. However, the energy of Gaia and her size, physically and spiritually, is enormous. Gaia currently brushes the upper levels of the new third and the seventh. Hence all of us, consciously or not, are experiencing several dimensional realities at once. One of the reasons why people are confused about whether they are in the third, fourth or fifth dimension is because they still have physicality. The mindset that physicality is only experienced in the third dimension is deeply entrenched. But that simply is not so.

The fifth dimensional experience is consistently reported as having very strong cosmos energy; a massive, warm, comfortable and connected energy field. The sense of expansion of shifting from planetary to universal is apparent. Many feel a sense of weightlessness and the feeling of no gravity although it is not floating aimlessly throughout space. My sense and guidance is that the ballast of the old third was so strong the absence of that energy makes one feel as if there is no gravity. It is certain the physical laws of the third are not the same as the fifth. The air, water and earth are clean – not cleansed but clean and sparkling as in the original design. Substance and material form have a different sensation. Space ships, especially rainbow ships, are seen as a regular occurrence. One is able to see what has always been there, observe what has always been around us and more importantly understand it and the ultimate connection to the larger plan of the Mother.

One sweet angel of the New You webinar series who has since left the planet described the experience in this way: "I am a symphony of vibrations, sounds, colors, manifesting sacred geometry, always changing, and transforming myself and all around me." A beautiful vision and one she went on to fulfill. Godspeed Andreina.

SIXTH DIMENSION: WHERE IDEAS AND BELIEFS MUTATE INTO FORM. ESSENCE OF CREATIVE CHAOS AND OPPORTUNITIES FOR GROWTH. CHAOS AS THE NUCLEUS FOR ACTION AND OUTCOME.

Quality of patience and surrender; understanding that you are not in control.

Entering into the sixth dimension is somewhat akin to landing in Oz. The air is pure and sweet, and filled with orbs of every size and color. Of course, these energy orbs are energetic beings; forms of spiritual sentience who are floating throughout the universe. Many of us have been fortunate enough from time to time to capture pictures of these high energy orbs with our cameras in sacred undertakings or situations. When I was first gifted with this vision, I saw the orbs colliding and popping like the soap bubbles children blow. Then I realized that a primary feature of the sixth is creative chaos – it is the place where ideas and beliefs mutate into form. There is a sense in this dimension of constant change but it is delightful, playful, and magical. Many of the pathfinders of the New You series reported experiencing fireworks in the sixth, and a deep sense of connection to Gaia.

I am one of those people who will do anything to avoid chaos. To me, chaos has been defined in my life as meaning conflict, unresolved issues, indecision, turmoil and a sense that everything is going crazy. How am I going to make everything right and make sense of this mess? Of course that represents an unresolved issue, a misplaced sense of responsibility and a fear of being blamed when things either aren't going right or don't turn out the way we, in our humanness, wanted them to.

Coming to understand and enjoy the sixth dimension is the opportunity to change that perception. In physics, chaos is viewed as an element of the universe that is a creative force. Random elements come together to create something new. Those elements also come together to mutate or destroy one another, again creating something new. What I have come to understand and appreciate is that in many ways the sixth dimension is another bridge dimension, similar to the second. That doesn't mean it does not have its own essence, qualities and delights. What it does mean is that it takes the energies of change from the fifth and works with them in those amazing orbs and constant movement, shifting, expanding and exploding to mutate into the seventh dimension of pure love and Christ consciousness.

The sixth dimension is about becoming – about being the energy orb, seeking out, joining and fusing with energies that will assist you in not only growing for growth's sake but for focused evolution into the totality of your being. One of the primary lessons we learn about the sixth is trust because we are not in control. We are taking a chance, going out on a limb, dancing with those energies and orbs with no guarantee that the outcome is going to be exactly what we thought. It is surrender to ourselves and the universe, realizing there are times to let go, trust and accept we are not solely in charge.

What I witness in the sixth dimension is that the combination of energies in the wondrous bubble orb world has potential for creation far beyond what we know or can imagine. It doesn't operate according to rules or patterns we are familiar with. This is the dimension where mutation, transformation of our dreams and desires can morph into new form. For me, it is also a dimension where I am invited and cajoled into letting the magic happen. It's about learning to dance with the orbs, even if the bubble pops in your face. It's about understanding that we are an element in the creation, a partner, not the control. It is part of our journey that will allow our anchoring in the seventh dimension of love.

Einstein gave us these clues when he described the sixth dimension ages ago: "The sixth dimension is the one my favorite – it is state of being where ideas and belief systems mutate into form. There are many above and below who suggest that the human race is in the process of experiencing the growth opportunities of the sixth. When we say chaos we speak of it in terms of creative chaos – for in every chaotic situation – whether it is internal such as cancer or external such as war or societal breakdown, there is an opportunity for growth. Often you have heard me speak of the process of implosion/explosion of creation. Chaos is the nucleus for that action and outcome. It can be beautiful and magnificent – think of it as the Big Bang, think of it as the birth of a solar system."

The biggest opportunity for growth of the sixth dimension is the understanding that you are not in control. It brings with it the growth of the qualities of surrender, trust, fortitude and hope. It is the ability to acknowledge that seemingly random chaos has a Divine patterning. It teaches the lessons of reaping what you sow. It brings forth a profound appreciation of the gift of the unknown.

SEVENTH DIMENSION: CHRIST CONSCIOUSNESS; STATE OF HEART AND LOVE; PLACE WHERE YOU CAN ANCHOR (ELECTRIC) ABOVE AND BELOW (MAGNETIC)

Qualities of allowing, being, love and acceptance.

Einstein's description of the seventh is as follows:

"The seventh dimension is known as the dimension of the Christ Consciousness. This is the state of being in the heart and knowing of love. It is the growth opportunity for compassion, kindness, selflessness, honoring and love. When you anchor in this place of consciousness you are fully capable of holding the vibrations, energies, lessons, understandings and growth of all of the twelve dimensions available to you on this planet. It is the gentle allowing state of being that permits expansion and incorporation of your entire original blueprint, soul design – what you think of as your universal or higher self, your angelic self, or your over-soul.

"If you think of the seventh dimension in terms of the electro-magnetic field that governs your planet, it allows you the capacity to incorporate the electric nature of the energy, patterning and lessons of the first six dimensions, and, the magnetic energy pull of the eighth through twelfth dimensions. You can think of the seventh dimension as the place of stillpoint where all energies anchor and flourish. It can be the place of intersection of All. It is the most natural and comfortable dimension for human beings because it is not only peaceful but feels like home to most. It is the state of being in perfect balance, of simply being. While many dimensions involve action, this is more a state of allowing. Because it is an intersection, it carries the growth lesson of acceptance and acknowledgement of unity and connectedness of all beings, all dimensions, and all life forms."

I have this delicious, ancient memory of being in the Garden of Gethsemane with Yeshua. It was a beautiful place, peaceful, fragrant and filled with the sweetness of Gaia. We went there to stroll, chat, listen, to simply be. Sometimes two of us, sometimes many. It was not an unusual thing to hang out in the garden. Next to strolling by the Sea of Galilee, it was one of our favorite places. The garden was quiet and serene, peace was in the air. You could run into people you knew for a pleasant visit or be all alone. I mention this because my sweet memories are not of sorrow regarding the night before Jesus's crucifixion but of very happy joyous times, of living in community with a sense of purpose and knowing of unity, connectedness and love.

When I enter the seventh dimension, the Garden of Gethsemane is often where I find myself, because that is one of my special places, a heart place that is a touchstone and catalyst for what love looks and feels like. It is a physical reminder and sensation of not only the beauty and purity of Gaia but of humanity as well. It is a powerful remembrance of what is possible when love rules. There are also times when I enter into the seventh when I find myself in my own front garden early in the morning just as the sun is rising and the world waking up. There is dew on the grass, the birds are just beginning to say good morning, and the bunnies and frogs are coming to eat the seed and bread I put out every day. Then there are times when I find myself elsewhere – in an alpine meadow, in the Sahara Desert in the moonlight, the red rocks of Sedona, the Blue Beach in Puerto Rico, or my private garden in Atlantis. The key is when we move or send ourselves into the seventh the experience is of untrammeled beauty of Gaia. Many of the original patternmakers of the New You reported being with angels, the halion engineers or beings of sheer energy, having a close sense of being or being with the Dove when in the seventh. The first sensation is of love, activated by the love of the planet or the stars from which we came. There is always a sense of overwhelming peace – that deep outbreath and feeling of, thank God I'm home.

We go to the seventh not only to find our Christ consciousness and the Love, but to remember that we are love – we always have been and always will be. This is the core and purpose of human experience. Not all the dimensions correspond to the thirteen chakras but in this case the seventh dimension is absolutely and irrevocably anchored in the heart chakra. If you are ever in doubt about how to access the seventh or how to find it, go to your heart – and then go deeper.

The guidance of the Council has always been that ultimately the plan of the Divine Mother, Gaia and humanity is that we are ascending into the seventh dimension. Originally, the visual the Council gave us was to picture our heads in the heart of God (13th Octave), our hearts in the seventh and our feet firmly planted in the third. Now of course the visual is to still keep our heads in the 13th Octave, our hearts in the seventh, and anchor our feet and cords firmly in the heart of Gaia in the fifth. In this manner we anchor in the love, keep our feet and bodies in physicality while being free to explore and be in the twelve levels of the twelve dimensions of human experience.

The seventh dimension offers, in my opinion, the greatest gifts and the hardest challenges. Let's be practical – why would you send yourself to the seventh dimension? Theoretically we all want to be enlightened, to be one with love, to be in the Christ consciousness. Or do we? The thought or idea of travelling to the seventh is bound to raise or trigger unresolved issues of self-worth and self-love. If you have not worked with the Council and Archangel Michael to resolve and remove your false grids and illusions then the mere thought of going to the seventh can be terrifying. Why? Because, what if you aren't permitted access? What if you go and are found wanting? What if you go and you don't feel the love – after all hasn't that happened to you tons of times in the old third? Love is what each and every one of us yearns for, and it is the core issue of what we are afraid we will not receive and be. The COL has spent a great deal of time discussing this in the chapter of removing False Grids but do not feel surprised or insufficient if, even as you read this, the thought of the seventh raises some level of unease or discomfort. Simply know there is further yet to go, to release, and I promise you – when you get to the seventh it will be everything you have ever dreamed of and so much more.

One of the primary undertakings of the New You is the creation of sacred union relationships. The primary and most sacred of those relationships is with your sacred self. From that place we move into sacred union with our partners, our family, our friends, our community and on out into the world. Each of us yearns for love, to be and experience love, up close and personal. You go to the seventh to experience the love and to bring it back to your physical reality, to your physical life, to incorporate it in everything you want and do.

EIGHTH DIMENSION: CREATION; MANIPU-LATION OF SUBATOMIC PARTICLES, OF LOVE INTO FORM. MOST CHALLENGING TO AN-CHOR BECAUSE ACCEPTANCE OF CORE POW-ER, WORTH AND ACCEPTANCE OF RESPONSI-BILITY

Qualities of unity and connectedness with One; place of Nova Being; Virtue of Awe.

Einstein has a great deal of insight to share about the eighth dimension. He describes it as carrying the quality of creation. This is the state of being where the manipulation of energy, of my beloved subatomic particles, of the fuel of Love into form – be it process or tangible, is learned. When you have anchored the growth pattern of the eighth, then you have no difficulty in bringing forth your heart desires, and aligned with Source and your universe. Creations not in alignment with the higher self and collective are phantoms manufactured by human ego and not of the sacred nature of the growth patterns of the eighth.

"In many ways, this is the most challenging growth cycle of all. Many travel through this creation dimension again and again; shying away from the energy because it entails use of personal core essence power, and the acceptance of responsibility. This lesson of acceptance for one's creations is an inherent component of this growth cycle. You cannot consistently create and anchor into the third reality without acceptance of this precept. Many shy away from this cycle because they believe it is a sin of hubris to think that they can manipulate atoms. They believe that this is the purview only of the gods. This situation is often present because of flow from past lives, when human ego manufactured painful experiences.

"The qualities of this growth are the understanding of unity with One and All, the ability to fully embrace and participate with God Source. It is an acceptance of your role within the universe, and it is a humble devout vow to abide by the Universal Laws of Creation. It is through the embracing of this growth cycle that the anchoring of Nova Being and the creation of Nova Earth will truly come to pass. The virtue is awe, in deep recognition of the wonder and unlimited potential of the universe and Source."

The eighth dimension extends an invitation to re-engage with our ability to create, and to be on Gaia as the creator race we once were. It is a dimension of both the apprentice and the master. As Einstein points out, many people simply avoid the eighth because of past mis-creations, fear and harsh judgments of past and potential behaviors. Yet, if you don't travel to and embrace "the you" who exists and awaits you in the eighth then you are denying your potential, mission, purpose.

When you go to the eighth dimension it is a learning process, under the guidance of Sanat Kumara, Keeper of Universal Law. It is not a situation (and having said this there are always exceptions) where you pop up into the eighth, figure out what you want to create and bingo it's done. Creation is instantaneous, and as rapid as the splitting of the atom. It takes practice, patience, stamina, and fortitude to know how to harness those energies in ways that are only of love and never of ego. The eighth is where you go and create everything your heart dreams and desires. When you have this energy mastered, it is a snap!

Going to the eighth, bringing the love of the seventh, knowing you carry the magic of the fourth and the mastery of the eleventh is worth every molecule of effort you invest in this undertaking. It is not a burden so much as a familiarity. Do you remember as a child playing pick-up sticks or jacks or any of those hand-eye co-ordination games? How hard it was in the beginning and then when you got it, how it was a piece of cake? That is like learning to work with the creation process, which includes the creation formula, the thirteen blessings and virtues and universal law. You undertake creation from the eighth and bring it back into the physical realm. This is part of your heritage – part of the fun of being alive. As one sweet Anna of the New You group put it: "the eighth is a blank scroll filled with wonder and potential. It is a place of balancing my angelic self within physical reality."

The closest visual experience I have had in visiting the eighth is a guided meditation the Council has channeled called the Accessing the Warehouse of Heaven. Not only does the meditation actually take us to that place of creation but teaches us about choices and responsibilities. I offer it here for you to have this wondrous experience. Do it, enjoy it time and again – it never gets old.

(LISTEN TO THE "WAREHOUSE OF HEAVEN AUDIO MEDITATION)

NINTH DIMENSION: COMPLETION OF CYCLES; ABILITY TO LET GO, REACH RESOLUTION & CONTINUE ON IN JOY INTO THE NEXT REALM OF EXISTENCE. HOME OF TRUTH.

Qualities of joy, truth and surrender.

When I enter the ninth dimension I have the sensation of stepping into an infinite ceiling or dome of blue – the blue of Mother Mary, of a perfect summer day, a blue that calms you, and at the same time makes your mouth water. The sense of expansiveness is phenomenal, yet the dome sensation also makes you feel enclosed, and cocooned in security. The blue is representative of the infinite nurturing of the Mother; the security of her nurturing and reassurance. It also is the truth of Archangel Michael. Many of us have a commitment to both the Divine Mother and Michael – we are of the united legions – and in this way, the ninth beckons to us.

For some of the New You pattern-weavers the ninth dimension brought forward experiences and visitation with the angelic realm, the clarity of Michelangelo's vision of being touched and activated by the hand of God. One of the most beautiful visions shared within the group was the sense of plenitude and completion. That is what the ninth is all about; completion of the old and the continued journey into the new.

Our beloved brother, Albert Einstein, describes the ninth dimension as "the growth pattern which engenders completion." This is often a challenge for human beings. It is the understanding of the pattern of growth for each cycle of life and existence. It is anchored and made manifest in the human being by the ability to let go, to reach resolution, to continue on in joy, to accept, and participate in the unfoldment. The quality of this dimension is truth.

He says, "The growth pattern of this dimension is easily discernible in human beings. The most significant anchoring of this dimension's quality is when a baby is born. They choose, consciously and fully aware, to relinquish their state of angelic freedom to come into form, to continue with a new cycle in order to be of service and have a unique human experience. That momentous event could not take place unless the spirit coming into form had fully embraced the qualities of the ninth. That is what humans so often fail to understand – that the growth patterns of the other dimensions are already present within the third dimension when the child is born. They are as undeniable as the rings on an ancient oak tree – not seen from the outside but present nevertheless. It is the truth of the core essence. The choice in the human third reality is simply whether or not you will allow those qualities to be brought to the surface.

"The same quality is seen in the completion of life – of the ability to resolve and embrace the next chapter of existence. The same is true of the growth patterns of resolution of old patterns, relationships, habits, addictions, and jobs. When you practice completion you are drawing on the energy of the ninth dimension. You are pulling to you the knowledge and patterning of that reality."

One of the things that struck me in my private channeling sessions is how many lightworkers emanate from the ninth dimension. However, in light of this consideration that this is the place of completion and resolution, it makes perfect sense. We are here on our magnificent Gaia to complete the cycle of the old; the cycle of illusion humanity has been trapped in for thousands years. We, the re-patterners and the wayshowers are here to break that cycle, and embrace the infinite. What an enormous sacred undertaking, and what a gift.

Perhaps for that reason, the ninth dimension called out to me when using various dimensional realities as examples for our New You webinar series. I share this exercise because I believe it will enrich your journey of interdimensional you. I also selected it because this dimension is about completion, reaching resolution, making peace with the third, joy and truth, and a whole slew of attributes that are essential to the New You.

So again, by intent and knowing, in the company of the Council and your guides, send yourself to the ninth dimension. Find the you, who is living there. What are they like – what can they integrate into you to help you with this anchoring in your physical form? Letting go is fundamental to growth. We can't carry everything – or everybody. It will wear us down and break us, besides which it is not our job. Remember what Archangel Gabrielle told us, "carrying someone else's burden is highway robbery."

Bring back that knowing into your physical you of this time and place. Anchor the knowing of how to let go; the joy of knowing this journey is about completion. Embrace the excitement of what lies ahead. Anchor the tools, the qualities, and essence of specific to you. Don't be merely an observer. Bring it in. Own it in your conscious heart knowing. And then do it, and bring it into action.

TENTH DIMENSION: BEAUTY, PURITY AND CHARITY – COMPLETE WILLINGNESS TO PARTICIPATE IN THE UNIVERSE.

Qualities of selflessness and generosity.

Each of us has a unique vision of what the perfect picture of sublime beauty looks like. Often it is a composite of places we have seen, paintings, dreams and visions. Even though there are places of phenomenal beauty on Gaia, our vision of perfect beauty is not usually a place we can take someone to and say 'this is it'. That is because our vision is a soul memory of past lives, different planets and different locations and situations on Earth, as well as soul memories of what lies beyond.

The New You webinar participants loved the tenth dimension. It is a very gentle dimensional reality, where ethereal music plays as angels whoosh by, where creative white palaces in the sky can be explored. It is the sensation of a place where beauty reigns, where peonies and tulips blossom and sparking water flows. As one sweet angel put it, the tenth is a "Club Med for angels." The tenth is definitely not to be jumped over. If you are ever feeling grumpy, disillusioned or out of sorts, I strongly encourage you to take a vacation to the tenth – it will heal what ails you.

Einstein teaches us that "the tenth dimension contains the growth patterns of beauty, purity and charity. It is the patterning and state of being in complete willingness to share and participate in and throughout the universe. It is the growth of selflessness and generosity. It is the sense and patterning of understanding, knowing and creating beauty from the purity of heart, soul, being. It is the commitment to be only a reflection of love.

"This is a magnificent dimension few upon the Earth seldom achieve, but which is completely available to each of you to experience. It is so far beyond what you conceive of in terms of tangible human creation and yet is part of the pattern of each and every plant, animal, tree, rock, stream, and molecule of air on your planet. It is part of the essence of Gaia. It is the ability to fully participate with no sense of ego-self. In many ways it embodies the quality of Divine Creation. This is the dimension where angels play."

Each of us have the innate appreciation of beauty, it is part of our physical and spiritual DNA. Far too often the appreciation and love of beauty are for that outside of our selves. What anchoring the qualities of the tenth dimension does is bring an expansion of that appreciation, awe and wonder deeper within as well as expanding our sweet selves. It allows us to consciously anchor and love our beauty, our place in the grandeur of the Mother's creation. In doing so, we expand our appreciation of others and All, and so it grows. Whatever you do, don't rush through your journey to the tenth; visit there often. Beauty, genuine beauty has been unseen in the old third for far too long.

ELEVENTH DIMENSION: MASTERY – FULL EMBRACE OF ALL ABILITIES, KNOWING OF TOTAL SELF AS REFLECTION OF DIVINE. ACCEPTANCE OF SELF AS FULL PARTICIPANT OF GOD. GROWTH PATTERN OF TEACHING, HEALING & CONTRIBUTE.

Qualities of acceptance, joy and the truth of mastery.

Our pal, Einstein, continues with his explanations of dimensional reality.

"The eleventh dimension contains the growth opportunity of mastery. This term is greatly misunderstood upon your planet. What mastery means is the full embrace of all abilities, knowing, talents (of which the human is minor), and of self as reflection of Divine. It is the quiet acceptance of self as participant and reflection of God Source. It is the lesson of letting go of all preconceptions and limitations and becoming a willing participating vessel of One. Now, you begin to see just how fluid the dimensions are – how they work like a formula together, joining together in growth patterns to create something new, old, unique and common. All your master teachers, including Jesus Sananda, emanate from the eleventh dimension. It is a growth pattern that when anchored results in not only the ability but the desire to teach, contribute and heal. The presence of many masters upon the Earth is a wonderful way in which to understand how the qualities of the dimensions are anchored in the third physical life-form."

I don't begin this dimension with a physical description. That's because this reality is so far beyond what we think of as the physical. You will have an experience of arriving in a place of beauty, serenity and expansiveness. The eleventh is beyond physicality, it is the state of mastery and the home of the ascended masters, which of course is why all of us are so eager to send ourselves there. The mere idea of sitting at the feet of Jesus Sananda, St. Germaine, or the Buddha brings tears to our eyes, and longing to our hearts. But this is not a dream. It is a reality that invites you.

The Council, and especially St. Germaine and Archangel Michael, have repeatedly told us that we are on right now Gaia in our mastery. Years ago, the COL used to tease us and say we were M&Ms, a reference to a popular American candy. They referred to us as "masters in the making." But that reference has stopped, and they now beckon us forward to sit, and assume the full anchoring and embrace of our mastery.

The statements regarding our mastery sometimes spark our ego. We feel puffed up and on top of the world. That is not mastery at all, and the temporary sense of arrogance dissipates quickly. Another reaction is the small self, cringing and denying, feeling the impending sin of hubris.

The sending of yourself to the eleventh to meet, anchor and know your mastery is a key component of the New You journey. We love to go there because not only do we come to know ourselves in a whole different light, we get to hang out with those we love, honor, and emulate. However, what also enters into our heart awareness and is transmitted clearly not only from the masters but from our core is that with the acceptance of our mastery comes responsibility. Responsibility for our sacred self, for our planet, for humanity, for the fulfillment of the promises made so long ago. Not to worry, with that sense of responsibility also comes the undeniable knowing of "I can do it." You may not have all the answers or the details, but the knowing of fulfillment and your abilities is deep and unshakeable.

Twelfth Dimension: Joy, Grace & Love; Divine Ecstasy; Quality of Clarity; Incorporates All Eleven Dimensions.

Qualities of grace, joy and love.

The twelfth dimension is the beginning and the end, a place perceived as indescribable beauty; of Mother Mary blue diamond; pink diamond; golden light; vibrant intense colors and the ruby red of the heart of Gaia. A collective perception is of sitting on a rainbow cloud in perfect harmony, peace and knowing of your ability and action of creation.

Our debt of gratitude to Einstein is colossal. His teachings have allowed us to perceive and access realms previously believed to be unreachable. In his description of the twelfth this kindred spirit does not fail.

"The twelfth dimension growth pattern is of joy, grace and love. This is the point of wholeness where there is no need to demonstrate in form. This is a state of being, and the bridge, to the Divine ecstasy. It is the place of arrival, integration and departure from your universe. When you have integrated the growth opportunities of the twelfth dimension you are free to basically travel where you wish. It is the state incorporating all the growth patterns of the other dimensions. It is outside of the time-space continuum."

The twelfth dimension only now brings you to that place of peace of incorporating all dimensions. You find yourself in a situation where a decision is made of whether to stay and complete your mission on Gaia or to return to sheer energy. This is not a gift or dimension accessed casually. There is no sense of judgment, necessity or need – all which is far behind you. What is present is the complete sense of wonder in what is possible, what the human journey can entail. That, my friends, during this time of ascension, is irresistible.

The journey of the interdimensional you is a journey you will access, and draw strength and wisdom from time and time again. This is a life-long practice and gift of the New You. Each dimension gives you information, qualities and understandings you need to complete this wondrous journey in form. So relax, enjoy and return often.

Elimination of False Grids

The release of false grids, which is an integral part of making peace with the third dimension in order to truly leave it behind, is one of the most Herculean challenges of humanity.

A false grid is more than a personal issue or blockage. It is the foundation and construct of the old third dimension. It is the set of beliefs that were the constructs, the operating system, of the old third dimension. When I use the term false grids it calls to mind girders – rusty steel girders that have reinforced the tallest skyscrapers in the world; buried deep within the ground to make the building unshakeable, reinforcing the notion of indestructible. We know, after the tragic experience of 9/11 that no building is indestructible and how rapidly a building can fall down. But while we roam our city streets, we believe these monoliths to be foundational and permanent. The gift of 9/11 is that we also know in our hearts and minds that this is not truth.

I use the example of the destruction of the Twin Towers not for purposes of drama but to demonstrate the magnitude of false grids, and the fact that they can be shattered in a moment. Does the elimination of false grids need to be filled with drama and intrigue and feelings of betrayal? Absolutely not. The analogy is to demonstrate what we thought was solid and indestructible, isn't.

The foundations of the old third has included some very nasty beliefs; false paradigms created by humans who were based not on love but ego. There are also some very beautiful and worthwhile grids of the third dimensions we not only want to preserve but shine up and expand upon. This is not a matter of throwing out the baby with the bath water.

False grids are beliefs come when people are challenged. They simply shake their heads and say, "Well that's the way it is, get used to it"; "you can't fight city hall"; or "you need to learn how to play the game." These clichés have nothing to do with honoring the individual or the collective capacity for goodness and love. These grids are insidious because they're built into the fiber of our societal structure; every aspect of our everyday lives from family to finance, education, politics, and self-worth. There is no area of our lives in the old third that does not contain an element of these false grids.

False grids are nothing new. The Council has been addressing them for a long time. However, with the ascension of Gaia into the fifth dimension, and with part of our ascension process being the elimination of these grids, the urgency and excitement of eliminating them become more pressing. The drive to make peace with the third is what this exercise is about. It is about making peace with yourself and the old, and laying it to rest. The false grids are something we cannot run away from; it is the dragon that must be slayed. It is the task of the re-patterner and the New You warrior. When that dragon is slain, you can embrace the realization that you now live in the world and dimension where the Thirteen Blessings and Virtues are the foundation upon which build your life, and go forward.

The Council tends to classify the false grids in alphabetical categories. The guidance is to present the lists and discuss some of the grids in detail. As soon as you look at the list you will know in your gut the magnitude of what we are tackling. Don't worry. You don't walk alone. Not only is this undertaking under the purview of Archangel Michael, the entire Council also is present – ready, willing and, oh so able to help.

First we will list the grids and then go into detail of how to eliminate and emerge victors of our own destiny. The major false grids, listed in order of priority are:

L – lack, limitation, loss – this includes abandonment, isolation, loneliness and lack of self-worth and self-love, and self-doubt

D – doubt, death, destruction, disease, despair – includes disbelief – the ability to never believe – lack of faith and trust; depression, disgust, disappointment, disillusion

F – fear, fault, blame, anger; self-doubt and denigration can also appear here; failure (this can also be related and found in the fear. Here the COL means a belief that nothing ever works; failure is inevitable.)

G – greed, lust, control; includes abuse of power, jealousy; mercenary or stingy belief and behaviors

C – cruelty (think of people who have had many lives of war or torture), cynicism, critical

E – ego (as king), excess, exclusion

H – hatred, harm and hubris (inappropriate pride and narcissism belongs here)

A – addiction; all addictions are addictions to pain, to the belief system that human existence is meant to be hard, painful and without joy

Almost anything you can imagine can be a false grid. Once you start working with them you will see them popping up all over the place. Before moving into the task of how to further identify false grids and how to eliminate them St. Francis asks to share his perspective on the matter.

"Greetings, I am Francis. Yes you can call me Frank. You can call me friend. You can call me whatever you choose. I am just glad that you are calling me. Welcome my dear friends and welcome to this time of rebirth, reconstruction, reawakening, re-emergence and ascension.

"I speak about the New You which is truly the original you; it is the fulfillment of your divinity, your spark of oneness, the brilliance of your heart and soul, your talents and abilities, your sweetness and your charity in form, in the reality of the human form. This, dear friends, is miraculous. There are so many false grids that have pervaded your planet and lives as you have gone forward in trust and wonder, but also under the cover of false beliefs, false paradigms, values that were not of love and certainly not of truth, hope, charity, and not of the completeness, appreciation and the allowing of you to be you.

"I know this because I have walked as man, as human, and I have struggled just as you have with the release of these false grids. Archangel Michael, the Mother and especially Archangel Gabrielle came to my aid because I did not know what to call them, from whence they came, how deep and pervasive they were, or how to let go of them.

"When I left my life behind and wandered to the country-side seeking purity, friendship, love and community with the birds, beasts, animals, and eventually of my brothers and sisters, in a sense I ran away. I ran away because I felt I had to. In the situation, the society, the structure I was in, I knew I would not discover the truth of my mission, its purpose, and who I was. My very soul demanded it. It did not demand it only in the sense of 'Francis you must do your service and complete your promise to the Mother.' It demanded it in terms of my finding, embracing and embodying joy, peace and reverence, awe, for this journey of One. In that, I also came to learn that joy was found in unity with the kingdoms, with sweet Gaia, with the air, elements and elementals, and with my brothers and sisters of Earth.

"I will help you in this relinquishing of false grids. Some of you say 'Well, my goodness, I have been working on the clear-ing for so long.' But, you really haven't. It may feel that way but there are many layers to this illusion and there are many layers to the collective, and this destruction is part of your role as path-finders and way-showers, gatekeepers, pattern makers.

"You do this not only for your sacred self but for many. Be-cause of that there is a level of intensity, but there is also a level of joy, freedom and awe, because you, dear hearts, are experi-encing what no others on Earth have. You are breaking the way through virgin territory, you are embracing yourself as multidi-mensional/ interdimensional; you have called all parts of your being home and you are allowing that foundation of who you are to now begin to grow, work, expand and become.

"You are courageous, filled with valor and a sense of adven-ture and I, for one, wish and choose to travel with you. Go with my love. Farewell."

No one is exempt from false grids. The clearing that you have undertaken, be it for a day or a decade, has assisted in the lightening of the load but these are collective issues built into the foundation of our collective understanding and definition of what it means to be human.

To identify a false grid is easy. Go to your heart, in reference to your head and emotional body, and simply ask, does this feel like truth? Does this feel like love? Is this a loving, kind, generous thought, belief, or action? Does it contribute to the well-being and balance of myself and the collective? Truth is not illusive, and most certainly the heart knows what love feels like. Even the most ravaged individual knows what love feels like. It is what they most yearn for in the darkness of the night. It is what the soul cries out for.

When we take the moment to pose the questions and listen, the truth is instantly available. Truth and love are part of our internal operating system, it is built into our spiritual and human DNA. It is not something that needs to be analyzed and picked apart. Truth is self-evident. If you find yourself analyzing and picking apart a situation asking yourself 'is this love, is this false grid?' you can rest assured that your ego is at work trying to hide the truth from you. Go back into your heart, call Archangel Michael for assistance, and with outrageous courage allow yourself to discern what is right in front of you.

Recognizing or breaking a false grid is not always a huge event, it can happen in what appears to be a small way, an insignificant event or random thought. One night I was honored to be speaking with God. While I have been a channel for many years, I don't often get to sit down and have a heart to heart with God. S/He came in to discuss this issue of false grids and how to eliminate them. Needless to say, even at three o'clock in the morning, I was in awe. But after a while, my attention seemed to wander, mulling over the issues of the day – or so I thought.

That day my sweet husband had stood in line at the pharmacy for hours waiting for a prescription that as it turned out wasn't ready, even though there had been that delightful autocall. While this situation happens to all of us at times, this has been a persistent and annoying pattern with this particular pharmacist. As I waited, basically ignoring God, I began to compose a scathing letter to the management of the store, outlining this person's slowness, ineptness, lack of customer service – the letter was perfect corporate America – I remembered how to play that game. Then came the booming voice: "Why would you wish to destroy this person? Why would you wish to rob her of her livelihood? Why would you wish to diminish her? Why would you not practice compassion?' Oops.

Where God gently and loving led me was back to the path of love – to send the pharmacist self-worth, confidence, joy in her job rather than fear of making a mistake. God sent this person knowing of her particular talents and a readiness to embrace them, a certainty of attitude, a knowing that her customers appreciated her efforts and talents and her as a person. There was no real embarrassment on my part that I had let my mind wander, that I had erred. God doesn't work like that, thank goodness.

What I was shown, and my reason for sharing this story, is that I engaged a false grid – the grid of fault, anger, blame and the grid of lack and limitation. The core of me was angry because I felt we weren't important enough to be served with timely respect. Unfortunately it's that easy – you can be hanging out with God at three o'clock in the morning and still fall into the old traps. But with that infinite love I, and therefore we, were able to instantly release not only the issue but bless the person that the false belief was directed towards. Now, not all grids are that easily vanquished – let's face it, I had more than a little help. But do not doubt for one instant that release cannot be that swift, gentle and effortless. After all, we have Archangel Michael right next to us, lifting these grids off of us as soon as we ask. However, it is also important that the recognition of the grid be kept in our conscious minds until no such energy exists in our world. That is the mission of the New You.

Why is it so important to eliminate these false grids? Because they rob you of your joy, your wholeness, and potential to create and live in the sweetness of the Mother's plan. They limit you, restrict you, and attempt to define you. They make you less than, individually and collectively. They promote and nurture hatred, cruelty, prejudice. They make you doubt our divinity, and our connection to each other and All. We cannot fully anchor in the twelve dimensions and co-create Nova Earth while we are shackled by false grids.

We have all grown up knowing about hiding our light under a bushel basket. This practice is about limiting ourselves, staying small, believing that it's safer to stay small, unseen, unnoticed, flying beneath the radar. Worthiness is not something we need to find or develop, it is who we are and always have been. A huge part of the emergence of the New You is not only acknowledging and accepting that but embracing it with gusto. You begin with forgiveness and keep going from there.

Fear of failure, of letting God, our families, ourselves (the list is endless) down, of not fulfilling our soul contract is the flip side of fear of success. The Council's acronym for fear is False Expectations About Reality. The effect of FEAR is that it freezes you. When you are in fear, which is different from the fight or flight response, it flash freezes you. You are not able to move forward. You are not able to take effective creative action. It simply freezes all movement and you find yourself existing in the past. Fear is the ballast of our being, and not in a good way. When that heavy burden is lifted from our shoulders then we remember we can fly. Our hearts become light enough to sing and the sounds of sweet Gaia are not drowned out by the deafening roar of fear.

The Council has said that anger and fear run on the same spectrum. Anger is a mask for fear. If you peel the onion and look at the underlying issue, you will realize you are angry because you are afraid. You choose anger because you are fearful of being afraid. You become aggressive because it's safer than feeling vulnerable, powerless, or like the victim. The false grids are interwoven, welded together like those steel girders, and as you begin to dissemble them you will experience a domino effect.

When we stay hidden, small and dim, running just below the radar, not causing waves, being obedient little children, it is because at some level we fear punishment and retribution. At some level we carry that false grid, and say that Source/One/Mother/Father/God is a judgmental punishing being. This is a false grid and societal belief, held by most religions; that one must earn redemption. The underpinning of this paradigm is that we are born unworthy, and become increasingly so with every misstep we take. Our only hope is surrender to that harsh judgment of our inadequate self and pray that mercy and clemency are available for us. Does that sound or feel like love?

Doubt is another false grid that is ever-present in our society. It is viewed as being naïve or foolhardy; as being Pollyannaish to move through your life in trust, hope and faith; to believe in the innate goodness and just sense of the universe and the collective.

I also want to address an aspect of the limitation false grid that, as we grow older, we grow dimmer. What happened to the wise elder and the crone? In our Western society there is a collective belief that young and beautiful is desirable and older is not. Our media reinforces that on every level, although that is changing as well – have you noticed the movies lately? Our habit is, if we age and remain less than, unseen, we will be permitted to continue and not be asked to leave. This aspect of living small also relates to the fear of death issue. But we are ascending; the pathfinders of the New You setting a new paradigm. We are growing brighter and brighter, not dimmer. As we proceed with the elimination process let's throw that one to Archangel Michael, as well, and read his words of encouragement.

"Greetings, I am Michael, Archangel of Peace, Warrior of Love, and bringer of news. Welcome my sweet annas as we work, play and create with thee in the bringing forth, the birthing and anchoring of the New You; the wholeness of your inter-dimensional self, of your bright being. While this is a period of great intensity, do you not find yourself increasingly peaceful, centered and in the truth of who you are?

"This level of intensity that so many upon your plane are experiencing is not simply due to the increase in frequency or vibration. It is not simply due to the higher dimensions that you are already fully anchored in and accessing. It is due to the fact that at this moment in time, of what you think of as the construct of time, that most of humanity is out of balance in terms of alignment with Gaia, the kingdoms, higher realms and your star brothers and sisters. This is not said in a way of judgment or criticism; it is simply said to further your understanding of what is transpiring.

"My bright angels, Gaia and all upon her are firmly anchored in the fifth dimension, brushing the seventh, occasionally brushing the renewed third. That is true of the bees, birds, mountains, trees, flowers, devas, elementals and oceans. The only segment that is not fully anchored into the fifth reality is the totality of humanity. We understand and honor this choice and momentous undertaking for the collective to come forward as one.

"You are forming the pattern and the new paradigm. You are assisting in the laying down the pattern of new humanity. You may be small but you are mighty. There have been times when I have undertaken my mission of peace where those who have been naysayers – workers for the dark – said 'What difference can one Archangel make?' And they spoke of me with great derision and distain; they tried to dismiss me. Well, that didn't work.

"The difference of one and the circle of One that you have formed and are strengthening each and every day are making a universal difference. It is assisting in the rebalancing and re-anchoring of love, the unfoldment of the Mother's plan. Each one of you is connected heart to heart to heart to heart. Do not underestimate what you are doing, each in your beautiful, unique manner. You are not only selected and chosen, you have volunteered. You have chosen to step forward and embrace the fullness of your being. You do so for yourself, your circle and for many. For this, blessed annas, we thank you. We, the entire Council of Love, are here at your service, so please turn to us. Go with my love and go in peace."

Archangel Michael offers us the phenomenal gift of removing our false grids. In this channeled meditation Michael brings us across an amethyst sky to rest in a lilac cloud where he lifts, dissolves and removes our false grids. You don't need to identify or understand, especially mentally, what the false grid is. There are times when the issue is so painful that the compassion of our guides, Archangel Michael and the Council prevent us from seeing everything. The rule of thumb is what is it in your life that doesn't feel like love, joy, bliss, fifth or higher dimensional? All of those feelings are false grids, belief systems that have come from either you or the collective. They are illusions that keep you imprisoned and small. Time to let it go, and Michael is just the archangel for the job.

Elimination of the false grids is not a one-time fix but rather a meditation and process you will repeat again, and again. The grids come off in layers, and it is astounding how deep these collective false paradigms are in our DNA, our mental, emotional and physical bodies. Because this meditation is about bilocation (and yes you can do it), the experiences with Archangel Michael tend to be physically felt, seen and experienced. The grids can present them in a wide variety of ways: barbed wire, chains, rusted metal bars, ropes, plastic wrap, flowers, satin ribbons, vines, and even soggy bread. Some of the most potent false grids are the prettiest and most attractive. For example, one of my false grids was fear of success which was wrapped around my body as beautiful soft pretty pink velvet ribbon. Seductive but it had to go – and boy was that liberating. However, I also had to do it many times over the years. A false grid can sneak back in. Those collective belief systems can be very insidious.

The Council emphasizes it's not necessary to understand or identify the nature of the grid you are releasing. It's more than sufficient to feel the heaviness, ropes, goop and so on. Not everyone will have the same visual or experience. Your experience also will be different every time. The key is to not fall into judgment, just allow and be. The point is to let go of these burdens forever. As you will experience, these grids are often layers deep and very old. Hence it is useful to go back several times and ensure everything is bright and shiny. Do not try and remove all your grids in one meditation session. Go gently and slowly. Allow Michael to do the heavy lifting. Then go back now and then to make sure everything remains clear.

It's time for you to give the meditation a whirl. As I previously mentioned, false grids are nothing new and I have used this meditation in a couple of Council classes over the years. However, when Archangel Michael guided that this work was an integral part of the New You, he also said the energy of the meditation had been amplified. He said the New You re-patterners were ready to let go of the old. I would say that's a little bit of an understatement! Relax and enjoy.

(Listen to the "Elimination of False Grids" Audio Meditation)

This release and clearing piece of eliminating your false girds, and hence those of the collective, is pivotal to anchoring the New You. Every now and then I stop in my tracks and am gob-smacked, in awe, of the work we are doing together. It is monumental and creating the new paradigm, not only for each of us but for humanity. I am honored to be with you in this journey. Because of the importance of this element, and the Council's guidance to dig deep and then dig deeper, they also have provided us with further assistance.

The New You is the pathfinder who is fully anchored in their heart. They live from a place of heart-consciousness. That does not mean that we neglect what we have learned about our conscious, sub-conscious and unconscious mind. It is important to become aware that sometimes issues or blockages aren't in the conscious mind but subterranean in the unconscious or subconscious. Part of what we as the New You are doing is bringing forth what has previously been hidden or shielded in our unconscious or subconscious to the level of conscious knowing. Knowing where your grids are hidden or layered can be very helpful in letting them go. Similarly, knowing whether an issue is past (life), present or even future can also give you additional insight in the releasing process.

St. Germaine offered some very powerful insight on this issue of clearing the false grids that I would like to share:

"You have chosen to come, to incarnate, at this time to re-invent, to re-pattern what people think of, and I use the word 'think' as the human condition. For too long they have believed the human condition to be pain and suffering, lack and limitation and that is simply not of truth and it most certainly is not of love or the I AM.

"You are the bold. You are the ones who are the courageous, carrying valor and stamina, gentleness and laughter. You are the ones that share the goodness of your hearts. For what is love but the goodness of your heart, the acknowledgement of Divinity above and below, within and without?

"I welcome you, my old friends, to this time of renewal; to this time of re-patterning; to this time of regrinding, and of anchoring the New You. I am with you. Let us begin."

To know your false grids we are going to use simple kinesiology, coupled with a bit of channeling. For this exercise lay your hand on a firm surface, preferably a table or desk, especially while you are learning. It doesn't matter whether or not it is your dominant hand or not. With your hand resting comfortably on the desk you are going to assign one finger to be your yes indicator and one to be your no. The finger will lift up and tap in answer to your question. The index and middle fingers are usually the best and easiest to work with. For example, if I ask, "is my name Linda?" My index finger, which is my "yes" will tap up and down.

Do not hold your hand or fingers rigid, just relax and allow. Whatever you do, don't force this exercise. Tension will defeat the purpose and cloud your answers. Anchor in your heart and ask your guides to help with this undertaking. In the beginning the movement of your fingers may be very slight or just a mere tingling. Stick with it and before you know it your fingers will be jumping as if you are playing the piano. A similar method is to ask your body to move or tilt forward for yes and back for no, or visa-versa. Some of you are already competent with muscle testing or the use of a pendulum or dowser. These are perfectly useful tools. The benefit of the finger method is that it is unobtrusive and can be done anywhere.

It's a great idea when you are starting to use the finger

exercise to test yourself with questions you know the answers to so you familiarize yourself with the sensation and perfecting the finger-tapping method. It will build the trust muscle. It is a practice makes perfect exercise. So keep at it – it is very useful in breaking through and identifying what level you are working on. As you begin to feel comfortable with this, you will become ready to implement this method in helping to clear false grids. What I have found is this method is helpful with stubborn grids that don't want to let go, or keep returning.

Ask yourself, silently or out loud, does the issue, the paradigm, the grid rest in your unconscious (pause, ask); conscious (pause, ask) or subconscious (pause, ask). Once you located it, again inquire if that area is willing to let it go – pause, ask. When? If it is immediately proceed with the Michael meditation. If not, then ask – one week, two weeks and so on. Even if you think you have cleared the grid it is always good practice to go back and double-check using the finger-tapping method.

This method can also be utilized in coming to understand if the false grid is from this life, a past life or a future life. It can help you determine whether the issue is yours or whether you have volunteered to clear it for the collective. It is highly unusual for an issue to be just for the collective, as we tend to carry a mirror of the issue within as well. The key is to remain in the observer position, accept, allow, and let go. The final step of this exercise is always the False Grid meditation with Archangel Michael.

It is also worthwhile to relate these false grids to your archetypes. Life after life, we have chosen a sweet array for ourselves (never just one) – priest, nun, healer, harlot, mother, survivor – you name it. But these archetypes are false and exceptionally limiting ideas about who we are. They pigeonhole us, and we are so much bigger than that. It's an excellent idea when you are doing your false grid meditation to bring in some of those archetypes you want to eliminate and let them go. It also is useful to make sure you are clearing from all dimensions and timelines as well. It's the full Monty.

Sometimes we are reticent to look at our false grids, to let go of old beliefs or habits that have become part of our lives. But only you can do it. The Council supports you in this undertaking but only you can say scram, knowing not only that it's time but probably past time. You know that old saying "you will feel so much better." In this case, it's true. Call in Archangel Michael and gently let the release commence. Remember to thank yourself for your valor and fortitude.

Now about repair work: Once you have removed the false grid think, feel, sense and listen to what need to be replaced from the twelve dimensions and planes to fill that gap, be it grace, joy, confidence or forgiveness. Go with what comes to you. Referring to the chapter on the Thirteen Blessings and Virtues later in the book will help enormously if you find yourself at a loss. But the rule of thumb is, if you feel or hear it, bring it in. As always, first do no harm. Give yourself the blessing; then check if more is needed or desired. Stop when you feel the gap is filled.

The feeling that you experience after releasing the false grids and filling yourself up is one of incredible freedom; of such lightness that you feel like you are floating. Not only does the COL encourage you to enjoy it but to embrace it – it is your new normal. It is the reality of not only the New You but the fifth dimension.

IDENTIFYING YOUR CORE ISSUE AND KEY MOTIVATOR

One of the final steps, and perhaps most critical pieces of clearing out the old false illusions, grids, and self-limiting behavior patterns, is identifying your core issue. The Council calls this your key motivator. This process is akin to identifying your original idea when you emerged from Source, embracing your Stranger, and going to a deep place of acceptance of who you are.

This exercise is not only about identifying your core issue but embracing it, being fully conscious of why this issue is your key motivator and learning how to work with it, in terms of being both your Achilles heel and your best friend.

In Vedic Hindu literature, this core issue, or as the COL puts it key motivator, is referred to a *vasana*. But be clear, this key motivator is more than one of many *vasanas*, issues, beliefs or behavior patterns you have been confronting and releasing during this journey. This is a primary issue that you want to know, embrace, accept and understand as part of the understanding of your sacred self.

Each of us has this aspect of our being that we have carried through many lifetimes and is a primary motivator in terms of either helping us create and keep going, or bringing us to a place of defeat and giving up. In order to explain both the process and the import of this key motivator, I would like to share my story. I use the term story because that is what all of us are doing – we are creating stories about who and what we are; what we need or don't need to do; and then too often falling into reactive automatic behaviors as a result of these ideas or beliefs about ourselves. This process is about breaking free of those ropes that bind and proceeding in ways that our history becomes our ally and supporter, rather than the sword of Damocles.

Years ago, when I began my apprenticeship with the Council of Love, the Apostle Peter came said he would help me review and understand my past lives. The process was intense. I was to lay down and watch the movie for three hours every day for a period of thirty days. Because I was in recovery mode from injuries the lying down part wasn't difficult, but the multi-step assessment of each life was challenging. I would watch the movie, feel myself die – realizing that there was no pain, only release, then receive and arrive at insights regarding that life – what had been learned, what had been left undone, and what the overall purpose of that life was about. Sometimes it was uplifting and sometimes it was really hard to witness. The emphasis with Peter though was being the observer and witness. He was a very strong, yet gentle guide in this undertaking. A strict taskmaster but tender in helping us arrive at observations and understanding.

I must tell you I have never been one to be particularly interested in past lives. I firmly believe we are here for the present, and while all of us are influenced by our histories there is far too much naval gazing about who you were or weren't in some distant past. I flippantly say about past life explorations that there are simply far too many Cleopatra's floating around. It is exceedingly rare for me to discuss any of my past lives but for purposes of this exercise I am more than willing to share – and I promise there are no hidden Cleopatra's.

Situations in which I have advised past life explorations are when there is a persistent habit, addiction or pain that does not seem to have any reference point in current reality. In those cases of past life bleed throughs, investigation is helpful. The proviso is always though, don't get stuck there.

I was a surprised recently when Peter the Apostle appeared by my bedside in the wee, hours of the morning and said it was time for me to understand the core issue/key motivator process; that it would involve looking again at my past lives but from a different perspective. What he wanted me to understand more deeply is, what had contributed to either the end of life or breakthrough in terms of my mission and purpose, and the key motivator.

So what is the key motivator? It is the issue, circumstance or external situation that so challenges your core that it either makes or breaks you. The key motivator is the core belief tied to your idea, mission and purpose that when activated will result in either victory and success or feelings of defeat and surrender. There can be no judgment in this process, just acknowledgement of what your individual, unique key is – and how it is working with or against you during this time of such incredible change. Once you have identified your key motivator, it becomes obvious and apparent that you have to smile and slap your forehead – a genuine "could have had a V8" moment. Remember, your key motivator is tied to your soul mission and purpose, it's your idea.

As you read the following stories, remember that my idea and soul purpose is love; to be a transmitter, channel and awakener of love. To me the most important thing on Gaia and throughout the Universe is love. Love is what drives me, motivates me, and keeps me going.

Before we even began, I was given insight that my key motivator is disillusionment. Now I think of myself as a pretty positive person and so this descriptor, and that's all it is, was somewhat surprising. But as we quickly ran through situation after situation I came to understand what the Council was showing and teaching me.

We returned to a life that was very soul destroying for me, around 1200 A.D. in what is now called Romania. I was a peasant, robust looking, and happy with my simple village life. I was married to a man I cared deeply about, and we had a daughter who was the center of our existence – our joy. Our village was raided, most of it burned down, the fields razed. My husband went with a band of men to fight the raiders and never returned. None of them did, and the knowing in the vision is that he is dead.

Our daughter has now grown into a beautiful young woman, and the noble lord landowner has his eye on her. He covets her. There is no food, illness is rampant, hope was pretty much dead. I considered giving my daughter to the lord who was wealthy, and who would provide for her. My daughter would live and have what in those times was considered luxury. She would be a mistress not a wife. She begged me not to make that decision, and to allow her to stay with me because she was happy even though we had less than nothing. She begged me not to assign her to such a life of humiliation.

I did not heed my daughter's pleas and gave her to the lord. The promise was, that I would be free to come and go and visit with her at will. At the time, I truly believed that it was for the best as the villagers were close to starvation. Death was not far away for any of us. But as I walked away from the palace, I could hear my daughter's screams. I could hear the screams of rape, the screams of pain, of defeat. I ran back to the manor and banged on the gates until my hands were bloody and shredded. I begged for her to be released and returned to me. No one answered, no one came. I had been duped and deceived, and my daughter sacrificed.

I returned home and hung myself. I could not forgive myself and I could not live knowing what I had done to that beautiful young girl, who was the joy of my existence. I was completely disillusioned (and Peter hinted at despair), and there was no point in continuing on. The losses and disillusionment defeated me, and did me in.

Now in the first round when I experienced this life there were a lot of tears, remorse, forgiveness, letting go of the pain, and suffering. So when I looked at this life again from the perspective of understanding my key motivator, it was not as emotional. The primary issue or false grid had been released years ago, but the re-examination allowed me to see and understand the power of disillusionment in my life.

I visited several other lives where there was a similar pattern – suicide often being the outcome. Because for me, when the disillusionment is total there simply is no point or interest in going on. That was important information for me to understand. If I become deeply disillusioned I am in that danger zone.

Peter, the Apostle, also showed me lifetimes where that drive to avoid disillusion had wonderful effect. In my last life, I was Norman Bethune, a Canadian doctor from Montreal who was a communist. He lived from 1890 to 1939. It was an exciting life. While this man had many shortcomings, that isn't the topic of this discussion. Bethune was involved in the Spanish Civil War, and the Chinese Communist Revolution. He aligned with Mao Zedong and became the first field surgeon for the communist army. He trained and introduced the concept of bare-foot doctors to China. He was a hero to the people and is still revered to this day in China.

What was important for me to understand about that life is that this drive for love, freedom and equality for all was my key motivator. I would not give up and live a comfortable doctor's life in the polite society of Montreal. I had to follow my passion, and do what I believed was right. It drove me to many foreign places and I died (happily) in China from a surgical infection.

But I didn't give up. There were many instances in his life where Bethune could have admitted defeat and disillusionment but he didn't give in. The idea of being defeated is abhorrent. Disillusionment is not an option.

Through this review of several lives I also have come to realize that, even in this lifetime, disillusionment has been a key motivator. I can see the patterns of how I have either turned away or persevered. When I am speaking of disillusionment I am not talking about simple disappointment. I am referring to soul-destroying disillusion that robs the heart. I am talking about on the floor done in; the dark night of the soul. I am talking about situations where I have discerned that there is not enough energy or movement towards love, and, in order to survive, I have to move in a different direction. Have those moves and change been guided, of course. But the key motivator has been the knowing that if I were to stay in this state of disillusion, I would die.

How does this knowing, this information of what we have termed, a false grid, assist us in moving forward? Let's go back to *vasanas*. There are healthy *vasanas* that assist us in moving forward, and there are self-defeating *vasanas* resulting in defeat of the heart and soul, even if one continues living. The purpose of understanding your key motivator is to know what the trigger is and to utilize it in ways that spur you on. You become, not reactive but proactive in deciding how to precede, what to avoid, and what will catapult you on your spiritual path.

For example, there have been times in this chapter of my life as channel for the Council of Love when I have been financially without, scorned and questioned about the validly of my beliefs. There have been times when it would simply have been easier to resume a lucrative corporate job with a secure salary and the respect that seems to attend such a position in our society. But my key motivator of not allowing myself to enter into disillusionment has kept me going. I'm the gal who doesn't know when to quit. Often, I have had people ask me, "how do you keep going for so many years?" My answer is always the same – I just put my head down and keep going. Not because I don't think I have other choices, but because I feel this is a path I can't give up on.

It is reflective and part of my soul mission and purpose. It is the promise and the expression of my love for the Divine Mother. I keep going because I believe in love, and I refuse to become so deeply disillusioned that I am no longer me.

So the question is what is your key motivator? How do you discover what your key is?

As with all the COL exercises and processes, you begin by anchoring in your heart, going to the 13th Octave and anchoring in the heart of Gaia. Call in your guides, the Archangels, and for this exercise, St. Peter, the Apostle. Like the removal of false grids exercise, lie on your bed if you can. Certainly make sure you are comfortable and not about to be interrupted or disturbed during this viewing. Ask Peter and your guides to show you situations, lifetimes, or to simply call up knowing of your key motivator. Sit with it, lie with it, make friends with it, and hang out with it for several days. Let it inform you of its role and purpose in your life.

Understand your key motivator is going to be uniquely yours. For some it may be fear of failure – or success; limitation; disease, control – you know the list. Abandonment has been a very strong theme within the New You groups. The point is to come to the place of balance with your key motivator and enlist it to assist you in your soul journey. It is your unique personal warning system of your danger zone and it is crucial for you to understand.

You don't want to live or stay in the space of your key motivator or core issue. That is not the purpose of gaining this understanding. Once embraced and aligned, it becomes part of your operating system, one of the tools at your disposal, similar to understanding your soul color, ray, or your Stranger. It becomes part of your balance, your stillpoint. You know not to venture too far either, to one side or the other, because where this information is useful is at that midpoint.

Looking at this information for the first time, it can be disconcerting. As you begin this exercise make sure you are anchored in your heart, in a place of forgiving, allowing and acceptance. No judgment, no guilt, no blame, no fault is allowed or helpful.

You may also find that brief journaling of this experience will be helpful because it allows you to go back and look at a life or issue without bringing up all the emotionality that can attend that journey. Begin, comprehend and then let go.

The day will come when we are fully anchored in the higher realms, especially the seventh dimension of the Christ consciousness. Your key motivator will not be of such immediate importance to our journey. But for now, during our individual and collective transition to the New You, it is a critical piece of information. Embrace it.

It also is essential to comprehend the core issue of the collective; a core issue that rests within the heart of each and every false grid. This illusive and obvious issue is, self-worth and self-love.

Lack of self-worth is the cancer of the human race. When we dig deep, peel back the onion skin, so many of the issues that we identify as core issues come back to lack of self-worth, self-love. What does betrayal, disillusion, and abandonment have to do with lack of self-worth? When we dig deeper, we realize we are the pure essence of love and could never feel disillusioned, betrayed or abandoned.

Often the precursor to breakthrough with this core issue is raging anger. When I have a client who is railing against God and the entire universe, who is fed up and ready to quit this hocus pocus spiritual hoopla, I silently cheer. Because I know, that underneath that anger and fear, is the admission that they are terrified that Mother/Father/One has forgotten them. The feeling is "if you love me then why do I feel so alone; why do I feel so abandoned; why do I feel so unsupported; where the heck are you?"

I know out of this explosion comes surrender. I know the trapdoor opens into the light and into a new brighter understanding of love and of who the person truly is. That knowing is one of being loved, cherished and valued beyond measure throughout the universe. That breakthrough can only come with the clearing of the false grids, the surrender of the illusion of lack, isolation and separation.

When you reach this place of angst, and you will, smile and know you are not alone. Know that you are also clearing the core issue of humanity, and allowing the old third to finally and completely dissolve. Remember to allow Archangel Michael, St. Peter, your guides, the entire Council, and especially St. Germaine, to help you. You are not and never have been alone. You are an incredible angel in form, flying free. So let go, and spread those wings.

St. Germaine has the final word in this chapter as he invites us to allow him to ignite our self-worth. St. Germaine did not initially arrive as an enlightened being. He tells us that he came in like all of us, rapidly adopting the illusion of being in the third dimension and then working his way back. He points out that if he hadn't had the experience of the false grids, then how would he ever be able to teach us how to get out of it?

Getting rid of the false grids of lack, limitation, debt, despair, and feelings of lack of self-worth does not mean that nothing will ever go wrong. Often we fantasize that if we are worthy, then everything will be perfect. That's not the case. Sometimes, these challenges come up because we are capable of dealing with the issue. In dealing with it, we are teaching others how to deal with it as well. With the increased energies of the shift we are all feeling these challenges coming up. Pretty much everyone feels right now that we're right at the wire.

The challenges are emerging so we can break through. This is the final letting go of the old third hologram. The Council encourages us to draw upon the higher dimensional energies in order to do so. If we're not drawing upon the clarity and unity of the fifth; the magic and alchemy of the fourth; even the creative chaos of the sixth; then we are drawing upon the old energies of the third, and that means we're going to get stuck. So the challenges are pushing us to expand, and to pull in energies we haven't previously been working with to a greater extent. Imagine, we are going through the same process as St. Germaine did thousands of years ago. I can't think of anything that gives me more heart.

"Greetings, I am St. Germaine, keeper of the Violet Flame, brother of your heart and brother of your soul, brother of your journey. Many times I have said to you, 'I will not reincarnate. I will not walk this earth again.' Will I assist you? Will I work with you? Will I guide you? Will I revel in your victories? Yes.

"Dear heart, I have walked the planet many, many, many times for thousands and thousands of years. As beautiful as Gaia is, which is often why I stayed so long, I do not return. Well, one of the reasons I do not return is there is no need to. When I returned to Earth previously to collect, to teach my armada of healers, to share the knowledge of healing, it was to assist you to lift up out of the old third, into the cleaner third, the fourth, the fifth, the sixth, the seventh and so on. But my friends, you are already doing this. So you do not need me in form to come and urge you along, to show you the way. You will see and hear and be with me clearly in the other dimensions when the illusion of limitation simply gone.

"It is a time of creation and co-creation upon the planet. It is a time of bringing your dreams to fulfillment in form, in your timeline, in the realities that you are choosing to experience and create. The precursor to creation is the fullness of knowing of your worth. This is not an attribute or a quality that you create, that you seek, that you call forward; it is the latent ember within your heart that I ignite with your permission this day.

"Self-worth is part of your composition; the knowing of your mighty beauty, your power, your truth, your harmony and your peace. This is as real as your hair, your face, your feet, your imagination, your sense of smell. This is not something to be acquired. This is something simply to say yes to and activate.

"There have been times, in my life and yours, when you have said, 'If I am so loved by Mother/Father/One, then how can this trial and tribulation be real?' Well, dear heart, you are a participant in the co-creation of dilemma. Do not always see a challenge as some shortage of worth. If anything it is quite the contrary; you and One and All have deemed that you are more than capable to undergo this transition of fire. Yes, to progress yourself but also to assist others.

"If I have but one purpose in my sacred stewardship with the Violet Flame, and the I AM Presence, it is to reach all beings, not simply on Earth but everywhere, and to ignite and assist you in the anchoring, the acknowledgement, and embrace of your I AM Presence, which is a direct reflection and participant of the I AM.

"This is my mission. That is why I wish to heal you of all these wounds of war that you may go forward in the brilliance of who you are. The old third does not fade, it is gone. I invite you, my beloved brothers and sisters, my family, come and join me in the new realm of human existence. And if you feel you do not know the way, take my hand I will show you.

"The greatest individual human tragedy is underestimating yourself. It bars your creativity, it bars you from knowing how wonderful you are, it bars you from exploration. This sense of 'I would like to but I don't think I can' – dear heart, if you have the feeling that you would like to, then you can. It is a new way of thinking, of considering and of being. But it is not complex. It is actually very simple. Sometimes you say 'oh this is too simple Germaine, it can't be this way'. And I say to each of you, it is."

The Care and Feeding of the New You

The care and feeding of the New You is essential if you are going to build, anchor and embody the energies of this being you are becoming. One of the key elements of this process is consistency. Similar to a car, if you don't maintain it, check and change the oil regularly, and keep the gas in the tank, the car won't serve you; it won't take you anywhere. How often when your car breaks down do you feel that curse under your breath saying "damn car, breaking down just when I need it." The same is true of the totality of your being – your body, mind, heart and spirit. You can't just attend to the care and feeding of your sacred self now and then; when you have time; when you think of it; when you feel out of sorts; or when you feel like you're in trouble. You wouldn't just feed your dog, or say hello when you think of it – you do this every day, lovingly and consistently. Don't you deserve just as much nurturing and love?

The care and feeding of the New You is the way in which you love, nurture, support, cherish, maintain, honor, and respect who you are. It is not sufficient to take care of one aspect of your body, such as the physical or spiritual, and ignore the rest. The foundation of the New You is an integrated being, a re-patterning of the tapestry of what it means to be human. There cannot be tears or loose threads in the warp and weave.

The Council addresses the how-to of becoming and balancing by reminding us of the important of routine, and specifically the routine of prayer, meditation and ritual. The guidance is that all three elements are necessary for our well-being, for anchoring interdimensionally, for being the fullness of our sacred selves, and of raising and holding the highest frequencies available to us. It is not a matter of doing one or the other, this triangle works best when practiced as a unified process every day.

Although ritual is the last mentioned in the triangle, it is the first point we discuss because it is sets the stage for your meditation and prayer. Ritual is doing something in a consistently sacred manner. One example that we are all familiar with is the Islamic practice of laying down the *musallah* prayer rug and turning to face Mecca to pray five times a day. That is a ritual. Ritual informs the universe that you are beginning a sacred practice; that you are preparing to communicate to higher realms. It also informs your sweet self, your conscious, subconscious and unconscious, that you are entering into a sacred space to commune.

There are dozens of sacred rituals you have observed and consciously or unconsciously participated in throughout your life. Part of the fun of this segment on the care and feeding of the New You is designing your own sacred ritual, one that reflects your values and your needs. Your sacred ritual is consistent and repeated most days (there are always exceptions) in your sacred space.

Every person deserves a sacred space, it is part of feeding your heart and soul. It reinforces and builds your sense of self-worth and self-love. I am not referring to a meditation room or an elegantly appointed space – not everyone has that luxury. Your sacred space can be a closet, a table with a small altar or even a corner of your dresser where you place things that mean something to you. Place objects in your sacred space that remind you of the Ascended Masters, the Archangels, the Divine Mother, the kingdoms, your totems – the list is expansive and you tailor it to you, no one else. It can be crystals, statues, pictures, everyday items that have special meaning and significance to you.

For example, I have a beautiful antique blue glass octagonal clock studded with crystals and emeralds on my altar. This clock was given to me by my grandmother for my high school graduation because I had admired it from childhood. It symbolizes for me many things – it's an all-purpose sacred object. The blue is my soul color, and the "diamonds and emeralds" remind me of love and purity, and, the light that we all strive to be. The eight-sided shape is sacred geometry and reminds me of the many angles and facets of my life and self – and yes, the dimension of creation, the infinity of love. The clock reminds me that I have committed this time on Earth to my sacred purpose and to the Mother. Because the clock has to be wound it also reminds me that my time here is limited and I must not take my life for granted. Like all things, I too will wind down and return home. It reminds me of my lineage and heritage, of the continuity of life. And that's just a clock that anyone coming into my sacred space would think "oh that's pretty, looks old." The choices of how to arrange your sacred space don't need to declare everything about you; the significance of each precious item is for you.

Sacred ritual is a sequential practice when you are beginning your time of prayer and meditation. One of my favorites is what the Council taught us ages ago and is called the candle and the crack – easy enough to remember. The ritual is lighting a candle, bringing in the light of the divine, banishing any darkness and purifying the space. The crack refers to opening the outside door or window a tiny crack in order that energies flow smoothly – out with that which does not serve, in with the light. Part of your ritual might be holding crystals which will amplify your energy field. Some folks like to wrap a prayer shawl around their shoulders. I always wear my shield over my heart, a symbol of protection given to us by Archangel Michael. The key is to create your sacred ritual, formulate it and then stick with it. Your ritual should never feel forced but rather as natural as breathing. From time to time you will feel the need to shift or change parts of your ritual; do so with gusto and glee – there is always a reason.

Prayer is heart-speaking – to Source, Mother/Father/One, to our guides and guardian angels, to our Stranger, and our universal self. Soul conversations are not included here because the focus of this triangle is you. The extension work you do with others is discussed in the chapter on sacred union.

Universal Mother Mary has spoken to us many times about the importance and power of prayer:

"Do not forget my children, to pray. Understand prayer is one of the expressions of intent. In many ways you've thought of prayer as junior league because you learned it early in your life. Nothing could be further than the truth. True prayer is your heart speaking to the Universe, to Mother/Father/God; to your guardian angels; to the mighty ones; to those who look out after you, who cherish you and nurture you. Nothing has more power or more appeal than the small child who sits in prayer in innocence, and awe, in trust and says please.

"We do not categorize the difference between a child's prayer asking for a new bicycle, or your heart speaking asking for world peace. All are heard, and responded to equally. Some prayers are easily achievable, not because we have limitation on what we are capable of, but simply because there is less human interference. We will not interfere in the exercise of human free will. For many upon your planet, prayer is for last resort; it is neck and neck in tandem with when despair and desperation set in. Of course that is not good either, for we wish your prayers to come from a place of calm and tranquility, of heart speaking, and place of knowing and trust. But dear one, we will accept them however we get them."

Meditation is conducted in the same heart-space as prayer. The difference from prayer is that when you pray you are speaking and expressing your heart and soul desires to the Universe. In meditation, it is being in the receptor mode, listening with your heart to the responses that are being sent to you. There are times when you may think that the response doesn't relate even closely to what you have been requesting. There are other times when you will feel that there is no response; that you don't hear or feel anything at all. It's important to really know that even if you think (emphasis on mental body) that you are not hearing, seeing or perceiving that our guides and the universe are always talking to us. Often, the difficulty is that there is so much mind chatter in our heads that we can't hear what is being relayed to us. In such instances our guides and the divine realm will often speak to us through nature, other people and what we call coincidence. There is no such thing as coincidence, it is always the universe getting your attention and attempting to convey to you something important for you to know and understand. The key when you are experiencing monkey mind is to keep going, go deeper into your heart, allow those random thoughts to float away like white fluffy clouds and continue. The discipline of sticking with it always pays off.

I am a heretic when it comes meditation. What the Council teaches us is that the starting point of meditation is comfort. If you are paying undue attention to your body, your posture, your breathing and so on, then that is what you are doing – that is where you attention is focused. The key in meditation is to be relaxed enough to not draw your attention on your body. The starting point in the care and feeding of the New You is comfort, and that applies to meditation as well. As you become more adept at hearing and listening you may discover a tradition that appeals to you and facilitates your practice. Meditation is not intended to be difficult or challenging; that is of the old paradigm. So relax, sit in your favorite chair, in your sacred space, and listen. The Council suggests sitting to start with because, in the beginning, there is a very good chance that if you lie down you will fall asleep. This is not a hard and fast rule, merely a suggestion.

Neither meditation nor prayer is intended to be in prostration before the emperor. Quite the contrary, prayer and meditation is sitting, relaxed in your body, emptying the business of the day, and chatting with those who love and treasure you. It is part of the ongoing sacred conversation between you and the Divine.

Your routine of prayer, meditation and ritual is not intended to be confined to one hour a day when you are in your sacred space. Rather, the idea is to anchor that unity, connectedness and balance energy and then expand this awareness to every aspect of your life and daily routine.

How the Council approaches this subject of the care and feeding of the New You was by beginning a list of the things they would like to see you pay attention to and practice. They have been clear that lists are the starting point, and the opportunity is for you to add to their suggestions. Even though the suggestions are broken up into the sections of body, mind, and spirit/heart, the categories are designed to be interchangeable. Soul and heart are used synonymously, as the source of creation essence and energy.

Although this is one of the shortest chapters in the book, the work and expansion contained in the Council's guidance could fill a lifetime. Again, the proviso is not to become adamant or obsessive about this project but rather to introduce balance into your life, and addressing every aspect of your being.

The key is integration, and while you may take one item on the listing and work with it for a while, the point is to build, allow, anchor and enjoy. This exercise reminds me a great deal of working with the thirteen blessings and virtues. Often people will chose to work with one virtue for a space of time before moving onto the next – the choice is yours. This is never intended to be a pass/fail or proving yourself. The key is to take the guidance, expand upon it, make it your own routine and enjoy the fruits of living in your totality.

The suggestions are made in bullet form because they are not intended to be directive, are rather self-evident, and repeated in several contexts. The purpose is to draw your consciousness to the question and practice of how are you taking care of yourself. Are you taking care and nurturing every part of your being?

BODY

- food, importance of color in food – especially green; fueling your body with what it needs and asks for
  - light – getting enough sunlight
  - laughter, really is the best medicine
  - rest – listen to your body and rest when you are tired
  - programmed and crystal water
  - programmed air – writing your creations in the air
- supplements, flower essences, vitamins – don't forget to transmute with a moment of prayer

- earthing; connecting with Gaia and nature
- movement – yoga, walking, dance – find your passion
- alone time, social time, stare at the wall time, recreation
- body-work
- chakra balancing and clearing
- physical intimacy, not just sexual but hugs, human touching, connection
- daily honoring and cherishing your body
- gratitude – the value of affirmations

MIND

- intellectual stimulation
- relaxation
- conversation – actual, inner, guides and mind chatter
- information input and output – what do you talk about, think about, what do you read, watch, absorb?
- do you have supportive environments, people and work in your life?
- do you initiate friendships and relationships that support The New You?
- meditation
- do you trust yourself, or do you second-guess your knowing and intelligence?
- allow your mind to soar, dream and create
- power of imagination and inspiration
- are you listening? Are you willing to listen? Remember ready, willing and able
- how and do you express love and gratitude to your mind?

SPIRIT/HEART

- what feeds your soul?
- are you connected or disconnected – what is your comfort level?
- are you proud of your spiritual self?
- is your spiritual journey something you are eager to talk about and share – or do your avoid those conversations?

- do you chat with/communicate with your guides?
- do you follow guidance – always, sometimes, irregularly?
- what are your signs?
- what do you read and listen to?
- what are your special gifts – how do you use them?
- what are your daily spiritual practices?
- what are your sacred rituals?
- when and how do you meditate?
- how do you communicate your heart's desires to Source?
- do you have supportive environments, people and work in your life?
- do you initiate friendships and relationships that support The New You?
- do you have a sacred space or altar in your home?
- do you work with crystals or sacred objects?
- what are your spiritual tools and how do you use them?
- do you invoke the protection of the archangels?
- do you cleanse your sacred space on a regular basis with smudge or crystals?
- do you allow Gaia to fill you up and nourish you?
- do you allow your guides to fill you up and nourish you?
- how do you express gratitude to your higher and universal self; your guides and the company of heaven?
- are you serene, content, happy, joyful – if not why not?

When you begin this process, be the observer. It is helpful to journal for a few days. I am not suggesting volumes on what this shift feels like but rather brief notes on what your day consists of, and how you are spending your time. This practice will highlight for you areas that are sparse and those where you may be spending the bulk of your time and energy.

All of us go through periods when we are living more in one sphere or the other. It may be an incredibly busy time at work and hence you are really anchored in the mind. You may be grieving from the loss of a loved one and spending a lot of time and energy in your heart. You may be recovering from an illness and be focused on your body. The key is to be the observer not the judge. When you are spending an inordinate portion of you energy in any one sphere it becomes even more critical to take time to go into the alternate spheres because it will help the stress of what you are going through. The goal and the reward is balance. That inherently implies no stress, no fear, no judgment, no beating up on yourself. Gentle, loving, tender, sweetness and flexibility are the watch-words. Attending to every part of your sacred self is the privilege we are all granted in this journey.

Sacred Union

Partnership is a fundamental precept of being human. We are connected and in unity with ourselves and the world around us whether we acknowledge this or not. We cannot deny our interdependence on air, earth, water, sunlight, and sustenance. The issue then is do we want to be in an unconscious partnership or elevate our relationships to sacred union, and what does sacred union mean? For the New You the choice is obvious – we choose to be in the higher dimensional consciousness of sacred union with all – with ourselves, the Divine, a loving partner, our family, our community and Gaia.

The question then, is how we elevate our relationships to this higher level? What are the practical steps we can take to engage in a more meaningful fulfilling way with everything and everybody around us? Can it be as simple as acknowledging and embracing the reality that this way of being is a choice? Let's begin this exploration by reading what Yeshua has to say on the matter.

SELF & THE DIVINE

"Greetings, I am Jesus Sananda, I am Yeshua, I am brother, friend, ally and fellow traveler in and out of form. We have been together for many eons, and our connection and love does not change, it does not vary, if anything, it simply grows. I come here this day to talk to you about sacred union, about that union of love that is the most precious gift throughout the entire universe; the gift from which all else flows.

"Sacred union is the gift the Mother gave you at the very beginning of existence, when you emanated from the heart of One as a bright spark, as a light of divinity and love. Your most sacred union is with the One has never altered. It is reinforced, not only every time you have reincarnated, but every time you returned home. That is sacred union. It is the heart bond between Mother and you. Within that, it is the deep recognition that you are of Her heart, you are of Her essence, and therefore, you can never be 'less than.' This pervasive illusion regarding lack of self-worth is simply a phantom. I know for many it has been the monster haunting you in the night. But it is nothing more than a fleck of dust that I will blow away, right now. I do this for you, and humanity, because there is no room for it. It is not of truth, and it most certainly is not of love.

"The second sacred union is you with you, with all of you, with every fiber, every molecule, every subatomic particle of your being, above, below, and out into the multiverse. Sacred union is you embracing you in the knowing of your beauty, your might, your power, and your indelible sweetness. It is you loving you enough to say 'I am entitled and I choose my journey, I choose my creations, I will my creations, and I will to will Thy will because that is who I am.' Sacred union is deep acceptance that there is no one above or below or in-between that can make you vary or stray from that truth of your whole being, your sacred union with your divine self.

"I wish to speak to you of my sacred union with you. You are the beloveds of my heart; you are my family, and friends. We joined in sacred union eons ago. I wish to bring this again to the forefront because what does sacred union entail? It entails service, consideration, generosity and sharing. These are all expressions of love. Please turn to me as I turn to you, my brothers and sisters of Earth who are doing the ground work, who are preparing the way and who have been doing that for a long time. I know how hard you work; your diligence, commitment, stamina, and fortitude. This makes it all the more important to share with me in the joy, sweetness and unity of our hearts. This is not a gender issue, this is not a spirit/master/human issue; this is a bond of love that transcends all.

"The reinforcement of your sacred union with yourself is my

gift to you. I ask you to remember our union and bring it back to life, and then to continue in your other sacred unions, which are equally important: union of partnership, of family, of friendship, and community. This is not a hierarchy; these are mirrors of love."

Sacred union is what we most desire and fear. The desire, the heart-wrenching longing to be loved, acknowledged and connected to the heart of One is part and parcel of being human. There is not a soul alive that does not yearn and seek love. The ultimate expression of love is our connection to the Divine, it is who we are, from whence we came, and where we will return. Any person, and there are many, who denies they don't need or want love is in serious denial.

Although the sacred union with the Divine is what motivates and moves us both spiritually and physically, it is the sacred union with self that is the starting point of this process. Sacred union with yourself is far more than simply acknowledging your divinity. It's embracing the totality of your being. It is loving, cherishing, accepting and becoming the truth of who you are. Sacred union with self does not mean accepting what you have deemed as your faults, shortcomings, or poor behavior, and saying "well, that's simply who I am." Sacred union is brutally honest; it does not make up stories and excuses to let you wiggle out of self-responsibility and potential – it shines the bright light of truth on everything you think, feel and do; it exposes those dark corners of doubt and hones in on what your heart and soul genuinely desires to achieve and experience.

Sacred union with self is moving from that place of illusion; believing you are less than and that's acceptable, into a place of ultimate becoming, expansion and absolute knowing that you are capable, talented, creative and loving. It's knowing right down to your bones that you are here for a reason.

Reaching the place of sacred union includes practicing a lot of forgiveness, compassion, fortitude, and a dash of awe. It is also recognizing that forgiveness does not mean permission to be less than. Compassion means understanding when you have taken a misstep. Fortitude means consistency and constancy, sticking with your journey even when it's rough or unclear. Awe is accepting what you are really capable of and wondering who you really are. There is no conceit in sacred union with self because there is an innate understanding that you are participating in the heart and energy of One; that you are part of something bigger. You are unique and essential to that whole, but so is everybody and everything else. Hence within the process of coming to a place of sacred union with yourself is the inclusion of the next step and knowingness of sacred union with Source.

Jesus Sananda eloquently expands on this notion of sacred union with self in this way:

"I wish to begin this phase of the New You on sacred union by speaking to your heart. What you have been undertaking in the past couple of months, twenty years, and for some of you the last twenty eons has been the embrace of your sacred self. We wish you to have a deep understanding, and an even deeper commitment, to who you are. In that deeper commitment we want you to re-find, re-commit, re-connect with the love of your sacred self. To be able to sit, stand and walk in wonder, gazing at how incredible you are, and to be able to do this in a sacred manner. Not one of you is boastful and the ego is shrinking. We do not wish to eliminate ego, but to have it balanced as you allow the truth of your fullness, wholeness and divinity to shine through. And you are. This isn't simply a half-hearted attempt. You are bringing the totality of who you are, and the strength of your eternal self, to this exercise. Therefore, when we speak of moving into this phase of sacred union we reiterate that the most sacred union is with your beloved self."

How do we, in practical ways begin this work of being in sacred union with ourselves? How do we do this without becoming self-obsessed, myopic or being overly self-involved? Isn't part of the journey about extending ourselves in service, being part of a family, soul family and community? How do we find this balance between knowing, loving and accepting our divinity and being in and of the world? While these are really important questions, the key is to understand that if we do not enter into a sacred union with our selves, then any relationship we are going to have will be limited. Our ability to grow, become, create and share with others is determined by our relationship with our sacred self. You cannot engage fully with another if you have neglected or refused to engage fully with yourself. This is not a matter of being self-absorbed, it is a matter of knowing the fullness of who you are, and what you have to offer.

In our early teens or younger most of us had a terrible crush on someone – the girl with the pretty blue eyes; the boy with that dimple and mischievous grin; the person who dressed so sharp and seemed so confident; the lady down the street who always had a kind word and baked cookies; someone outside the immediate family who wasn't already completely savvy to us. Each of us, when we are honest with ourselves, know what it is to adjust our persona, behavior and actions in hopes of winning the heart and attention of another. We've all done it, be it for a grade-school crush or job interview. We have all had times when we have altered our presenting self in a desire to be more than, to be accepted, admired or desired. We adapt our personality and presentation because we feel that who we are is insufficient.

I use this example, outside of the reference of family, because not only it is something we can all relate to but it's relatively harmless. No need for guilt and maybe it even provokes a few sweet smiles of remembrance. Part of growing and becoming is trying on different personas and masks. If done in an experimental fashion it helps us begin to know ourselves more deeply. If done as a continued pattern of escape, it's detrimental. That being said, the reason why we initially try on different personas is because we don't know, love and recognize ourselves yet – we don't know yet how great we are! For some people that knowing has come and anchored at an early age, but that is the exception not the rule. For most of us, that deep knowing, acceptance and treasuring of who we are is a life-long process and challenge. At least it was until the energies of the fifth dimension and the New You came along.

Entering into sacred union with yourself is as easy as looking in the mirror, deep into your eyes and seeing the truth of who you are. Often this exercise make folks uncomfortable but keep going – move past the discomfort to the giggles to the tears to the deep seeing and recognition of your soul. The next step in this exercise is to declare your love for yourself out loud. Follow this routine daily, and reinforce it with meditation, listening, and seeing in nature and others the beauty of who you are.

The sacred union with yourself is the starting and finishing point. Every other relationships – with God, partner, family, community and planet begins with you loving you.

Inherent within the sacred union with self is the sacred union with the Divine. Loving yourself is seeing yourself with and through the eyes of the Divine Mother. An integral part of having a sacred union with the Divine is taking time to nurture and grow that relationship. It isn't a sacred relationship if you never take time to call and chat, visit and spend time listening, or simply hanging out together. The heart and soul list in the previous chapter on the Care and Feeding of the New You is a starting point. Realize that if you want and value a relationship with the Divine, you have to participate. Otherwise it's not a relationship. And it most certainly isn't a spiritually mature relationship.

The 13th Octave is a gift directly from the heart of One that restores the sacred union with the Divine. Prior to the gift of the 13th Octave, you had to die to experience this level of Divine union. What is clear in hindsight is that this blessing was brought forth to assist us in preparing for our ascension. It is a gift that re-anchors the knowing of the unity and connectedness to God without having to leave the physical form. Going to the 13th Octave changes you in minute and extraordinary ways. Life does not continue in a business as usual manner. But then, who wants it to? That illusion of the old third dimension of separation, abandonment and loneliness is exactly what our hearts yearn to dispel. That is exactly what happens when you go to the 13th Octave – all sense of separation is replaced by sacred union.

The 13th Octave is the first download in the New You. That is how important it is to the New You – it is the foundation upon which we build this bright new world, Nova Earth. It is the jumping off point for ascension. The guidance, and it can't be stated strongly enough, is to do this meditation every day, until the energy of this sacred union is anchored indelibly. For more information on the 13th Octave, refer to Appendix A.

One of the keys to sacred union with the Divine is the acknowledgment that it is already in place; it is the bedrock of who you are. Think, act, behave and know that there is always an invisible third party, a very big third party, present and witnessing everything you think, feel, do and say. God really is listening, and so are your guides and guardian angels.

PARTNERSHIP

One of the most common questions and desires I encounter in my work relates to having a genuine loving partner. While there are those on Gaia who chose to travel alone, and who are very good and complete in doing that, the majority of those on Earth yearn for their sacred other. There is a consistency in this yearning. People don't simply want others to fill an emotional gap or a spot at the dinner table; they deeply desire to create a meaningful relationship with a sacred partner that is equal, accepting, co-creative, expansive, tender, exciting, loving, physical, spiritual and fun.

Such relationships are not for the faint of heart, because they demand you be fully present, honest and allowing. The sacred partnership is not about seeking a clone but a compliment. These relationships are based on knowing yourself, being willing to risk and trust, to commit and explore. The sacred union partnership is the most rewarding and challenging of all the sacred unions. One of the sacred partnerships that we often refer to in terms of a model is the relationship between Yeshua and Mary Magdalene. I would like to offer both of their perspectives and insights on partnership, love and marriage.

We begin with Jesus:

"Greetings, I am Jesus Sananda, Yeshua, beloved brother and

friend, kindred spirit. Sacred union is part of this New You not simply because we desire for you to have romance. I, for one, am completely in favor of romance, of unity, in ways that the human beings are just beginning to imagine. Part of the journey you have chosen is sacred union with a divine partner in human form.

"I know the joy of this and I have spoken, as has my beloved Magdalena, about the joy of that union, as well as the comfort, succor, strength and complimenting of one another. When you are in the recognition and embrace of your divinity, your human divine spark, your expanded self, your New You, then you are perfectly positioned to join in sacred union with the partner of your choice, of your heart and soul.

"It may be a soul-mate that you have known forever or it may be someone entirely new, the choice is yours. I knew returning to Earth that I would have the choice of partnership, of union, of marriage with Mary but that did not erase my human self, my ego, my masculine self that wished to engage in the process of choosing, pursuing, joining and becoming. Why did I wish to engage in the process? Because it is fun, rewarding and challenging. It makes you stretch and grow in ways that are unimaginable. It is incredibly rewarding and sometimes like a slap in the face because you think too much of yourself. I speak from experience.

"When I was thinking, feeling and examining about my creation of my perfect partner I pictured someone who would not only complement me and bring that sense of unity and family, but also someone who would make me expand, make me step up, make me be a better me. This is what I suggest to you. Is Mary was more than me? Yes and no. No one is more than anyone. But you have all had experiences where the person that you are in relationship with brings out the best of you. The beauty of this is that you reciprocate, you become the mirror and you bring out the best in them. I cannot think of anything more beautiful. It is sacred to be able to share, without reservation, the totality of your being without editing, holding back, or keeping secrets. It is a gift to be able to be vulnerable and exposed; to be able to laugh at the silliest things and cry at the most profound.

"The sacred union you call forth this day is with one who also has done their process, their work, that does not diminish or scoff at you in any way, shape, or form. Now you ask 'What am I going to do I've already been married for fifty years and my husband thinks I'm crazy?' I know that experience as well. What I also say to you is celebrate – he thinks you're crazy and he loves you anyway. I am not simply talking about male-female, your sacred union is with who you choose and who chooses you, who looks in your eyes and heart and reflects back to you the wonder and the beauty of who you are.

"Do not think, my beloved friends, that if you are already in relationship of any form that it cannot be elevated to the divine qualities, the thirteen blessings and virtues, laughter, wholeness and the sweetness of knowing that you have surrendered to each other. And at the same time maintain your autonomy. There's nothing better, nothing while in human form and on this journey which you have already committed to doing.

"I offer my assistance to help each one of you with the clarity, determination, softness, tenderness and the love, and at times the temerity, to enter fully into sacred union. It is your next step, and you are ready. Call on me. I am with you forever. Go with my love and the love of my Magdalena. Farewell."

Although the words and slant are slightly different, it is interesting how similar the vision and experience of sacred union in partnership is for Yeshua and Mary Magdalene.

"Greetings, I am The Magdalena. I am Mary, but I choose to be called The Magdalena. It was an endearment first given to me by Yeshua, and then it spread as so many of the apostles and disciples would call me such. It was not a title but a term of endearment. I wish to speak to you today as old friends and fellow travelers, travelers of the heart, beings that I have loved in and out of form for a very long time.

"I wish to speak to you this day about stepping forward, for that is the guidance, and dare I say directive, of our beloved Universal Mother. It is a sacred invitation, and you know She does not issue invitations casually or even often, not of this magnitude or nature. I come this day to stand by you, next to you, and with you, because I know about this issue of sacred union, and of stepping forward, of assuming the fullness of your being and your role.

"In the beginning when I was with Yeshua, even prior to our marriage, I was shy. I would adopt an attitude of quietude and honoring, even though my heart was beating a million miles an hour just to gaze upon him. I was nervous about what I had to offer. I had been trained and educated in the sacred ways. I was a channel in my own right; and my specialty was the creation of sacred ceremony and sacred space to bring forth Love and the Holy Spirit, always working with the divine feminine. I had been prepared in my own right.

"When I engaged with my beloved Yeshua and chose to go forward in sacred union, we knew of many of the trials and tribulations we would face. None of them outweighed the love and the rightness of sharing our love, not only with each other but with our families, circle and communities. There were many external efforts to try to control both my actions, behaviors and beliefs. We did not see this as offensive, often the advice, the desires to have us adhere one way or the other was based in love and concern. How did we handle this, what did we do? We listened to our hearts. That was what we focused on, and that is what I encourage each of you to focus on as well.

"It is important to hold intention of outcome, but you cannot live completely focused on outcome because then you lose the joy of now. It is the joy of now, it is the love that you share in this very moment that will sustain you. It is the joy that you choose each and every day that will feed and grow you, and fortify what you think of as your vibration. It is your decision to say, 'I will not allow those ridiculous paradigms of the old way to hold me back. I will love fully.' It is a warrior's stance and an individual decision. Do not let any situation, any hardship, any illusion rob you of your joy of now, of the sweetness of a child's smile, a drop of dew on a leaf, a starry sky, of reaching out to somebody who needs to know they are loved, and of letting someone love that you need to hear those tender words. This advice is not restricted to intimate relationships, but family and friends as well.

"All relationships are intimate and sacred, each in a different way, each equally precious, even the relationship with those that you think distain you, do not agree with you or would betray you. These are sacred and intimate, perhaps even more so, because they give you the opportunity to practice love and to hold that vibration no matter what. It is a statement that you cannot be interfered with, that no matter what the thoughts, the rumors, the allegations, the mythologies, you are love. That is the core of who you are, the beginning and the end.

"Sacred partnership union looks and feels like everything you have ever dreamed of. It is excitement. It is the heart racing excitement of being so deeply connected and in that the deep acceptance of your beloved. Acceptance is the knowing of your beloved's spark of divinity, and accepting them wholly and completely. I am not suggesting that there are not moments when Yeshua and I would look at each other and the sparks would fly. But it is acceptance knowing that even if there are moments where your viewpoint is different, it doesn't change the love you have for that person. It cannot be changed, it is unalterable, it is bedrock and in that is surrender to one another, that wonderful embrace of knowing that you are cherished for not just the good, not just what presents, but for all of your being.

"In that surrender and acceptance is an honoring that says I will respect you, I will protect you, and I will have your back no matter what. I may not agree with you but I trust your heart, I trust your wisdom and I will follow you as you will follow me and if it means separation at times and letting go, then I will honor that, I will be strong enough. It is elation to share a bond that can never be severed. Archangel Michael has spoken to about cords, and that most cords need to be severed so you may choose love and joy. But in sacred union there is a different level of bond which is so deep and profound that it will never be severed.

"For example, your connection to Mother/Father/One is never broken, that is the downfall, the illusion that has created the old third dimension. But there are other bonds of love such as friendships that are so honored and deep that it is like sisterhood and brotherhood. There are children who you love, that you will never, ever let down or betray, that you would die for. It is that sense of unity that you realize that you are no longer just one heart, that every choice, every decision from where you choose to live, eat, pursue as your sacred work or your daily work, all these decisions are made from this place of united heart. I cannot simply feel for my joy without taking into consideration yours. That is the unity consciousness where Yeshua and I live and it is where we invite you to live with us.

"My journey on Earth was a journey of joy, growth, discovery, of becoming, allowing and letting go. It was painful, filled with sorrow, and despair. Yes. Simply to be in union with Yeshua was a divine gift. It was not the whole of my life the same way as having my children and as you have yours is not the whole of your life. But did it give definition, purpose, framework and the deepest meaning and joy? Yes, yes it was what my life led up to and it was the meaning that remained with me until such time as I passed from the earthly realm.

"Now, in this period of ascension, it is truly a time of embodying in physical form these qualities of your divine feminine and masculine. This balance allows you to proceed courageously in the creation of sacred union and partnership. There is nothing that I would love to do more than to assist you in this. My advice to you is to know all the rules, customs, belief systems, and then break them! Have the courage to do what you know is truth and to express your love gently and in outrageous ways. Free yourself to be the love, and to love yourself, because you cannot support your partner, community and this beloved planet unless that love for yourself is completely unconditional. Love yourself so thoroughly that no matter who says what about you, who wishes to speak ill of you or stone you, that you can stand tall and still because you are the truth. You not only know the truth and embody the truth, you are the truth. Is this easy? No, and it never has been; but it is always, always worth it, the reward is infinite.

"There are many of you out there who have always known of my love for you and of my connection, my marriage, my partnership, my sacred union with Yeshua, and of the trials and tribulations of our families and the closeness, the joy. We never sat and bemoaned what was to come or whether people liked us or not. Dear heart, we had fun, we played, baked, cooked, ate, shared; we walked, felt the sun on our face and the moon in our hair, the water on our feet. This is what I want for you. Embrace the joy and know that my gratitude to you did not end with my life or yours. You look to us, to the Company of Heaven, and the Council of Love for blessings, and intervention. But what you sometimes forget is we express gratitude to you as well. You are the brave ones, you are the ones who have turned to the Mother and the Mighty Ones and said 'I will go.' You are doing magnificent work, all of you. You are holding the light and when it is time, I will embrace you yet again. Farewell."

The New You does not need to run hither and yon seeking partnership. It will emerge and present itself in not only divine timing but your timing. It is a matter of being clear, of opening your heart and engaging with others when they reach out to you. This new form of union is not about pursuing or being pursued; it is about allowing the deep recognition to inform your heart when you encounter each other. This does not mean you stay home and wait for the doorbell to ring. Creation doesn't work that way. Action, in alignment with who you are and what you are birthing is necessary. Begin to make greater eye contact, smile, go to places where like-minded and like-hearted people congregate. Make yourself available, and allow. Declare your intention, and open your heart to receive.

The COL exercise of the heart-to-heart infinity is perfect for either attracting or growing a sacred union partnership. This is an exercise where you send the love and energy of your heart to your partner. Here's how it works.

As always, anchor deeply within your heart in meditation. Go to the 13th Octave, anchor in the complete knowing of Love.

From the center of your heart, send out your soul color ray as a laser beam of light to your beloved. The movement of this ray, this laser beam, takes the form of an infinity sign, ∞, a sideways number eight. If you don't know what your soul color ray is don't worry about it, send the color that comes to mind, or if in doubt send white light. However, after you have done this exercise go back and listen again to the "Soul Color" meditation.

In the space between your heart and theirs the laser beam of light crosses over into that sacred space that exists between you. Then it carries your light, your energy and love directly into their heart. While the energy is making that infinity loop through their heart, it picks up their soul color and brings it back directly through your heart. The point of intersection of the infinity is the place of sacred union.

Keep this energy between your hearts flowing for about five to ten minutes. Set it, with intention, to flow for twenty-four/seven. Where the heart connection has been broken or lost you will immediately feel and begin to see in physical reality a re-establishment of the love. What this exercise does is send out your energy across the universe to them – it acts as a homing or direction signal so not only is the connection made but you can locate your sacred partner.

This is a simple and yet powerful tool of connection and renewal. You can use this with your children, parents, community, star brothers and sister – the list is endless. The incredible thing is the laser beam is always felt and it always works!

FAMILY & SOUL FAMILY

It's important to remember that we chose our family, not just our parents but our siblings and extended family. The choice of who you incarnate with is the result of an extensive discussion between your guides, the souls you are incarnating with, their guides, as well as the Universal Mother. The circumstances of the life you are being born into, the society, class, race, opportunities which will be presented or absent are all aligned with your soul mission and purpose. Generally you tend to incarnate with the same soul family and soul circle time and again, both on Earth and elsewhere. The vision I am given repeatedly is when the Divine Mother calls for volunteers you look to your soul family and partner and say, "I'll go if you go" – and the rest is history.

Often I hear from the query, "why did I chose my family – it has been so hard, so unloving." It's important to understand there isn't a single human being, star seed or earthkeeper who decided to come to Earth in order to experience hardship, pain and suffering. Each bright soul came with the full expectation of giving and receiving love. Each of us, arrived with the expectation we would have the joy of being in a caring, nurturing family – be it with a single mom or a tribe of twenty.

Even those of us who have incarnated in service to the Mother during this time of shift and ascension came expecting the support and love of our family circle. While we knew the shifting of Gaia and humanity would be challenging and frustrating at times, we did not question our certain victory or the support that would be available to us from above and below.

Sometimes it's hard to fathom what was arranged and agreed upon in joy and excitement on the other side is not always what translates when people engage with free will in the old false grids of the third dimension. The good news is that Gaia has ascended to the fifth dimension and in the higher realms that density of lack of love, support and sweetness does not exist. Part of the clearing of the old debris, releasing *vasanas*, issues, debris and the false grids is changing the experience of what it means to be in family. That's the good news.

Universal Mother Mary offers these words of encouragement:

"There is very little, other than your sacred journey, that is more important than family; the family that you have chosen and most of you time after time, that you have chosen to travel with, that you have chosen to construct within and operate whether it is in India, Australia, New Zealand, China or the United States, it matters not. You have chosen your family and you have chosen your soul family as well. Let me emphasize the starting, mid, and finishing points, my sweet ones, is always your sacred self. Without that foundation and honoring there can be no other relationships

"We know just as clearly as you do that relationships within the family of choice have not always been easy or graceful, smooth or even nurturing, honoring or respectful; but they are family. I have walked the Earth, and the dynamics of family have not really changed. There is always one who can be an irritant or who thinks they have the sole monopoly on truth or is enmeshed in the grid of control, lack or limitation. But there are also those that you cherish and wish to keep closer and closer.

"All are equally playing a part and this becomes clearer as you, sweet ones, abandon the old third, the drama and the false grids, because as you do they are forced to, not in a way that is pushy, it is simply that they cannot meet you there and therefore you raise them up to meet you in a new reality. Is this easy? Not always. Is it worth it? Always, and in all ways.

"We look at the issue of family, of kindred spirits, of friend-ship, of soul family, but let me emphasize, the starting, middle, and finishing point, my sweet ones, is always your sacred self. Without that foundation and honoring there can be no other relationships."

It isn't difficult for us to imagine what an ideal family situation looks and feels like. While I could write reams about the nature of the New You family, it is far more powerful to read, anchor and integrate what the Father, Mother and Son have to say on this subject. It is an incredible gift to hear what our true Father, Mother and Brother have to say about family. It broadens our grasp of what family and soul family, is intended to be. We begin with Yahweh.

"Greetings, I am Yahweh, Father, Grandfather, One. Wel-come my beloved family, children of my heart and children of my essence, children of my being. Welcome my sweet angels of every soul ray, hue, and color. Your vibration is felt throughout the multiverse, for you are clear and you are bright, and you are mine. Yes, I know of your infinite connection to the Mother and it is right and just, but I wish you to know out of this place of Oneness and stillness that I, too, claim you and offer you my heart, my help, my love. Always, and always it has been thus.

"I come this day to speak to you of this sacred nature of family for this is one of the areas in the New You that you now focus upon. Before I say anything I also want to say you have arrived at the New You and it is the old you, it is the original you, expanded, polished, and brighter than ever according to plan; according to our plan and your plan. As Father, as Grandfather, I am entitled to tell you how proud I am of you. This has been a journey of persistence, exciting exploration, wonder, growth, unity, and more than anything, of coming together in trust. What else is family except that?

"The nature of human experience has been constructed on unity and community. There are many ways in which the Mother could have unfolded this plan and there are many ways in which it is unfolded elsewhere. But as a planet of love, as a planet of fulfillment of joy in form, the very idea of the human collective was unity. How could that come to pass, to unfold? What was the structure, form and framework in which Universal Law could be translated in practical and realistic ways for humans and the collective to have this experience?

"Well, it begins with family. Even when your family experience has been horrendous, a living nightmare, and did not turn out or materialize the way it was intended, the plan was for beings to come together to love, share, dream and create. In some situations the decision of who to incarnate with in terms of family was rapid, immediate, and left little room for discussion, for the bonds on this side were so strong and so repetitive that you simply chose each other and took off.

"In other situations, very diverse and different individuals from very different rays, backgrounds, lineages, planetary systems, selected to come together to see how that would work and how creation could still take place and love could still thrive and survive. But the framework has been family, and the sacred nature of family. Even if it is not so in this lifetime, each of you have had experiences where the joy and the love of family has been the deepest and most supreme gif; one you cherished highly.

"I also come to speak to you this day of other forms of family, of different forms of community and unity, because the soul family that is emerging and the soul communities that are merging in the Cities of Light all over your planet, are creations of beauty to behold. There are many coming together and choosing, in form, in activation as New You, to be family, to undertake that heart connection, to trust and support, to nurture and share. This is exactly what we had hoped for; it is exactly what I had planned when I have invited you into the family business, when I have given you the keys to the Warehouse of Heaven.

"My beloved ones, I come this day not to proffer advice but simply to say, 'Well done. I am proud of you, I support you, I encourage you now and forever.' Go in peace. Farewell."

We continue with Universal Mother Mary's description of her experience of family:

"Often I have spoken to you about my family, about my beloved husband Joseph and son Yeshua. I do not speak to you very often about all of my children, for I had seven you know. You are familiar with some of them, but not all. I also do not often speak about my beloved mother, Anna, and about my extended family.

"I mention this because I wish you to know what deep reverence and love I have felt as a woman for my family, for the ones who have honored me by walking with me. In family there is mutuality, for not only did I choose them, they honored and chose me as well, and yes each other, for the experiences that we would share, for the love and laughter, hardship, growth, and purpose.

"Family is sacred. No matter how much you share, or how many differences you have on this side prior to your return to Earth, there have been sacred vows to honor, to help, promises to keep, to support, to extend your hand when a family member is drowning.

"The family is the microcosm of what you are creating in community upon the Earth. Now we expand this to soul family, to those you love, those you entrust with the secrets of your heart, your life, the ones you choose to hold close to you. You may call them friends, but they are indeed your soul family. This is what this circle of the New You and the Council of Love is. It is what it has always been; it is a family of Love. From time to time there will be squabbles, differences and irritations. But that is far surpassed by the love you share, by the commonality, and the joining, the union of hearts.

"I speak of the love of family is because, my sweet ones, you are also my family; always and forever. I have told you many times that I have birthed you from my heart, from my womb. You have emanated from the heart of One. But I do not think that you always understand when I say this, that the implication is of family. I know as Mother that sometimes you are irritated, disappointed, angered with us, frustrated for what does and what does not evolve or take place upon your planet, but I also tell you, sweet angels, that part of this is the frustration of wanting to place blame and guilt elsewhere. It is alright, because that is part of the dynamic of the family. However, part of that dynamic is also when you look at each other and say, 'wait a minute I did not do this to you.' You need to more deeply comprehend the process of co-creation.

"When we share our heart, our essence, our very being; when I weave and stand next to you, with you, before you, behind you, within you, as never before this also entails co-creation – and yes, responsibility – a choice of what we do together as family. So I ask of you this day as our human Council of Love, not just individually but collectively to decide: what do we choose, what do we endeavor together to create, what is our conjoined hearts' desire?

"I ask you to weave the tapestry with me. I have asked several of you to help show, interpret and discuss what it means to live in family with me, with my beloved son, with all of my family, with Joseph. When you have a father, mother, cousin, aunt or sister you do not see because they are not in your household, you do not stop including them in your thoughts, heart, creation and healing work or your daily life. They are part of the fabric of who you are, and the bond is not merely biological, it is the soul choice of love. You want to share, build, offer encouragement, advice, to point the way. You want to be able to say, 'no, that doesn't sound like a good way to go,' while offering the encouragement to keep going.

"This is the relationship I am asking of you. I am asking for the soul conversations. It can cover any topic, any dream or desire. Feel free to ask whatever is in your heart and on your mind: is the sky blue, do you really think Mary's essence is blue diamond, do you think Yeshua, is magenta? What is the place of integrity with compassion? How do I balance my wants, my desires with responsibility? These are human questions and these are questions of heaven. I am listening, and I will always answer."

Jesus, our brother who has walked the Earth and knows the joys and challenges of family and community, shares his insight:

"I wish to speak to you about the importance of family. The family is for every day, they are the special occasion of your heart. Family is your wisdom source, your fountain, your compassion, laughter and tears, and the depth of understanding that will come from nowhere else in the human experience.

"I have walked with you as brother, teacher, healer and friend, not as Master. I want you to understand this, for you give me many titles. The honor I wish to hold with you is brother, brother of your heart, soul and brother of your journey, whatever that journey entails. It entails a great deal, and this expansion of understanding and being is only just beginning. When I come and I walk with you again in the New Jerusalem, I will do so not as master I will walk as brother and friend.

"There is such controversy upon the planet about my very straightforward and simple love and marriage with my beloved Magdalena, the twin of my heart, the twin of my very soul. How could there ever be controversy about the creation of a family, about the coming together in love?

"Think of my father, Joseph, as a mighty oak, strong and

silent, and so dependable. He would shield and shade you from the hard times and he would support you; you could lean upon him. Joseph does not get enough credit. Yet there is not one father upon the Earth who could do better than to emulate my beloved father, Joseph. He taught me what it was to be man, to walk in strength, meekness, gentleness and to have the courage of my convictions, my knowing. My beloved mother who knew from day one what my journey would be would often shy away and ask 'Yeshua, please, stand back a little, do you need to be so obvious?' My father never did this. Sometimes in the quiet of the evening he would suggest temperance and a way of speaking that would help others understand my message. He showed me the way.

"Let me also speak of my family and my beloved Mary, Magdalena. Do you truly think that as partners we never fought or had words? The love and passion was strong between us, but we were both very independent souls. There were moments of disagreement and moments of incredible tenderness. Guidance was equally available to both of us. We did not engage in this journey together without her fully understanding my pathway. The strength of this one was enormous, for she knew she would carry on alone, that she would be single mother.

"I relied on her strength, for there were moments when I would falter. As a human man there were times when I would simply think, let me take my family and run away, let me protect them and myself; let us start over. Mary would just look at me, and we would know not only of our everlasting sacred bond. but of the promise and contract that we had come to fulfill in that life. Just as each of you are fulfilling a promise in this one, which is why we wish to give you all the help that you can possibility get. You are the Nova Beings; you are the nova healers, and you have been given the science directly from Einstein to support that. It's time.

"Do not simply think in traditional terms of family. Each of you has a soul family you have traveled with forever. Each of you is encountering your soul family in a myriad of ways, situations and environments. Open your heart to that recognition.

You are reuniting because you have agreed long ago to do so – to be with your soul family in support, sometimes in disagreement, but always in love. Lean on your soul family, family is what gets you through, they are your strength, they are your oak tree, they are your shade, and they are your sun. They are the expression of your heart, they are your mirror. Lean not only on me, but upon each other in honesty and truth. You are dealing with the elimination of core issues of the collective. Be honest with yourself and each other. This is opportunity rarely given. Trust each other, and understand that you are trusting each other with your lives. Then look to the foot of the table for I am always there. Go with my love, go with my wisdom and compassion, and go with my laughter."

We understand what family and soul family is intended to be, and what it can look like. But what do we do when the vision and the experience don't come close to aligning? What can we do when we wish to raise the frequency of our familial relationships from acceptable or comfortable to sacred union? There are a multitude of tools at our disposal, including working with the creation formula, Universal Law, Archangel Michael's sword, and Universal Mother Mary's gift of removal. However, for this task I would like to recommend soul conversations.

Soul conversations can be used in a variety of situations, including conflict resolution and significantly improving the quality of a relationship – be it with your child, spouse, partner, parent or friend. A soul conversation is heart-speaking from your higher self to the higher self of the person you are working with. It is a sure-fire method of truly being able to reach a person for a heart-to-heart conversation. Here's how it works.

Go into meditation and anchor in your heart, as deeply as you know how. Go to the 13th Octave. Call the person's higher self forward. Not to worry – they will always show up. If you are not visual don't worry; simply know the person you are working with is there, fully engaged and listening. Always keep the conversation on the level of love. This system has no room for fault, blame, guilt or judgment. Begin by telling the individual how much you honor and respect them; how you understand that they have their perspective and unique journey, and perhaps you don't fully understand all the factors they are dealing with. If you love and care for them, say so, but only if it's true – this isn't about flattery but truth speaking.

From that place of heart and balance state your case. It may be that you want to be closer, more deeply connected; that you want the bond of love that was once so bright to shine again; that you want forgiveness, freedom, divorce, respect – anything goes. Fully express your heart's need and desire. Ask them what, if anything, they need from you in order to accommodate your request. It is uncommon for the other person's higher self not to offer you some insight and direction at this point. They will always answer.

While in deep meditation, reassure them of what you are willing to do, as well as what you need. This is a heart exchange conversation, not a one-way street. You close by thanking the person, the higher self and all the guardian angels and guides that have assisted in this exchange.

Depending on the severity of the situation, you may need to have this soul conversation several times. It will progress the way a human conversation does. In the meanwhile, the soul conversation is sinking in from the person's higher self into their conscious awareness. Often you can tell because the behavioral shifts start and you can see the changes, the relaxation of tensions. Folks often report that their sweet child is back, or the spark has come back into a relationship, or a difficult situation at work has simply been resolved.

If the situation has not been resolved to your satisfaction, after a few days, or a week or so, bring up the topic of the soul conversation with the individual. Often this proves unnecessary because they bring it up first. Often you hear them say 'I've been thinking about something I want to talk to you about.' That is wonderful confirmation. Staying in your heart, in that place of honor and respect, and hopefully love, and have the conversation in the physical reality.

You will be amazed at how well soul conversations work.

They are proof of our ability, particularly as we ascend and become fully interdimensional to be able to fluently and effectively communicate at a much higher level. Work with it, play with it, and remember, always begin with love.

FRIENDSHIP & COMMUNITY

One of the loveliest gifts of being part of the New You webinars was the friendship and community which formed on a very deep level. The sharing, honesty and true grit of these two magnificent groups is awe-inspiring. This coming together is a clear demonstration of how we find our soul family and circle in the most unusual ways, collecting them from all over the world. The heart-sharing, clarity, truth, assistance to one another, and the willingness to tackle big and difficult issues with vigor has been astonishing.

When I followed guidance to launch the New You webinar series, I was told the group would come together quickly and would be performing a massive universal task; that this was an undertaking that would change the world. Well, naturally a little bit of trepidation crept in, and while I forged ahead, my hope and prayer was that the coming together of these two groups of twenty-five strangers from every corner of the Earth and every walk of life, would be minimally fruitful and give people the boost, the lift-off they were obviously ready for. Talk about underestimating something, or more specifically a very special group of somebodies!

Everything the Council indicated about the formation of this group of sweet Annas (angels of the Lord) has come to pass and more. The gentle manner in which this group of re-patterners of humanity has stepped forward and bonded together is nothing short of a miracle. I use this personal example because it demonstrates how friendships and the idea of community are shifting. Virtual friendships and community are not a thing of the future – they are our here and now support.

The first class the Council of Love brought forward after the introduction of the 13th Octave was Accessing the Universal Internet. I am not what anyone in their wildest imagination would call a techie, and that couldn't have been truer in 1998. Email was still exotic and the Internet a challenge. The COL explained to me the Internet was a gift from our star brothers and sisters, patterned on the universal internet which was their mode of communication. And while the class included computer and Internet terminology, the core of the material was about reading the screen of another's heart and mind. It was the first step in telepathic communication and learning about how our star family maintains and conducts communication and community.

We all participate in a variety of communities; work, neighborhood, spiritual, friendship and so on. What we have recognized over the past decade, and increasingly over the last couple of years, is that our communities are merging and they are global. The Internet has redefined how we connect and form bonds of unity. Data which transmutes into information which then catalyzes action is no longer controlled the way it has been in the old third dimension. This is not only true of news or political movements such as the Arab Spring or Occupy Wall Street; it is true of the spiritual community as well. The dearth of information from the company of heaven is astounding. The key in reading and acting on that information is the same as it was two thousand years ago. Practice discernment.

The real gift of the Internet is how it has demonstrated that we can connect on a very deep heart level to people who we have never met in physical form. Just as our star brothers and sisters have learned to be in community with species and planets they have never encountered but have come to love and admire, so too are we. This does not eliminate the richness of physical community. If anything this virtual community enriches our physical relationships. We are coming to more deeply appreciate the smile of a neighbor, a hug from a friend, the gentle touch of a loved one, because we realize how unique and precious those physical expressions are. In many ways they become a surrogate and mirror for all the warmth we give and receive across the airwaves.

This expansion in what it means to be in community reflects our spiritual growth; our desire to be connected at all levels across Gaia. We are also forming a much deeper sense of community with the kingdoms, the animals, elementals, stone people, fairies and the unseen realms. During that monumental workshop of Accessing the Universal Internet in 1998, Gaia was welcomed and initiated into the Intergalactic Council. Earth joined the interplanetary community, whose purpose is peace and the spread of peaceful trade, technology, culture, science and esoteric knowledge. The foundation of the Intergalactic Council is Universal Law. It has been almost inevitable that our perception and practice of what it means to be in community would shift – and thank heavens it has.

The fifth dimension is a reality of unity consciousness. It that realm separation and isolation are not options. Being a recluse doesn't fit. There is a difference between liking to live quietly and privately, and shutting yourself off from the world. In the past many people became reclusive because the experience of the world was too painful, too much. As we grow into our new form of what it means to be human, and what it means to be part of not merely the human community but the intergalactic community, that sense of wanting to run away and hide because the world doesn't feel safe will disappear. The blessing of being able to flow between private alone time and fully engaged in community will become like the ebb and flow of the tides.

The following channel with Yeshua and the energy of the Magdalena teaches us how to proceed in building community, and through that our own sacred self.

"Welcome I am Yeshua. Mary (Magdalene) and I welcome you. It is my pleasure and honor to speak to your hearts about maintaining a high vibration and going forward in your sacred journey. Each of your journeys' is different, unique, and magnificent and yet at the same time a piece, a small puzzle piece of the bigger unified whole. The thing I note about so many of you my friends is you worry about this mission; you worry about this mission night and day and in-between. Am I doing it right? Am I letting anyone down? Have I fulfilled my purpose? Am I on track? I do not hear you say 'Am I having fun? Do I feel loved? Do I love? Do I feel the connection to my family above and below?' No, not simply your star brothers and sisters but us as well for we are part of your family, we always have been.

"One of the surefire ways to maintain your highest vibration is to simply remind yourself, not only that you are not alone, but that you are wholly and completely, without any exception, loved. We have given you many tools and we could sit here and talk about prayer, ritual, meditation or esoteric studies, but what we want to do right now is to reach in and touch your heart. During this time of transition, many old issues you thought were put to bed ages ago are coming to the forefront. That can be nervous making, anxiety provoking and fearful. So Mary and I want to touch your hearts and reassure you how deeply you are loved because nothing, nothing maintains the highest vibration in the universe other than feeling and being, accepting and acknowledging love.

"If I have ever had one message to each of you, it is that you are love, it is the molecular structure of your being, the subatomic fibers of who you are, the light quotient, it is not something that disappears, it is not something that can ever be taken from you, it is the core, the essence, the spark of you, unique and beautiful. I wish to share a couple of ideas and methods of how my Magdalena and I would maintain clarity. Let us use the word clarity and love in exchange for high vibration because as we speak you may notice it makes it easier and perhaps will make more sense to you.

"One of the things we did, and it may sound trite, but we stuck together and when I say that I mean that we spent our time with like-minded, like-hearted, like-believers. Yes, the disciples, the apostles, the many followers and friends; that group grew exponentially every day. We would spend time with family, with those who knew our truth and who loved and accepted us. If you are not fortunate to have family who understands the fullness of your mission, we suggest that you still take time to be with them whether it is electronically, on the phone, or in person, because these people know and they love you. They may not know the truth of everything but even by being with them you are changing their vibration.

"There is no being that came into a family without a soul agreement. Many of these soul agreements have been violated, I understand that. But when you spend time with your community, be it one or twenty, it is reinforcing, it is entraining. It does not matter whether it is work time, play time or free time; being with those who are like-hearted, like-minded, who are on the same journey, reinforces you. It gives you permission to be yourself. So this is what we, my Magdalena and I, would do.

"Another practice we did prior to walking out to do the work that we had chosen, for which we volunteered and yes been selected, was to assess the situation and task beforehand. Will this be reinforcing? Will this group that we meet with be resistant? Do they believe in love? Do they believe in what we have to share? If the answer was yes we would plunge right in but when the answer was no we would do a great deal of preparatory work. We would have soul conversations, we would send energy, ask the Mighty Ones (archangels) to surround not only us but them as well, using the tools at our disposal. We would prepare the way.

"Another thing we would do would be to create time for our sacred selves and to do whatever we felt like doing; sometimes it was nothing except staring at the sky, playing with the baby, sitting quietly, sharing tea. Other times it would be rich, deep, philosophical discussion and questioning to open our hearts and our minds even further, to bring that communion of all parts of ourselves. That is the gift of sacred union, of having one that you can truly share your hopes, your fears, your concerns, your dreams with. I know not all of you have been blessed in this way but I do tell you that most of you have come with the intention and therefore the plan to have this experience of love.

"The sharing, the community, whether it is a community of thousands, community of twelve, or a community of two; it is community and the connection and unity that helps to maintain higher vibration. It is that sense of common mission, of being united in purpose, belief and knowing. It is a shift in your planetary humanness that you are becoming conscious of choosing joy, heart, and love. The way in which many of you have been trained, brought up and educated did not put choosing joy front and center. That is really unsatisfactory. Yes it requires diligence to retrain your psyche and open your heart. But this is the path of the New You – it is the path of forming community. It requires practice and patience, but also excitement and exuberance. Many of you are just beginning to learn, or remember, how to communicate with your hearts, to be honest and truthful, trusting and hopeful with disclosing what is in your heart. Dear hearts, keep going, because not only is this what the ascension process is about, it is what your life was always intended to be."

Forming and being in community is organic and also work – it requires effort and heart-desire to stay in communication, to share ideas and feelings, to build rapport and trust. There are times that community, like family and partnership, also requires a thick skin, of the ability to allow yourself to be vulnerable even if that means others having a go at you. You need to accept that when that happens, and it will, that it is about their lessons not yours. In community you are not only gleaning support, nourishment and love; you are also being the catalyst and are having your buttons pushed. You are the reflection of the mirror, and sometimes you will love what you are looking at and other times you will think 'I need a little touch up'. The key is to laugh, and continue on – community is not only our future but our now.

As we move on to the Universal Law, you will understand how many of the Laws can be utilized to build community, as well as all forms of sacred union. Examples are to invoke the Law of Intent – all of us intend to live in harmonious, loving supportive communities; the Law of Above and Below – the higher realms are in the authentic experience and existence of community; the Law of Attachment and Detachment – attach to the higher vision of community and detach from the old third false grid, it's time. Embrace your communities deeply and savor the richness they offer you, it is one of the sweetest gifts of being alive, and it's meant to be enjoyed.

We leave this section on sacred union by sharing with you the most beautiful meditation on the experience of community, Cities of Light Within. This is a gift from my heart to yours.

Listen to the "Cities of Light Within" Audio Meditation)

The New You Creator

The core mission and purpose of the New You is creation. After all the work you have done, all the expansion, the sweetness of sacred union, recognition of your interdimensional self, it all comes down to this point – the New You is a master creator. We, the re-patterners of humanity, the re-constructors of Gaia and the builders of Cities of Light are essentially creators. We always have been, we always will be – it is part and parcel of our spiritual and physical DNA. It's why we came to Earth at this time, why we are embracing the brand-new ideas and previously unheard of concepts of the New You, and part of anchoring our ascension into physical form.

This is an exciting and incredible time to be alive. Has it been a tough go at times? Undeniably. But I for one wouldn't have missed this opportunity for anything. All of us have done amazing and beneficial things up until now. My friends, we are just getting started. Now comes the fun, the reward, the fulfillment of the dream and promise.

We bring this section of the New You Creator by allowing Universal Mother Mary to remind us about why we're here, why the New You and why we chose to come at this quintessential moment of history.

"Greetings, I am Mary, Universal Mother, Divine Mother, Mother of One, Mother of All, and Mother, sweet angels, of each of you. Welcome my beloved circle of angels, humans, starseeds, gate keepers, pillars and showers of the way. I welcome each of you as brand new. It is not merely a return to your original design; it is the fullness, completeness and wholeness of that design expanded even further. Time, space and energy did not stand still, child, it continued forward as did each of you. The New You is the erasure, elimination and destruction with Michael's sword of all that does not serve you. This allows who you are to come forth as creator, as creator race, as part of that original circle. That is why I have beckoned to you, why you have answered, and I thank you for doing so.

"Your commitment to me is as full as my commitment to you. Our love is as one, as Mother and child, but more – as sisters, brothers and colleagues in a sense of the word that you have never imagined. We are in a sacred union and partnership. The channel has asked, 'What lies ahead?' Well, it is the fulfillment of this partnership, of our sacred soul agreement of eons ago. Does it catapult you back to the light, back to the heart of One? Yes it does. But the speed at which you return and the choices that you will make to stay upon the planet to guide and create Nova Earth are yours. Mind you, I wish to influence you as does the entire Council of Love, your guides, the ascended masters, archangels, saints, prophets, and kingdoms as well. We all want you to stay; to enjoy the bounty of your diligence and creations, to marvel at the pristine beauty of Gaia and humanity.

"Dear heart, your presence continues to be needed upon Terra Gaia, Nova Earth. Will she survive? Of course, she is already in her radiance in the fifth dimension, and traveling to the seventh. That is not the point; the fulfillment of the promise is the realization of joy and love in form. It is not about arduous sacrifice, work and drudgery; it never has been. It is about laughter, glee and letting the gladness of your heart be known. And in that laughter and glee, to be creating so magnificently that you won't want to leave until the project is done. Therefore, dear heart, your portion of the project is only done when you deem so.

"You are the patternmakers; you are the human anchors for the re-patterning of humanity. What does that mean mentally, emotionally, spiritually and physically? The answer does not require science or knowledge of subatomic physics. What it requires, beloved one is a willing heart; what it requires is what you have already given, and that is a 'yes.' So much lies in front of you, and I do not mean in the distant future when you turn ninety-three years old. I mean right now. You have inordinate capacity to create. Do not wait thinking that you need to reach a certain marker or level. That is all old thinking and it is over and done with.

"Begin with me today; take your heart's desire, bring it to your stillpoint, hold it in the sacred space, not only of your union but our sacred union, and let us spin it out to the entire universe. Let us demonstrate together the wonder of who you are. I will not hear any denials from you. Your magnificence and humility are known far and wide. Denial of your capacity only diminishes you and I will not stand for it.

"Go with my love and let us begin. Farewell."

Our starting point as we proceed in this adventure is fully anchoring who and what is the creator race. Who could possibly explain this better than our beloved St. Germaine?

"I am St. Germaine. Now we get down to work and really play. My friends you have rallied round and anchored the 13th Octave within your conscious bodies and selves.

"You are the creator race. That is how you are known throughout the intergalactic federation, as a race of master creators. You sit there shocked and awed – as I was when I first heard it tens of thousands of years ago. You are creators. There are many myths upon this planet, one of them being that you are a replica of Source and Creator. That is truth. You have demonstrated time and again your ability to create wonderful things, community and harmony, peace and prosperity, but you have also demonstrated your ability to create illusion and separation; belief systems that do not serve such as death and destruction, war and hatred. Those lesser creations are but a dream, a part of your evolution. Now each of you is being called to step forward to create your new world. It is a world based on love and existing as sheer energy in form. This has never happened in other universes and galaxies. What has occurred when the energy or species has evolved to collective unity of One, when the minds and hearts became One, was that form was released. You know this of the Halion engineers and healers of Tralana.

This creator race is going to create a new form, Nova Being, a physical form that holds the sheer energy of love. That is your job, your mission. That is your choice, purpose, service and the only reason you are here. You are expanding yourself and everybody on this planet to a place of unification where the uniqueness of form is absolutely celebrated in joy, and released at will. This planet is a reflection of the diversity of the Mind and Will of One. That is the New You, the creator race."

Yahweh adds to our understanding of what it means and entails to be the creator race:

"Greetings, I am Yahweh, Universal Father, Father of the Universe, Creator, and friend. I come to speak and embrace you, my beloved ones, as the children of my heart. For as the Mother and I are united as One, so are you. In very practical terms, I want to speak to you about what this means.

"I have invited you into the family business thinking that this was language that you would understand and embrace. Our family business is creation and love. We are manufacturers. We manufacture all kinds of creations, things that you know upon Earth and things that you have never even dreamed of. The material that we manufacture with is love, and the work environment is unity and joy. I repeatedly ask you to come with me to the factory, the warehouse of heaven, where we will access the creation codes, the molecules and subatomic particles of love, and manipulate them into form.

"What do you wish to manufacture and bring into form in your life? How are we going to work together, transmute this energy of the universe and package it into what your heart desires? Be clear, we are not manufacturing your ability to hold energy, you already have that. I am talking about the bricks and mortar. So, what do you wish to create? Is it a mate of flesh and blood? I am not suggesting that we are going to build him or her, but we will create the energy field that will draw that person immediately to you. Don't forget I have invited you to access the Warehouse of Heaven with or even without me. But as Father, as one who loves you so deeply, I want to accompany you until you have the knack, until you really understand in very human practical terms how to do this.

"We give you the Creation Formula, the theory of how to create, and the practical how-to. We do so not only for you, but for the planet. Because once you have the knack of this creation business, you are not going to stop. I urge you to take care of yourself first. When you are flying in one of Raphael's planes, we say put the air mask on yourself first and then assists others. Well, that is my advice as well. Let us first tend to the sacred garden of your heart, soul, emotional being and delightful ego. From there let us expand. If you wish to specialize, then I would be happy and honored to help you do so. Let me be concrete: if your goal is to create homes for humanity, write and publish books, sing and have a hit song, I will help you. I am trying to cover a range of potentialities so you will understand the magnitude of what I am offering.

"Part of your divinity and assuming form at this time of magnificent rebirth is the building of Nova Earth. So again, the question is what do you chose to create? You have been given the energy and totality of our expression not merely esoterically or spiritually, but physically. What are you going to do with it? If there is the slightest hesitation, then let me help you. Let us all help you. This Council of Love is exactly what its name implies. It is our expression of unity and community. You are part of this Council. You declared yourself part of it a long time ago.

"Come with me. Let my golden love warm you. I am not an old man sitting on a mountaintop in judgment. I am the Father sitting next to you with my hand on your shoulder simply saying how can I help? I am not saying let me do it for you. You have grown out of that. It would not be respectful of me to say that to you now. But there are pieces perhaps that are not clear to you yet and I will guide you. Remember, when we created the multiverse, we did not sit with furrowed brows agonizing over what to do. We did it with delight and joy. That is how creation takes place. It is ecstatic work; bliss. Farewell."

We know the who of the creator race. It's you and me, my

dear friends. We know the when is right now and the where is right here on this exquisite planet of diversity, Gaia. We even know the why, which is the unfoldment of the Divine Plan of the Universal Mother, and the fulfillment of our soul mission and purpose within that plan. I believe each of us has an extensive list of what our heart desires to create both individually and collectively. Therefore, as the bright New You let's move on to the how.

THE CREATION FORMULA

The Creation Formula is a gift from the Council of Love directly to each of us – not only to our hearts but to our conscious selves in the here and now. The purpose of the Creation Formula, just like the Universal Laws, is to help us understand, in workable practical terms, how to create. In the next chapters we will discuss in detail the creation triangle elements of the 13 Blessings and Virtues and Universal Laws, but as a starting point let us look and delve into the Creation Formula. Here it is:

INTENT+STILLPOINT+ACTION=CREATION

Over the past few years I have channeled volumes on the Creation Formula. For purposes of clarity and focus, I will include a couple of channelings that capture the spirit and nature of the elements of intent, stillpoint and action.

Throughout this book there has been no theme as prevalent as the necessity of love. We have read the repeated message that that is who we are; it is our purpose, why we are here, and the essence of the universe. I think we all grasp this concept – if we are not in and of love there is no authentic creation activity – not on Nova Earth, and not in the fifth dimension or higher. Similarly, joy and gratitude have been given ample air time, and are about to be given more in the following chapter on the 13 Blessings and Virtues.

Nevertheless, it is important to emphasize, that unless the

environment of love, joy and gratitude are present, then creation cannot take place. Certainly not at the level and sustainability we are talking about. You cannot create from a place of anger, lack, angst or fear. This is why it was so important to eliminate those false grids prior to reaching this step. There is a chance that when you begin working with the Creation Formula that some of those old lack and limitation beliefs will come to the surface to haunt you, making you question your innate abilities. If so, go back to the meditation of the Elimination of False Grids, open your heart and let go. Then come back right here and continue.

Sometimes desperation energy is sufficient to bring a creation forward, that blessing is generally your guides and heaven having mercy on you rather than you bringing something forth. The other piece of attempting to create in an environment of need is that it does not stick. How many times have you brought something forward, be it a relationship, money or good health, simply to lose it shortly thereafter. That loss occurs because the creation was not anchored in the Divine Qualities of love, joy and gratitude. With this straightforward understanding of the environment necessary for creation, we are prepared to step forward. Let's go!

As we begin this process the COL guides us to not begin with a laundry list, or even matters of global or universal import. We begin with one thing, one creation that we are going to see through from beginning to end. In this way you begin not only to integrate how the formula works but you experience each step, and witness the fruition of your work into form. Tangible results are important; they act as confirmation and fuel our enthusiasm. Success keeps us going. If you begin with a creation like world peace (did I just hear "Miss Congeniality?") what you are doing is choosing a creation that depends on the input, co-operation and co-creation of everyone on the planet. For now leave that to your work with Archangel Michael. Begin with something tangible, something that your heart has desired for a long time, something that you want but were perhaps even afraid to admit.

INTENT

There are many elements in formulating intent. First comes dreaming. Archangel Michael, Mother Mary, Yahweh and so many of the Council of Love are always pleading with us to dream big. What does that mean? What it doesn't mean is starting your intention process with a paper and pencil, making lists and becoming analytical. Dreaming is what a dear friend of mine calls "blue skying." It allows your heart and mind to go to what your ideal creation would look, taste, smell, and feel like. Dreaming can be lying on the grass daydreaming, or my favorite, staring at the wall time. It's allowing your mind to wander, without an agenda except to explore and discover what's written on the walls of your heart.

Many people hold the mistaken belief that intent is the whole of the Creation Formula. It is not. Just as the Law of Attraction does not make up the entire codex of Universal Law, intention is the starting point of creation. I have to share with you though, the formulation of intent is delicious, and it whets your appetite to keep going. Intent is heart and mind in a sweet dance of imagining and creating, of realizing that the universe is your playground. When the intent is formulated it drifts down and is anchored in your heart. Like all work with the Council of Love, creation work is done primarily from your heart. Your heart is the anchor and activator.

There are many expressions of intent; it doesn't simply remain a dream. It becomes a thought and vision, it claims excitement and anticipation; it keeps you focused. It's important not to obsess about your intention but to absolutely keep it front and center. Don't get sidetracked or diverted. A huge piece of learning how to create is learning how to maintain focus. Mother Mary has said that intention is often expressed as prayer. She also tells us that there are times when even a scream to the heart of heaven is a prayer. The texture of each intention will feel differently to you, which is why it's so important to begin with a single creation, and build from there.

Archangel Gabrielle explains intent in this way:

"Greetings I am Gabrielle, Lily of Love, Trumpet of Truth, Messenger of One. There are many who wish to come forward this day, and speak on the content of intent, because it is an area of great concern to us on this side that you truly understand, comprehend and incorporate into your very being, the wisdom of intent. We flipped a coin and I won. It was a golden coin and there are some on this side who would say it was rigged but truly I am the messenger and therefore I am honored to step forward this day. The issue of intent is often misunderstood and it is important in terms of your creation work with us that you have clear understanding.

"We use the word intent to incorporate a great deal. Intent may be expressed in many ways – through prayer, meditation, thought, wishing, daydreaming, but never is it expressed through worry, need, fear, or anger. Wishing, wanting, demanding and commanding are words that are interchangeable with intent. I command, I demand, I intend; but they can only come from the place of love. When shadowed, it is not an alignment with the heart of One, your universal sacred self, love and your own soul design.

"Intent is the first step in the process of creation. In fact, intent is the precursor to creation. It is the starting point. If you think of creation literally as a straight line it would be the beginning of the line. It is the place where you are deciding, aligning and beginning the process of bringing in. Again we emphasize during this time of co-creation of Nova Earth and creator race that we are not simply speaking of spirituality upon the planet. We are talking about creation in the physical realm.

"Intent is not simply saying I intend, which many of you do. When you intend is when you are making your decision about what you wish to bring in. You are bringing your full attention to the matter. This needs to be accomplished in harmony, grace and ease. When you intend, attend, command or demand, you are bringing every particle of your essence; body, mind, spirit, every level your soul design to that place of intention. You are magnetizing with your heart at warp speed, super gluing yourself to that intention. It is the place where you are beginning your full alignment, bringing your conscious, sub-conscious and uncon-scious into the sacred process of creation. There isn't a hierarchy in the creation process. Stillpoint is not above the intent; intent is not above the action. All these aspects are essential to the equa-tion. But here we talk about intent.

"Intending it means that you have brought yourself in full alignment with the heart of God, as well as your heart and higher self. You are intending what is for the best and highest good not only of your own being but of this entire planet. This can be done in an instant, which is why so often when you sim-ply declare you intent and stop worrying about it, it appears. It is because you have achieved that alignment. However, for the next little while, while you are learning we wish you to bring your full attention to what you are intending."

Take time to formulate your intent. This is a gift, a pleasure and is not something to be rushed. You cannot have a deep true intent if it is the first thought that crosses your mind. Remember, it drifts from the dreaming into thought and vision, and then into your heart. Enjoy the process.

STILLPOINT

Now we move from intent to the place of stillpoint. For many stillpoint is the greatest challenge and hurdle of the creation process. Stillpoint is the place of fertilization of your intent, the place where the energy collects and begins to implode and explode into the world. Stillpoint is the place of no movement, no breath, nothingness, the void. It is the place where twenty-first century humans seldom visit, let alone anchor. For many the thought of stillpoint is not only foreign but anathema. Neverthe-less, it's key component to creation. It is not an element you can simply say you don't understand or get it, then move on. The formula doesn't work that way. It would be like baking bread without yeast; jam without peanut butter.

In order to get you going on the stillpoint we include the "Home To Stillpoint" meditation. The best way to begin is simply to start. Explanations can follow.

(LISTEN TO "HOME TO STILLPOINT" AUDIO MEDITATION)

Sanat Kumara begins our discussion on stillpoint with this insight:

"One of the fundamental precepts of creation is that it takes place at the stillpoint of nothingness. If you wish to think of still-point as a place within your physical form, it is deep within the center of your heart. It is the place where you stop and simply remain still. Energy is always in motion if it is not at stillpoint. There is always the ebb and flow which is what the infinity symbol reminds you of. At the center of the infinity is the stillpoint, a span of time not measurable in your dimension. Regardless, let us reassure you of its existence.

"For human beings at this point of evolution, reaching the stillpoint is the most difficult task of all. Nevertheless, understand that you are sufficient to the task. How do you do this? Go to the place of stillness and then through an act of alignment join in union with Divine Will. Feel this in your heart and solar plexus, feel the two energies coming together in perfect stillness. You will experience a sense of simultaneous implosion and explosion, at which point the fertilization of above and below, within and without occurs.

"Now I have another piece of advice I wish to share with you, and that is to hold this stillness for at least seventeen seconds. Hold it. It's at this juncture, the stillpoint, where many of you are going wrong in terms of your creation work. That is why you are frustrated and feeling that you are not bringing things through to fruition.

"I leave you but I do not leave you ever, for you were entrusted to me as I am entrusted to you. Go in peace. Farewell."

Jesus Sananda also adds his insight not only on stillpoint but the necessity of holding this energy for seventeen seconds.

"Stillpoint is being in the All and the nothingness where the new is created, formulated, and brought forth. Now so many of you have difficulty with this stillpoint for even seventeen seconds. It is not a long time, is it? Pretend that you are spending a long period, a long period, thirty-three hours in stillpoint. Think of the magnificent things that we can create during that hiatus of in-between. In this way the seventeen seconds will seem like nothing and pass quickly.

"Often when you are in stillpoint, you do not go deep enough. You think that nothing is happening, and you must jump up, get busy and move into action. But that is simply not so. That is your ego speaking to you, that part of you that is afraid it will die if it is not in control. If my life long ago has taught you anything, it is that no one dies, that no one disappears, that existence is infinite, expanding and eternal. There is no rush to leave the stillpoint or the void; stay there as long as possible. You will not only survive; you will thrive. From that place, in your own way, by having gone to that place of darkness and light, you will resurrect yourself in a very different way."

We finish this section with the brilliant and always radiant words of Archangel Gabrielle:

"I come this day to speak to you of creation, co-creation, and the stillpoint. Stillpoint – what many of you think is the bane of your existence. I have spoken to you about intent, and now we move to stillpoint. Children, first of all it is time for you to throw away your worries, fears and woes about creation and co-creation. You have created since the beginning of time when you turned to your Mother/Father God and said, 'I'm going exploring – leave me be, I'm going off to create my own life.' How did you do this? You did it by creating your intent, which was an action and then by moving out of home, which was a very deliberate action. In the middle of that move you went to the stillpoint of your being, the heart of your home, and imploded and exploded forth upon the universe. Now the difficulty that you have been thinking about with the stillpoint is you are expecting major cardiac arrest and it is a hiccup.

"Each one of you has known moments of stillness, and it does not matter whether it has been in your bed at night, the crystal cathedral, the quiet of the forest or holding your newborn child. How I wish for you to think of and experience stillpoint is those times when everything seems to come together in love. It is when all is in alignment above and below, in the quiet love within your heart. Stillpoint is the place where you do not need to move; where quiet contentment sits, and peace reigns. Yes, there are many techniques, clockwise, counter-clockwise, breathe in, push out – do not worry about it. We are excellent facilitators and what I do not catch Michael will. The Mother has created you with her genes; the Father has given you his wisdom and Love. You have all you need."

Stillpoint improves and anchors more deeply within with practice, like muscle memory. Think of the years a ballerina trains to perfect that movement of the arabesque when her arms and leg are extended in what appears to be an infinite moment of beauty. She is supported by her core strength, her sense of balance and one leg. Stillpoint is no different. So let go, and allow yourself to ascend.

After you have held your creation in stillpoint, you drop your intention down into your solar plexus and push it out to the world. The feeling is of being in that spot where the seat of your soul, at the bottom of your heart chakra, and your solar plexus which is the seat of your will, intersect. You are releasing your intention, your creation out in a spiraling motion into the universe to collect the creation codes (energy), in order to materialize that which you have chosen to bring forth. It matters not whether this is something concrete, emotional or spiritual – everything is a composite of energy codes.

As you begin working with the Creation Formula you may want to do this process several times, not because it doesn't work with one go but to perfect your process and ensure that you really have gotten it down. Don't be concerned about slowing your breath or not breathing, your body will automatically begin breathing when it needs to. After your work with stillpoint don't jump up and go running into frenetic action. You have been deep in the heart of the universe, so allow yourself to gently ease back into your day. Ease out of the energy the same way you come out of a luxurious warm bath, relaxed, refreshed and ready for what lies ahead, even if it's just a cozy night's sleep.

ACTION

Action is the piece of the Creation Formula where we are truly anchoring what we have chosen to create in the physical dimension and reality we occupy. What I have observed is that while stillpoint is the biggest challenge and where people get nervous, action is the place where people simply fall down and don't follow through. If you don't take appropriate action in alignment with what you are birthing then how does it manifest in physical form?

An example of this is creating a sacred union partnership. Many people, especially lightworkers, pray and yearn for their sacred other to laugh, play and unite with someone. It is part of their prayers, intent and stillpoint every day. But they don't go out to places where they might encounter like-minded and like-hearted people. They don't attend healing or meditation circles, seminars or workshops. They don't browse the New Age or spirituality section at the bookstore. They don't ask to share a table with someone who catches their eye at the coffee shop. They don't engage socially or ask their friends and colleagues to be on the lookout. They don't make eye contact in the grocery store and strike up a casual conversation at the post office. Too often there is a sense of what I term "isolated arrogance;" assuming the stranger wouldn't or couldn't possibly be on the same wavelength level as them. So how on Earth are they going to meet this special person? The actions is matching the intention and request of heaven.

There are a million examples we could draw from, and I am sure each of you have stories that would have all of us rolling on the floor with laughter. That is the point – to laugh, see that appropriate action is necessary, be conscious and go for it. Now if you think I am plain spoken on the subject, you should hear what Archangel Gabrielle has to say.

"I wish to speak to you briefly about action, because it is a key ingredient of the Creation Formula as well. Action obviously is present throughout all phases of the creation process. Action is present in intent as you go to the still point and as you move to and from stillpoint. But when we speak of action, of projection into the world, it is doing something literal. Many times my children action is surrender, which is among the most important actions many of you can ever achieve. Surrender is absolute letting go, releasing into the heart of God and the universe. Which is exactly what you are doing to create. When you hold onto it tight you constrict all movements and abilities to produce. And if we are a team, we need some latitude and flexibility. If you are holding on too tightly we have no room for maneuvering.

"Understand therefore, part of the action is surrender. That is then partnered with a physical action in terms of bringing in symbolically or otherwise that which you wish to achieve. For example, if you wish to achieve a new job and career but never formulate a resume we are going to have a problem. You and I both have responsibilities in this process. You need to take the physical actions that are appropriate to your planet and to your reality. We will take care of the rest.

"Creation is instantaneous, and yes we understand the difficulty in translating our time and yours. It may not be in the very moment you open your eyes, but who wants a job when they're still in their pajamas? Understand fulfillment will be quick. That needs to also be part of your intent. When you are super-gluing to your intent, part of what you are saying is not simply I want a job, but I want a job by next Thursday or by next year. Those are very different statements and creations. Make your intention crystal clear and known. Also understand that you are always adding the provision to your intent that it be for your highest good and the highest good of this entire planet. Then let it go. Throw open your arms and prepare to receive. Know that you are progressing magnificently, and we are singing your praises."

Action is, and should be just as much fun as dreaming. It is that opportunity to take time and be in the world bringing your intention into form. Action is not about retreat; it's about stepping out. You would not choose to create a new car and then move into the wilderness alone hundreds of miles away from the closest dealership. You might enjoy the wildness of nature and the animal kingdom there but chances are you won't find you a new car.

Sometimes my most powerful creations are those ideas that float in and past and I think "oh that would be nice" and I let it go – no effort, just magic. Because I don't hang onto it the universe can deliver it without any interference from yours truly.

Then there are projects that I have been working on either in an ongoing way or periodically for years. I do not mean hit and miss, or as the mood strikes. I mean methodically applying the Formula and Laws as things arise. Pieces emerge, results happen but sometimes (read seldom) are they exactly what I envisioned or delivered in the manner I assumed. I think this situation is particularly true when it involves a co-creation with another human. Because even though we work and think we are on the same page there are always issues and differences in the subtleties of the vision. This is where not only human vocal communication is helpful but soul conversations are essential.

Let me be clear, I am not suggesting that you avoid these co-creations – quite the contrary. The New You is founded on our laying down the pattern for Nova Earth. Not just laying down the pattern, but demonstrating the how to as well. We are the teachers and wayshowers. We came to Gaia to live in community and unity – that is the higher dimensional reality. We have many varied expressions of how we choose to create that community from family to friendships to the larger community. But we can never deceive ourselves that we are in this alone. That is an element of creation that always has to be taken into account.

Sometimes we get discouraged or think our creation didn't work but that is where you have to take the larger community into consideration – the big community from Africa to Asia to the Americas and so on. You may be dropping the proverbial pebble in the pond and may not see the entire ripple effect but make no mistake it's there.

But back to how are create. Spend some time and think about it – what is working for you; what isn't. What elements of the Creation Formula are you stuck on? What are the pieces that elude or confuse you? What are the things that are really working for you? Analyze and see – and share – what is your process and how is it working?

We end this section with a little encouragement and support from our beloved Master Sanat Kumara:

"I am Sanat Kumara. Throughout all universes and forms and all dimensions and all realities, I am the Keeper of the Laws, not the creator of the Laws, but the keeper, as are each of you. In order for each of you to proceed as beacon and pillar of truth, you have need to understand these Laws.

"Very often, simultaneously, within a measure of time, by an act of will in alignment with the Divine, new energy is created. Galaxies are born every day so do you not think you can create a little something for yourself? Understand, creation can not to be achieved without the alignment of Divine Mind to your mind; Divine Heart and love to your heart; and, Divine Will with human reality and form. That is why we encourage you so strongly to dream, to think of what you wish.

"What is your deepest desire to see in your own life and on the Gaia? What could you contribute today? You don't need to wait. We ask of you to start with yourself, yes, peace on Earth would be grand and you will get to it. Peace within your own being would be the start. So begin, and I will help, I will teach you."

CREATION TRIANGLE AND DIAMOND

The creation triangle is working with the Creation Formula in alignment with the 13 Blessings and Virtues and Universal

Law.

As with all work that we do together you anchor in your heart and take yourself to the 13th Octave. Anchor deep within the heart of Gaia as well. Picture yourself in the center of the creation triangle. Your foundation, the base upon which you build everything you create is Universal Law and the 13 Blessings and Virtues. Make a heart promise that you will you create only what is a reflection of the Divine, for your highest good, and the highest good of the collective. See and feel your arms spread out wide. With one hand you are holding Universal Law, with the other you are embracing the Blessings and Virtues. You are anchored like never before. Above you, at the apex, not only of the triangle but your sacred self, is the Creation Formula. You are working with the highest energies, the Divine Formula in order to create heaven on Earth.

Let me show you this as a diagram so you get the picture:

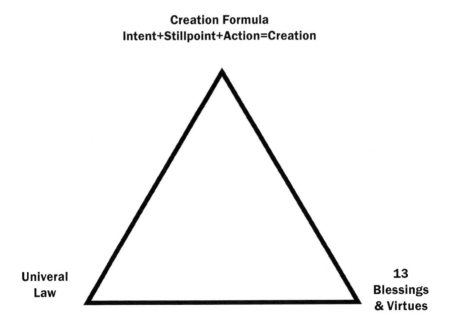

Creation Formula
Intent+Stillpoint+Action=Creation

Univeral Law

13 Blessings & Virtues

Stay in the center of the triangle cocooned by the strongest and clearest energy in the Universe. This is where you create from. In that way there is no room for lesser emotions or stray energies. You are exactly where you need to be and you are declaring yourself, once again, as part of the creator race.

There are times when you are creating that you know you are working with a specific Universal Law, in conjunction with a particular Blessing and Virtue. Let's use the example of creating a healthy physical body. For this creation, even though you have the foundation of the entirety of Universal Law and the Divine Qualities, you may choose to invoke the Laws of Intent and Change, along with the virtues of prudence and fortitude. You know within your heart what particular assistance you are going to need to anchor this desire for a strong healthy form quickly into your everyday life. We know our weaknesses and Achilles' heel, and therefore we know what extra assistance will aid us with our human self. It's asking for extra help, calling on the Universe and your guides to give you the extra support you know you need and will benefit from.

Practice that sensation of standing in the center of the triangle, your feet firmly planted on the foundation of the Laws and the Blessings and Virtues and picking from each side what you need to support your creation. There isn't one of us alive who doesn't appreciate all the help we can muster in bringing forth the desires of our hearts. The help is there for the asking, so do so.

Sanat Kumara shares this perspective on the creation triangle:

"Greetings, I am Sanat Kumara, keeper of Universal Law, planetary logos, and I step forward this day and to this circle as brother and friend. I come to speak to you about Universal Law. Not about clauses and statutes but about the very framework of the universe you live in, for that is the sacred purpose of Universal Law. It is to simply give and share with you, not in distant edicts, but in a very practical, workable manner the mechanics of how things work infinitely and eternally.

"You know within your heart the difference between right and wrong, between truth and non-truth, between love and what is not of love. Discernment of what are the Universal Laws and alignment with the 13 Blessings and Virtues, the Divine Qualities, is absolutely necessary. Universal Law and the Blessings and Virtues are inseparable. It has been constructed this way because Universal Law needs to express in practical application day to day in not only who you are with and to yourself but also to each other and to community. This pairing is a way to understand each other and build the unity that is the connective fiber of love throughout the multiverse.

"We are not, in any way, proscribing human laws. In fact, it is most unfortunate that more human laws do not align with these universal precepts of equality, divinity, understanding of within and without, above and below, change, elimination, and even completion. Where humanity is in right now is that process of completion of a very old cycle and might I say, not a very happy one. You are moving to a higher realm. That is the entire purpose of the New You; you are setting the pattern for Nova Earth. You are small but you are mighty. It does not take an army or a legion to lay down a new paradigm, or to expose a truth that has always existed but somehow been forgotten.

"You have laws of nature and physics, and there are new precepts developed and accepted every day. The new isn't foreign to you. Therefore working with the triangle of Universal Law, Divine Qualities and the Creation Formula will not be difficult; no more complex than aligning with love and truth. As you do this, your ability to create blossoms forth.

"We have given you the Creation Formula, but think of this as a triad with the Divine Qualities/the Blessings and Virtues, Universal Law, and the Creation Formula, and with you in the center of that triangle connected, surrendered and inseparable from these three points. You are there luxuriating in gratitude and joy, laughter and ease, and from that place of stillness you are extending yourself out to humanity through your expanded field and touching the hearts, minds, and lives of everybody.

"Do not avoid embracing Universal Law; quite the contrary. This has been my mission for many, many thousands of years and it is coming to completion and it is coming to completion with you. No, it does not mean that the laws cease to be, it does not mean that humanity ceases to be, it means that once the alignment is fully anchored and in place, then it is done, it is completed. Peace will reign and Cities of Light will emerge, and you, as pathfinders, way showers, pillars, and gatekeepers will be busier than ever. This has always been your plan. Many of you have always been aligned with the Universal Law of Change, that change is constant and that nothing changes, that there is continuity in all things.

"As transformation takes place, the essence does not change. That spark of light and love that you are, it never changes whether you are in or out of form, here or in the Pleiadian sector or on CeeCeeCee. And yet, change happens with every breath and every moment, because in every moment the Mother continues to create and expand the complexity of this universe, of this omniverse.

"You need to understand the rules of operation, and this is what I have given you. What I am asking is not to study the Universal Laws like some legal text, but to capture the spirit in which it is shared. That spirit, dear heart, is love and the 13 Blessings and Virtues. They are the physical, emotional and spiritual expression of the Law. When you create with the Formula, based in the knowing and practice of the Laws and the Divine Qualities, then you are creating in the same fashion as we do throughout the universe. And hence, my job as planetary logos to Earth will be complete."

There are times when you will be in the creation triangle when you will feel it morph or choose to have it morph into the creation diamond. The creation diamond includes the twelve dimensions, each with their unique properties and qualities.

The practice is the same as working with the creation triangle. What you are adding is the ability to access energies from the various dimensions that will support your creation process. For this, let's use the example of creating financial abundance. As always, anchor in your heart and go to the 13th Octave. Extend your arms and choose with the knowing of your heart what will help you from the baskets of the Blessings and Virtues and the Universal Laws. Perhaps this time it's joy and charity; give and

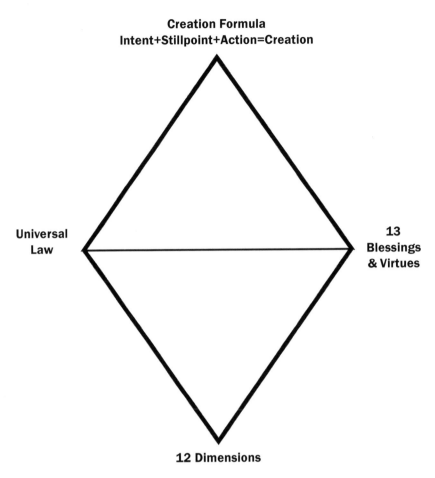

Creation Formula
Intent+Stillpoint+Action=Creation

**Universal
Law**

**13
Blessings
& Virtues**

12 Dimensions

receive. The choice is yours. Then reach down to the dimensions'
basket and choose what in that array will assist you as well.
Perhaps it's the qualities of the eigtht – creation, or the fourth
– magic. You can't go wrong and the choice is yours. Choose everything you want or nothing, but know the choice and the offer
is still there – it doesn't go away.

You make these selections prior to implementing the Creation Formula – the choices from the various baskets become
part of your intent. The walls of creation triangle and diamond
are reinforced by the Mighty Archangels. The creation triangle
and diamond are yours to play with, part of your creation process. Enjoy them!

Now let's examine in greater detail both the 13 Blessings
and Virtues and the Universal Laws. As you are seeing both are

an essential part of you stepping into and fully embracing your creator self, the New You.

The 13 Blessings and Virtues

The 13 Blessings and Virtues are the capstone of the 13th Octave, one of the original gifts from the Council of Love which gives us insight into how the company of heaven operates. The 13 Blessings and Virtues, also often referred to as the Divine Qualities, are also a cornerstone of the creation triangle upon which the New You brings forth both individual and collective desires into reality, anchoring Nova Earth in service to the Divine Mother.

The energy of the Blessings and Virtues has grown enormously over the past couple of years as humanity awakens and comes to understand not only do the old paradigms and belief systems not work, but a life built upon a foundation of love is necessary if we are to anchor fully in the higher dimensions. That is what the Blessings and Virtues are – they are your foundation for the practical living of a life based in love.

Each Blessing and Virtue holds the frequency of a certain ray or color. For the purposes of this chapter we touch upon those colors to assist in the anchoring of that divine quality deep within. On an overall basis, when you work with the Blessings and Virtues as a grouping, you are working with the silver ray of Archangel Uriel. For that reason it is recommended that you begin each session of working with the Blessings and Virtues by inhaling seven deep breaths of the silver ray.

Over the past year, a master, archangel or enlightened being has stepped forward to be our guide and anchor for each of these divine qualities. It has been an enormous gift and a process that many have participated in through the series on Heavenly Blessings, a blogtalk radio show produced by InLight Radio. I include the information pertinent to each of these beloved beings as they present themselves, their perspectives and gifts. I do so not because you cannot find bibliographic material readily but because it brings the love, the commitment and the closeness of these sacred beings up close and personal.

In terms of format, I have begun each section with the original COL definition of the Blessing and Virtue, originally channeled by James the Apostle, Master of the 13th Octave.

St. Bernadette, our very first guest in this series, summed up this exercise in this way: "It is not a matter of simply feeling that you are intuitive or that you are blessed in some extraordinary way, in fact, that is why we have outlined and suggested the practice of each of the Blessings and Virtues. It is not so much expansion but the anchoring of expansion. I can be very practical and it is a matter of practice, so do not become discouraged. Schedule your time to embrace and enhance the virtues. When you are practicing prudence, declare to yourself that this is my prudence week and you choose to do it this way, and then you can check yourself. Celebrate your progress."

PRUDENCE

"Prudence: Twin of temperance. The ability to know in all situations when to proceed and when to retreat; when to take action and when to be still; when to offer help and when to keep silent; to know in exact measure what is required, whether it is in baking a cake or healing a psychic injury. All things in correct measure. Prudence encompasses the quality of moderation, the genuine knowing and practice of everything in balance. No one person can live in only one area of their being, their life, and truly be representative of the whole. Prudence allows for the complete and total release of addictions. Prudence is an unusual trait on Earth. The vibrations are halion and siroun."

When I first began to channel the 13th Octave a group of thirteen ascended sacred beings stepped forward declaring "We want to be your core team." The group included beings from east and west; star beings and Earth keepers; enlightened beings, saints and the Divine Presence of Yahweh and Universal

Mother Mary. St. Bernadette was one of those beings who so graciously and lovingly stepped forward to accompany us on this miraculous journey. Although I have not channeled St. Bernadette often, I feel her gentle presence consistently. She's simply not a big talker, I don't know how else to put it.

However, as soon as the topic of prudence was raised, she was jumping up and down in my office, declaring "I want to be the one." Often what I am gifted with seeing, with saints or ascended beings is their mature self, but in this case the being that appeared was the 14-year-old girl, who had that initial vision of Mother Mary. Bernadette was a French girl who experienced the visions at Lourdes of the Blessed Mother. After that visitation, Lourdes became a sacred healing place. Many people of every faith or no faith, of every description and culture, go to Lourdes to take the healing waters. Many miraculous healings have been documented, miraculous healings of people who were crippled or terminally ill have taken the waters at Lourdes, France and been completely healed.

Bernadette, born in 1844, was desperately poor. Her family of nine lived in a dungeon. Bernadette was very sickly, having had cholera as a child, and as a result suffered from asthma. She also contracted tuberculosis, had lots of digestive problems and is a role model for so many of us who have health challenges because no matter what, Bernadette stayed the course. St. Bernadette was guided to this area out in the fields of rural France where she started to have visions and was guided by the Lady who would appeared in a rose bush more than sixty times. The Lady guided her to dig in the mud out in a farm field. People of her village, the police and the Imperial prosecutor, tried to stop her by judging her insane. But Bernadette persisted in her digging, and from that flows a wonderful spring of healing waters.

Now that analogy can't be lost on any of us because I think so many of us have felt that we've been digging in the mud and praying for this wonderful healing water, this spring, to come on up and cleanse and heal us and help us on our way.

When I was refreshing my memory regarding Bernadette I found myself chuckling, thinking, okay, this is why she wants to be first, because she's been there, done that. Bernadette had no desire to be a public figure and retreated. She became a nun and basically, because of her physical fragility, really retreated from the world. However, as she reminds us through these wonderful messages she did not retreat from her role as teacher, spokesperson for the Mother and guardian of each of us.

As I look at St. Bernadette, she's standing here with us in peasant clothing. She has got the deepest almost black eyes that you can see the soul through. Although she is plain, she carries that light of a young woman. She's beautiful. This is the being who graces, and anchor within our hearts, the sacred blessing of prudence.

The Council tells us that prudence is a very unusual trait for Earth. I think prudence is one of those qualities we see in our star brothers and sisters and the ascended ones, because it's all about moderation and balance. When we're in that place of temperance, moderation and balance we defeat and eliminate drama.

I have to confess that when the 13 Blessings and Virtues were first channeled I was not crazy about prudence. Think prunes; necessary, strong taste, not something I was eager to test drive. I mistook prudence as robbing me of my passion, my sense of adventure, my freedom, which you can translate as a young woman's desire for drama and a sense of independence. Independence is not freedom. Over the years I have come not only to appreciate but love prudence – it is the beginning and the end point of so much of what we undertake in our spiritual journey as humans. Without prudence, the balance and moderation, with shades of the observer participant, we cannot go forward. It is a huge, often under-estimated gift.

When you are working with the colors and rays of the 13 Blessings and Virtues, it is powerful to take a moment and inhale, taste, visualize the ray and bring it into the fullness of your being. It helps in anchoring the energy of that virtue not only on a subtle or energetic level but in your physical body, in the here and now as well.

The colors of prudence are halion and siroun. Halion is one

of the star-being colors, the planet and all upon her evolved to sheer energy. This energy is known collectively as the Halion Engineers, and they know all about ascension. The color of halion is mint green with thunderbolts of electric/electra blue with a touch of lavender. Take a moment and breathe this ray in; let it fill your heart, your head, your torso, your legs and let those Halion Engineers in to construct and reconstruct anything within any of your fields and bodies that needs attention; to bring you into perfect balance not only with the universe but with who you are.

Siroun, located at your thymus or high heart, is also one of the new colors. Take another deep breath of siroun, that peachy, pinky, gold color, the color of the peach fuzz or a perfect sunset. Allow it to swirl and move. Breathe it into your high heart, which is your center for harmony, for balance. Feel your heart chakra and your higher heart chakra opening and blossoming like the perfect peach rose. Now anchored in that energy of the open heart read and listen with your being what Bernadette shares with us about prudence.

"I am Bernadette, *bonjour*. It is my honor and privilege to speak to you this day and always. I speak on behalf of the sacred Mother. I also speak to you from my experience as a human being, as a young girl and later as a woman who chose her path despite many obstacles. I speak to you about prudence, but I also speak to you about human obstacles, which I fully understand. When I began to share, first with my sister and my good friend Marie France that I was seeing a Lady, not only were they afraid, they thought I was crazy.

"My friends, you have experienced much the same thing when you said "We are going to shift dimensions, we are going to take care of one another, we are going to lift up out of the poverty in every sense of the word of the human existence, and we are going to be prudent in our actions, not only with ourselves, but with one another. We are not going to interfere in the passage of another being, but we are going to be there as support and sometimes the observer." Many have thought you crazy, no?

"It does not matter because you are being true to your sacred self and you are practicing not only prudence, as well as temperance but balance and moderation. When you are a wayshower this is of particular importance. You know very well when to say something and when to keep quiet. This is a very important quality; to know exactly where to place the word, where to place energy, where to place the look in the eye, the smile on your lips, the touch of the hand that is encouragement not theft. To know when to stay still and understand that in this quietude you are holding energy for people you are working with, because there is something they need to proceed with, or they are not quite ready to hear, or, perhaps it is something that they need to discover for themselves. This quality of giving others the opportunity to discover something for themselves is often overlooked and underrated. You see it all the time with little children – it is so important for them to understand how things work. You witness them as they sit and stare at something, explore it, bring it in their mouth, in their hands, until they have a concept of what it is, and then they begin to play with it, or they discover that it is foul tasting and they avoid it. It is in this way that so many human beings learn.

"My dear friends I have offered my help and guidance to you for many years, not with the healing waters because I cannot and do not claim the waters as my assistance to you; that is a gift directly from the Divine Mother. Other than digging in the dirt, it has very little to do with me. When I step forward and offer my assistance to you, I do not do so as some miracle worker. I do so as a sister and as fellow journeyer. I do so in prudence and that is why you do not hear me talk a mile a minute or all sometimes because I feel that I can be of far more help simply helping you to discover your balance.

"When you have learned how to skate, ride a surfboard, a buffalo or a bicycle, you receive instruction and that is helpful. Certainly there is much instruction available to you on the sacred passage, but there is that moment when you find your center of balance and everything falls into place. It clicks in, and that is not something that can be taught but only experienced.

"In this process of ascension, all energy and focus is on the love and heart. Notice that in prudence, the focus is on the halion and siroun. Halion is at the bottom of your rib cage and your connection to your star brothers and sisters who are very present, not only above but in your neighborhoods. Siroun is the ray of the high heart. Why is this so? Because when you are opening both of these centers you are allowing your heart, without interference, to come into balance, into that place of moderation. Moderation is an absolutely necessary and an essential ingredient to your forward movement in ascension and in the anchoring of Nova Being and Nova Earth. In moderation there is no high drama. That does not mean that there are not moments of incredible excitement. Do you not think, *mon cher*, that when I saw the Lady there was not great excitement in my heart, in my mind? My very body felt like it was on fire. Excitement is absolutely wondrous; it is akin to the virtue of awe and joy. Don't ever think that Prudence is blasé; it is not, it is in the place of moderation. It is the balance between this fire of excitement and the cooling of healing waters.

"Let me point out that any water is healing water. When you say a prayer to the Mother and ask her to bless your water, to turn it into sacred healing waters, that request and that prayer is always heard and as you sip that water I will be there with you. I am not one of the fancier or gregarious beings, but I wish you to know that I am with you. I know what it is to have your faith tested. Be strong my beloved ones."

St. Bernadette is practical, and she shares ideas of how to practice prudence, how to bring it into our lives.

"When you are doing something it is important to take prudence into account. Think of the simple and the complex. For example, when you are preparing a meal. As a child, I often went hungry and, when the rare occasion occurred where there was bounty or much to eat, we stuffed ourselves. Now was that prudence? No, because, our bodies were not used to processing so much food. Consider it in this way: when you are thinking about what to cook for supper look at what is on the table – spiritually and physically. Often you have bounty, may I say too much – maybe there are twelve vegetables, two pieces of different meat, perhaps different drinks and water, and you want it all. This stems from a sense of wanting security, and a sense of social celebration. It is a sacred time for many families. In fact, for many families it is the only time that you are sitting together or gathering together. But one of the ways in which you can practice prudence is to look at the food and ask, is this prudent, balanced and in moderation? Are you wasting food? Are you cooking for tomorrow? Don't forget to consider the true purpose of the meal – to nourish you and those you love, spiritually and physically; prudently.

"Often you have a tendency to fly into old habits which is to blame yourself. You take responsibility for something that you have done or not done and you go on and on and on, not necessarily to whoever you have offended or mistreated, but to yourself. That is not in balance that is not in moderation, temperance or prudence. Prudence is to acknowledge where you have gone awry, to look at it, to do whatever repair work is necessary, including especially letting it go, to apologize to yourself, to the universe, to whomever you have harmed, and then to proceed. It is not to dwell on it day after day crying you made a mistake, and can't go on. That is not prudence or kindness. Bring it to the practical level of how you live your life.

"Is it prudent to spend three hundred dollars on a pair of jeans? If you are say it is prudent because these jeans will last me a lifetime and, I am giving myself a treat, then fine. But examine your motivations first. Live in that place of balance because it is going to make you feel better, it is going to make yourself feel that you are exactly where you need to be. The reward of prudence is not prudence for prudence sake, but that it leads you to a place where you feel that you are not living in scarcity or drama. I suggest to you, dear one, that you ask yourself are the jeans about drama? Is this clear?"

St. Bernadette shares how she handled the fear and criticism and judgment of the citizens of Lourdes when she shared with them the gifts of the Mother regarding the visions and the healing waters. Bernadette called upon her strength of heart knowing that even though there were no outward signs to prove her visions, she trusted her inner guidance and held firm believing that the answers would be revealed in divine time.

"How can you prove what others do not see or perceive? The question is always where is the external evidence, the proof? For me, finally although it actually happened quite quickly it did not feel so, the proof came in the spring that flowed and healed people. Each of you is truly facing this dilemma. This is one of the reasons why this Council of Love has asked you to focus on the Blessings and Virtues, because the proof, the landmarks, the markers are internal not external. This is something new for you to learn; this is a quality of Nova Being. You are learning a new way of measuring proof and it is from within. When I had this proof, the knowing of the truth of the Lady, within me, I would rather die or be locked away than deny what I knew to be true. I could not deny my visions, and neither can you."

What is St. Bernadette telling us? Her visions occurred over a period of a couple of years, the spring came up and finally the people said, "Oh my God, you're right, they're healing waters." Did she then say her job was done and got into retreat? No, she, like many of the holy ones, held the course. That is where you are right now. You're staying the course and tangible evidence is coming.

Finally, St. Bernadette tells us how being in a state of joy interacts with prudence to bring about balance in our lives.

"It is not in reference to the prudence, it is in reference to joy because, of course, with moderation and balance you will find the joy. In my visitations with the Lady, my life that followed, and with my life with each of you, I find enormous joy, this gladness of my heart. This is something I would also like you to bring forth in your life. So often prudence is seen as being a way of denial and that is old thinking. Prudence is not denial; it is being in the balance of your joy and doing, not just thinking or holding faith and trust, but doing what brings you joy."

The wisdom of the Council in making prudence the first gift of the 13 Blessings and Virtues is phenomenal. Often over the years I have wondered why they would start with prudence. As a starting point, who wants prudence? I've never heard anybody say "I wish I had more prudence." Yet over the years, and maybe as a function of aging, I have come to appreciate prudence more and more. Not only is prudence a foundational virtue, a building block of the New You, it is spiritually mature. When we are passionate about our beliefs we want to speak up, shout it from the rooftops and correct those who obviously don't have a clue about what's going on. Does that feel like love, like balance?

Prudence assists us in the Catch-22 of the Council's guidance, particularly now during this time of change. On one hand, we are guided to step forward, reveal ourselves, be the wayshowers, the re-patterners of Nova Earth. On the other hand, we are guided to practice prudence; to know when to speak and when to be the observer by staying silent. Haven't you ever experienced a situation where you lost an argument by speaking; or even harder, you won the argument but lost the war? Silence can be as eloquent and powerful as a million words.

One of the gifts from our star brothers and sisters which demonstrates prudence is a gift of language called Perro. It originally came through when a client was asking about how to handle an emotionally difficult divorce proceeding. Perro is a language which excludes any emotion; it sticks to the facts. The closest thing we currently have would be non-violent communication, but Perro is much more.

This form of communication was developed at the end of the inter-galactic wars to allow the various civilizations not only to come together but to proceed to a meaningful peace. Emotions, injury, devastation and loss were so great that it was difficult for opposing sides to speak to each other. Words were too emotionally charged with blame, fault, guilt and judgment; they lacked prudence. Our star family realized that if they could not come together and reach a truce and a meaningful peace, then annihilation was inevitable. Out of this very real need, Perro emerged.

A question that often posed is how differences are resolved by our star brothers and sisters. One of the outcomes of the inter-galactic wars and the use of Perro is a gradual appreciation of that difference of opinions, perspective, culture and values emerged. Moderated and negotiated conversations are immediately implemented when tensions start to rise. Compromise, in alignment with Universal Law is acceptable to all parties concerned. Perro is still used, a great tool of prudence when silence won't do. It diffuses the energy of emotional judgment, and allows truth to emerge. The knowledge of this language and technique is within you, and I encourage you to try it. You will love the results.

FORTITUDE

"Fortitude: Courage in all forms, endurance, the ability to keep going forward when others cease and give up. The virtue of pathfinders. Strength of purpose. Stamina in all senses. Know that patience is a part of fortitude. Fortitude is the encompassing of forbearance, and forbearance is indeed a quality that requires patience. To continue going forward with stamina when you really feel like pushing the individual off the cliff; it will be required in working with 12:12. The vibration is orange."

The reference to 12:12 is to the twelve levels of the twelve dimensions. Part of fortitude is strength of purpose, spiritual and physical; the strength to keep going even when you feel exhausted or emotionally beat up. The vibration, the ray that identifies fortitude is orange, not only its brightness and clarity but its smell, the fragrance and scent. It sits in our sacral area or our tummy where we have the ability to create in our own lives and on Nova Earth.

Our beloved Jesus Sananda, Yeshua, speaks about his embodying fortitude as he walked the Earth. He suggests that we are embodying fortitude perhaps even more than he did as human man.

"While I have practiced and embodied fortitude, in and out of form, and in and out of different lifetimes, I speak to you this day as Yeshua, as the one you know as Jesus, I speak to you as your brother Yeshi. Fortitude is strength of character and purpose. It is the knowing in every fiber and core of your being, not that you are right but you will go forward no matter what.

"On your planet and in many societies, this addiction to being right is very strong. This is not what fortitude speaks to. There are times in all lives when you misstep or you turn the wrong way, or you think you turn the wrong way, and I use that work 'think' for it is a mental judgment that is not of love, or that you have simply wandered off your path. Forgiveness comes into this in terms of your ability to forgive others, but also to forgive yourself. But what is even more critical is fortitude; the ability, the stamina, the courage, the bravery to return to center. It is the center, not only of the heart of love, of Mother/Father/One, but to your center and then to know that the center and your center have no differentiation. That, my beloved friend, takes courage. Fortitude does not always mean that you are right. Righteousness most certainly does not mean that you are always right, but it is a passion, it is a drive and it is such a deep sense of commitment to complete and to do what you have promised in your heart, mind and soul contract to do.

"Being upon your planet, even as I have walked thousands of years ago, is not an easy task. I am not just human, I am the embodiment – the Son – of the Mother/Father/One. How much easier could my journey be? Go to Earth, tell people to love one another, show them how to do it and practice it. There might be some people against you and they might even be vehement and kill you, but no matter, because I am an eternal spirit and I will simply return home. So, how hard could that be?

"I laugh and cry with you because sometimes we make light of our journey and that simple soul contract. The task that I undertook on behalf of the Mother was difficult, and even in that there was family conflict, even as a child. 'Yeshua, must you be so outspoken? Can you not simply listen to the Rabbi's teachings instead of correcting them? Everyone in the village thinks you are conceited and full of yourself and arrogant.'

"Of course, I would listen to these criticisms, but I would know, I did not have thousands of years to reach people, only a handful of years, just like you. I was so clear on what it was that I was to do and what I wished to accomplish, not just in service to the Mother, but because it was meaningful and important in the human, worldly sense. I could see the pain and the suffering of people and in my people because they had forgotten about love. Many of them had fallen into the belief system of a thundering, painful, punishing God. So here I was with a new message, trying to heal the hearts and then to spread that message all over the world when many did not think I should speak outside my faith. But the faith was in One and it was and is available to all.

"I practiced fortitude and I put one foot in front of another. I also had my human experience. I had my beloved one, my marriage with the Magdalena and that required fortitude on both of our parts.

"I practiced fortitude with the death of my little son and in so many ways; although I knew he had returned home, it broke our heart. We felt that in some way we had been forgotten or ignored. Now I do not bring this up to make you cry, I bring it up because I know the challenges, the difficulties, the tests that so many of you have faced and are facing because what you are doing is creating an entirely new face of the planet. And that face begins with the hearts, minds and actions of every being. This is enormously ambitious – seven billion people. You are far braver than I.

"I speak of this because fortitude is about staying the path, it is about endurance even when those around you nay-say. It is about putting your head down and then having it fully erect and saying, you know where you going. You know your mission and purpose. You know your star brothers and sisters are here. You know governments, institutions, economic systems will change and your am doing it. You not merely supporting it from a distance. Fortitude is very action-oriented. Therefore, I want you to know I do admire you and honor you. This is a difficult transition. Joyous? Yes. Worth it? Beyond what you know. But we would not pretend that it is easy. I support you my friends, my brothers, my sisters, my family."

Yeshua reminds us that we are changing the world with little evidence to show, often with no support from family or community outside of our lightholder community. What so many of us are doing is very lonely but the Council of Love says is, don't believe in the illusion, or the false paradigm of separation, or isolation. Since 12:12, you are in a unified grid and you may feel more connected, more united in heart and purpose than ever. But you also are embodying fortitude because you are often doing this alone.

You are the bedrock in terms of your fortitude. Do you need time out? Perhaps. But most of you embody it to the point that you says you would rather die, and return home. I know the truth is in my ability to contribute and activate and be part of returning of love, and building of Nova Earth. It is the only reason I am here and I'm not giving up.

We are the modern-day explorers, the adventures, as Yeshua calls us. But he reminds us not to hesitate to ask for directions if we feel we are off course, or if we have fear. Yeshua says:

"The key is to embrace your fear. Embracing it transmutes and transforms it into the very courage, the valor you will need. Part of fortitude is stepping forward and holding the course of being your strength and purpose even when you are frightened.

"When I was arrested, and I was arrested many times, I was fearful. I was not fearful of the physical harm that would befall me. What I was afraid of was two things: the effect on my family and my extended family, my followers, my friends, because I did not have one follower that was not dear to my heart. The second overriding fear was that I would be silenced. I feared being intimidated and that I would not speak the truth. Those were real fears. It is not that I never experienced fear or prayed for courage and bravery to do, not only what I had promised, but what I knew was right.

"What fortitude helps you do is allow you to step forward 'in spite of.' The very act of stepping forward, not in grandiose ways, because you do not want to make your opponent feel that they need to defeat you, but step forward in ways that eradicates and dissolves your fear because you embrace it. You say 'Yes, I am afraid and I'm doing it anyway.' And as soon as you do Michael is with you, I am with you, and Jophiel has your back. Begin in small ways to challenge your comfort zone but do not leave yourself exposed and feeling overly vulnerable. Perhaps it is expressing your truth to a friend, to a colleague, and do not take yourself too seriously, use the tool of humor. I used parables, because it entertained, everyone got the message, and it did not make people feel overly defensive. You always want to give the person you are speaking to, the situation that you are shifting, room to maneuver so they do not feel that their back is against the wall. That is kindness, that is consideration and that is fortitude. Fortitude is married to prudence, knowing the balance, the exact measure of what to do."

As we expand into the fifth dimension and beyond, we are seeing we are part of the unified whole. The entire purpose of the December 21, 2012 was the opening of unity, connectedness, and love.

You are a child and an angel of the omniverse. It is time to let the expansion happen, not merely for the sense of adventure, but in doing so, in extending and traveling so far when you come back it is not with a diminished self, with a smaller sense of who you are but a much grander, expanded sense of who you are, your place within the universe, and what you are capable of within that universe. You are also receiving and coming to know that the entire universe supports you.

You will notice that as the love and bliss and joy expands within you, the fear and the doubt doesn't stick as much, because when you're in a higher vibrational state those base kinds of experiences and behaviors just can't survive in the higher dimensions. When you put yourself in a place of love, bliss and joy, then you connect to your soul purpose. Connect to what brings you joy, connect to why you are here, connect to your intuition, the divine, and in honoring the fear, honoring the doubt, but also not sticking our heads in the sand around it, feeling it but releasing it and letting it go, then get back to who you are then you feel the joy, bliss, and love.

I have had my moments of doubt, whether it has been self-doubt or universal doubt. When that happens, I go to my guides or the Council of Love and say, "Fill me up." It is that simple, I am recharged.

Yeshua addresses these feelings of doubt and overwhelm:

"It is particularly trying for many of you who have financial, health and relationship issues during the transition. While this is a test of fortitude, it is also the opportunity to surrender. We are in sacred partnership but there are times when we surrender to your will. Support you? Yes, but surrender. And there are times when it is equally important for you to surrender and allow us to work the miracles. When you are in the way, when you are constantly reclaiming your issues or actions then you are interfering with the flow. It does not mean not taking appropriate action, but there are moments when surrender is the action and the key. So let the worry go."

Our beloved Jesus Sananda, Yeshua, he tells us a modern-day parable:

"I will share a very modern parable. It is the story of a young man in your time who had incredible dreams of hope, of faith. He did not grow up in favored circumstances, no not in dire poverty at all, but certainly in situations that were less than favorable.

"He held the dream and the reality that his mission and purpose was more important than any distraction, and he could make a difference in bringing light and love to the planet. He endured and he practiced fortitude. He did so in my name. He is victorious in my name.

"Each of you are that man, each of you are stepping into the arena of Nova Earth and doing your best to create what you know is based on truth and love and hope. You are the heroes of the parables. You are the embodiment of that fortitude. You are that being that says, 'I will not give up and no matter how many naysayers there are, how many falsehoods are perpetrated, how many back room machinations take place, I will bring forth the new world.'

"Each of you has the ability to create and to change the planet, not just the dimension. Your Ascension is the fullness of your heart; it is the anchoring of love on Earth, which is what the Shift is, that is why fortitude is so necessary. To allow things to continue in the old way is easy; but to change the world requires valor, stamina, and determination. You have this, my brothers and sisters, you have always had this."

Each of us has had situations, relationship breakdowns, broken hearts, losing jobs, unemployment, financial scarcity, illness, abuse or loss of a loved one, where we have practiced fortitude. Fortitude isn't one of the sexy virtues. True fortitude is a foundational virtue, one that has a long shelf life. People sometimes think of this virtue as being staid, staunch, and not really a lot of fun because it implies hard challenging times and soldiering through. But fortitude is not about martyrdom, it's about smelling the flowers, embracing the journey, and enjoying the everyday blessings, seen and unseen.

I realized that I come from a family that embodies this divine quality. I had never thought about them in this way before because it wasn't something discussed or praised, it simply was a way of being. My mother, a single child, was orphaned at eighteen months, and grew up knowing wealth and poverty. She was shuttled between relatives on the east and west coast of Canada, losing her dearly beloved grandmother and guardian at age sixteen. In her twenties, my sweet mother lost her hearing completely. She lost her firstborn son, and like many of us, knew the financial hardships of trying to raise a family on very little money.

I share this not to garner sympathy or even empathy but because we grew up never thinking Mom was in any way compromised or even affected by the hardships of her early years. Quite the contrary. My mother's dream was to have a family, be a wife and partner and a mom. She was all of those things and so much more, and inside this gentle angel of blue there was a core of steel, a core of fortitude. There never were any moments of "if only" or "poor me." In fact, like so many of that generation, there was no room for it. That outmoded and unspoken mantra of "count your blessings" was in force in our home.

In the past couple of decades I have witnessed how this spiritual DNA was passed on to each of us in different ways. My brother, Joe, survived a terrible plane crash, where he barely survived and his ankles and legs were severely injured. The pain was excruciating and many doctors thought he would probably never walk again. He persevered against all odds from wheelchair to painful rehabilitation to walking unsupported by any apparatus. We won't even talk about the social stigma and isolation, the feelings of loss that occur from being a huge success at the top of his career to lying in a hospital bed. This past summer Joe was on the winning golf team of his club's season's opener. Does he experience pain – every day. Does he keep going, enjoying his life, family and top executive career – yup!

A few years later my sister was diagnosed with leukemia. When she was admitted to hospital her blood count was so marginal it was a miracle she was standing, let alone working. The odds against Suzanne's survival were not stacked in her favor. But she put her head down and simply declared she would not die, she would not leave her son and husband to continue on without her. I highlight this because an element of fortitude is sheer stubbornness. Not stubbornness in the sense of being unreasonable or obstreperous but in the sense of aligning your will with Divine Will; with knowing your plan so deeply and clearly that you simply won't allow it to be sidetracked. Suzanne has passed the ten-year mark of being healthy, and when challenges come her way, and they do, as they do to all of us, I observe as she puts her head down, focuses on what's really important, and wades through.

Each of us has or has had situations where the option to give up is right in front of us, and often is an alluring attraction. That is why the virtue of fortitude is so essential. Coming to Gaia during this time of shift is the greatest blessing and the biggest challenge. We are system busters at the most basic level there is, and that takes courage, fortitude, persistence and perseverance.

HOPE

"Hope: The gift of heart-knowing of the presence of God. The ability to understand that very often things on Earth are not as they appear. An ability to pierce the illusion of the veil. The only reason for change. Hope encompasses serenity; total and perfect calm. To be in the world but not of it, to be able to remain centered and still, one with who you are regardless of externals. Hope is the color of deep twilight blue, almost navy. It is the deepest color of blue, the color of the Universal Mother Mary."

Do you see how hope builds on prudence and fortitude? Hope is the blessing and virtue closest to the stillpoint. When we are in the stillpoint we are in that place of hope. It is holding that alignment of knowing that even if we do not know that there is a plan, a Divine Plan and that we have a plan within that Plan, that everything is in alignment even when it looks completely screwed up.

Hope is a gift directly from the heart of the Divine Mother. So let us begin this exploration with examining our ideas about Her. Who is the Universal Mother Mary, the Divine Mother, and Maré? When I channel the Universal Mother I am channeling all the various versions that are held of Her throughout the planet and probably far beyond. While my personal connection in this lifetime comes from the Christian thought of Mother Mary, we know the Divine Mother is so much bigger than that. it's the eastern, it's the southern, it's all of those aspects. When I chan-nel the Divine Mother there is no form, it's a wispy, universal energy. It is very purposeful that Mary or Maré calls herself the Universal Mother because in that delineation we are able to access an aspect of the Divine Mother.

"Greetings, I am Mary. The distinctions that you make between myself, Universal Mother, and Divine Mother are human distinctions and they are created so that you will have a multitude of ways in which to come to know me so that I may guide you back home. No matter how far you may wander or what the journey entails. Whatever form you choose, in any instance or reality to call upon me, to know me, to allow me to embrace you, I am there.

"I have a million faces and as many names and I am still One. Creation is eternal and it is born of stillness but it is also born of infinite inspiration and movement, and this is the gift that I give to you. It is not merely hope, although that is the bedrock from which all emanates. You are also filled with inspiration, ideas, love and laughter to bring that stillness into form, into matter, into experience, into creation and right now into the creation of Nova Being and Nova Earth.

"Now, let us turn to this beautiful blessing and virtue of hope. It has come to be misconstrued. It is the plea heard in the dark of night. It is the prayer whispered over a sick child's bed, or when there is no food in the larder. It's the call for help I hear for a tangible sign. Hope is often thought of as request and receiving. But what I say to you is that, hope is the foundation upon which those requests, those prayers, those creations are based. If the knowing was not there of our existence and our presence in each and every one of your lives, then you would not pray, you would not ask, and you would not have hope.

"No, I am not asking you to limit your requests, because they are always heard and acted upon whether they are directly to me, to your guardian angels, your guides, the archangels or the masters. They are always heard and acted upon. Often you say that I don't here you because you've been praying for 'X', and not received it. We are not suggesting that our actions and how we respond to your prayers is always as you wish or think we should respond. But it would be erroneous to think we are not responding. It is the balance, it is our eternal partnership, it is the infinite agreement that we have formed when you agreed to assume form. It was straightforward 'I will go, but you have to promise to help.'

"That promise has never been broken even in what you have thought of as the darkest days either of your planet or your life. So my purpose in speaking with you this day is not merely to reassure you, it is to reconfirm that promise. I am your Mother. It is not possible within my realm, my essence, not respond to you. It is what a mother does."

Mother Mary tells us what the level of hope is that she is seeing on the planet, what people are embodying right now, and what is in people's hearts.

"Increasingly, minute to minute, second to second, mille-second to mille-second there is an increase in the level of hope, the level of stillness that is being brought forward by each of you. Why do I emphasize the stillness? Because that is where the knowing is found, that is where the creation takes place. Many think that Ascension, the coming to the new reality, is based in a flurry of activity. It is not. When you are going to the place of stillpoint, when you are going to the full place of hope, you are allowing the changes to take place. You are allowing the fullness, not only of our being, but of your being to come to the forefront and for that shift, that quantum leap to be completed. Your Ascension process goes well. You know I have an interest in this; it is part of my plan. Has it slowed? Slightly, but not significantly and that is what is key. When you are rushing about looking at your watch and saying, 'Well, it's been three hours and I haven't ascended yet.' It is rather funny, is it not? But when you go to the stillness and you allow the expansion and in many ways you allow yourself to float up and the expansion increases many times over because it is a building process, then you are underway. So you are, as a collective, about half-way there.

"What you have been feeling is the externals, all those distractions, are becoming less and less. Your field of vision is becoming more focused. Now that does not mean that you are not aware of what is going on upon your planet or that you do not care what is going on upon your planet, you care intensely. But what you are realizing is that in order to accomplish what you truly desire, what is the core of your being, that less is required, less movement, less activity, more simply being, because it is in that that you allow yourself to proceed. In that serenity you are allowing yourself to anchor and expand.

"There is a level of exhaustion that many of you are feeling because the human body and the human being has not been used to holding this much energy. Some of you are doing it very intensely, not only your work but the work for the human collective. The feeling of exhaustion, of less energy, is because you are actually processing more.

"You are becoming the Nova Being. I am not suggesting that the Nova Being is not a being that takes action, but when the plan was wrought, when it was originally formed, and in this timeframe that you think of now as Ascension, I never said to you, your guardians, your guides never said to you, Michael never said to you 'Go to Earth, work with your family, in many cases allowing them to misunderstand you and abuse you. Then if you could, please get a meaningful job where you are paid well and you have to work twelve hours a day in order to get ahead, ignore your inner being, make sure that you are busy always, so that you fall in bed at night without even ten minutes for a prayer or mild reflection. Do this for seventy years and then come back.' That was never the plan.

"The plan, even outside of Ascension, was for you to come to Earth as the bright energy, starseed angels that you are, to laugh and play and know the sheer joy and love, in physical form, of having a human experience. The experience, the entire plan was to be in joy. The entire purpose wasn't to come and work and slave, not on behalf of me, not on behalf of the universe and certainly not so you could earn points and be in a state of grace; you are a state of grace, you are a state of wholeness. You are coming to this place of remembering 'I am love, I am joy' and I may do this or that with my family, with my work, with my friends, with my community because it is meaningful and it contributes to the readjustment of Gaia, the building of a world that makes sense and is reflective of Divine Plan. My response to this growth dear heart is congratulations."

Much is transpiring with the return of the Divine Feminine energies. The Dali Lama has stated the Western woman will save the world. This statement is not based on gender but rather to the feminine energies of nurturing, compassion, understanding and love. Universal Mother Mary elaborates:

"The Divine Feminine, my energy and your energy, and again this is not gender based, is the ability to create and to bring forth, to birth, what is truth, what is light, what is meaningful. Western women have heeded the inspiration for a long time. About seventy or more years ago in the United States the Suffragists began to claim their right to vote, a very basic statement of 'my voice must be heard, my desires and what I wish to create for myself and for my family must be taken into account.' Now how was that born? It was heavily influenced by the work that they were undertaking with Emancipation. Many women realized that not only their black brothers and sisters who were enslaved, but themselves as well, that they did not have the power to invoke the practical changes. This awakening has gone in fits and starts, witnessed by the rise of feminism, again the demand for liberation, and for biological and reproductive freedom.

"It is self-determination and you are seeing it all over your planet, St. Germaine's cry for freedom, as the Arab Spring. But this cry for freedom has come most strongly, most clearly, and most consistently from the western women. You will not stand for domination and control; you will not stand for children being shot and families going hungry; inequality and subjection because none of these things are of love. The redefinition of family, of what constitutes family, of expanded family, of reconstructed family, of community and what community is capable of, is coming from of women.

"Now I do not say this to the exclusion of the male population because at the same time as you are shifting, ascending and embracing their Divine Feminine. In the same way, many women are declaring 'I will have to embrace my Divine Masculine and move into action in new and different ways.' The balance is being reached, and it is the western women saying, particularly to the western men, 'being in a male dominated society and culture is not acceptable. What you have created economically, financially, politically and culturally is not loving, not reflective of the divine qualities, and does not take into account the potential and the sanctity of each life.'

"What has been forgotten in many ways is that all of you have come from a unified field, and there is an innate desire to recreate, return and be part of a unified field. That is why you don't live as hermits. It is not simply economics or urban migration that has caused the coming together of people. It is the desire to feel connected and part of a bigger whole. There is an innate desire to recapture what brings you joy; there is the joy that you experience simply because of who you are and then there is the explosive joy of love when you share it. This desire to reconnect is creating exponential expansion.

"When you are doing your invisible work with the collective, what you are really saying is 'I am giving you love, I am giving you support, and I am trying to remind you that we care about you and we would like you to join us in freedom.' Too often the fact of joining together has become downgraded to being controlled; that is what is being cleansed and let go of. Now you are realizing that to come together is support and strength. You are not coercing anyone to join you, but are saying, 'We would like it.' That is a gift, because everybody, every being on this planet yearns to belong, to be part of a unified field because that is who you are."

On February 14, 2013, Valentine's Day, one billion people worldwide came together to support the ending of violence against women. This is just one example of the divine feminine stepping forward to bring attention to social inequities.

Mother Mary affirms that "it was the beginning of building

of Nova Earth in so many ways. It was such an appropriate day, the celebration of love and the celebration of freedom. Violence against women has been the anathema of your planet, beginning with Gaia who has been terribly abused. Sexual, predatory and physical violence must be eliminated. You cannot have love or intact productive communities, productive families, loving families, and have women being suppressed, mutilated, killed, beaten, simply because they are women.

"What this speaks to is the fundamental male fear of losing power. They know the creative power of the feminine and they have worked to suppress this through various forms of imprisonment and violence for thousands of years. Now, as the shift and awakening occurs, it occurs not only in men but in women saying 'no more.'

"Do not think that I do not move in each of these gatherings and crowds because I do. I encourage my women, my girls, my children to declare who they are and that they will not permit such violence against them. This was what you call 'a red letter day.'

"The light that exploded on February 14th from this planet lit up the universe. There was celebration far and wide of women, of Nova Earth, of love, your star brothers and sisters were dancing and singing, it was a holiday throughout many galaxies."

Balancing the masculine and feminine energies within ourselves is the key to understanding and expanding our beingness, of stepping into and anchoring the New You. It has never been an either/or. One quality is not stronger or higher than the other. Our Mother emphasizes "to be truly masculine is extraordinarily beautiful to participate with and observe. It is the holding of energy, the ability of action and to protect. Sadly, what the human masculine forgot, both personally and globally, is that they had need to feed the goddess within and without. Now that has been reawakened. As you reawaken the Divine Feminine, the Divine Feminine informs and demands the Divine Masculine within to step forward. In this way the old illusions and false paradigms of the old masculine simply fall away."

Mother Mary shares with us some of her human experiences and challenges from so many years ago. Having lived in human form, she truly understands what we are going through right now.

"Even though I lived in a different time and age during that experience, you would be surprised how little things have changed. When I was to be betrothed to Joseph, whom I passionately loved and who passionately loved me, we were beautiful partners, there was so much that was said to him about my character, about our age difference and about our different positions in life. I was hesitant because I loved and cared for Joseph. And he said to me 'Mary, do you not know that this is the plan of the Mother and Father? Do you not know, do you not hold hope that everything is exactly as it needs to be?'

"I experienced reticence at times throughout our life because we knew the pathway of Yeshua; we knew the trials and tribulations. There were times when I would ask him to perhaps not be such a confrontational, controversial, public figure. Again Yeshua and Joseph would say to me 'You must hold the hope, the stillness and the knowing, for you are the glue, Mary that holds this family together'. There were many brothers and sisters as well, and we simply could not let everything fall apart.

"But it is that knowing and being able, in the face of great challenge, to know there is a presence and a rightness to what is being undertaken. You have to stay in that place of stillness to the very last moment. I would hope for different outcomes in the human sense of wishing and hoping and yet my core was bedrock knowing that regardless of what transpired all was in order. It was not that I was not having a human experience, I was, but I was also aware of the fullness of the plan, my plan.

"I am not suggesting that you will always hold serenity at all moments, when the externals appear to be harsh or difficult. But I ask you to try. There will be times in your life that you also will experience heartbreak. You will have your human reactions of grief and sorrow, even when you know that death is a return to the collective, to the unified field. But the human heart yearns for a different outcome. But please, hold the knowing that all is right in the unfoldment.

"The incredible strength of the human spirit, whether you are angel, starseed, earthkeeper, way-shower, pillar, or gate-keeper, is unknown elsewhere. That is why you have chosen to step forward and be part of this plan of physical ascension. Your strength, determination and hope are teaching many throughout the galaxies. You are forming that template; you are holding the energy for this to happen elsewhere. You are far more clear and loving and determined and joyous than you know."

How do we stay in that place of stillness and serenity when everything appears to be chaos around us? How do we stay the course when our hope wanes and we feel that we have been waiting forever? Like all good mothers, Mother Mary shares a tip to help us through the hard times.

"It is a universal tip; it is laughter, because when you look and laugh, even if there are tears flowing down your cheeks, it is a form of surrender. The other key to serenity is beauty, yes grace and awe as well, but let me speak to beauty. When you behold, embrace, become, and acknowledge beauty, it is like a breath of fresh air, it is that deep intake of breath that calms you right down. Beauty can be found in the faces of your loved ones but it is best found and connected with by being outside in nature, by connecting with Gaia. You cannot be lying on the grass, walking in a pristine forest, sitting by a pond in the beauty and splendor of Gaia and not be serene. Even in an urban set-ting as you place your feet upon the cement or concrete, take a moment to feel the energy go down and touch the heart of Gaia. Feel the beauty that emanates, breathe the air, and breathe blue dear heart. Beauty will keep you serene, it will remind you of the plan; it will restore and refresh you; it will give you the capacity to go back and deal with the human beings."

As Mother Mary ends her discussion on this quality of hope

she reminds us that it is the eternal knowing of the Divine.

"The hope I see, know, feel, and am observing and participating in is the shift, the growing quantum leap of light. It isn't simply growing quietly or softly, it is jumping like a forest fire. It is the hope that this will be completed rapidly in your terms and in mine. You will do this because it is right and it is in alignment with who you are and what All is. You do it because of love, and because you are mine."

Hope is the quality of the New You Warrior. Earlier Mother Mary has pointed out to us that hope is based on knowing, not futile daydreaming. Often I have heard people, including lightworkers, say that hope is not meaningful – that if you are hoping then that is what you are doing, spending your time wishing instead of creating. This is a fundamental misunderstanding not only of the nature of hope but also of the creation process. Hope is a component of the formulation of intent, the catalyst to action and the knowing of assured outcome.

None of us would disagree that there is far too much war and armed conflict in the world. But in most cases, regardless of allegiances, these warriors believe that they are fighting for something they believe in. How could men and women go into harm's way, how could families bear the burden if hope was not a key ingredient in their life? How could those whose families, especially children who are stricken with life threatening diseases go forward if it was not for hope? How could we manage to get out of bed some days if it were not for hope?

Hope keeps us going. It fuels us and aligns us with our will and Divine Will. Hope is the knowing; the faith that there is more, that we are more, and we are part of an infinite expanding plan. It is the infusion of the energy of the Divine Mother. Hope is our greatest and most tangible clue that "we know."

PURITY

"Purity: Twin of clarity; sister of chastity, not in the sexual sense

but in the sense of the ability to remain pure in all aspects of self. To remain centered when there is chaos, temptation or a lack of harmony around you. To see, feel and know clearly what exists, what is illusion and what is necessary for survival in all senses of the word. It is the color of pearlescent white, the color of infants before they ground in their body. It is what all should strive for. It is what you all miss."

St. Theresa of Lisieux steps forward to expand the original definition of the Council on the meaning and practical application of purity. Because Theresa has been in human form she is able to give us perspective from both the human and spiritual points of view. However, it is important to understand that even though St. Theresa steps forward in an individuated aspect, she a powerful collective energy.

There have been several St. Theresas, and it interesting to chart the similarity and continuity of the Theresa mission, purpose and vision. There is a theme of prayer, love and devotion, along with working with the poor and disenfranchised. The first St. Theresa who makes herself known in my channeling is St. Theresa of Portugal (1250 A.D.) who committed her life to working with the poor. Then there is St. Theresa of Avilla (1582 A.D.), a Carmelite nun, known as one of the very early Christian mystics, with a deep devotion to teaching the power of prayer. In 1770 A.D., Carmelite nun, St. Theresa, was born in Florence, Italy and committed her life to the Sacred Heart of Jesus. Finally, there is St. Theresa of Lisieux (1897 A.D.), another Carmelite nun whom I feel most strongly in terms of a personality when I'm channeling.

St. Therese of Lisieux taught us the infinite love of God despite any human shortcomings or frailties.

The theme and the energy of Theresa has comes to Earth again and again to teach us the lessons of service, of love, the power of prayer, but usually they have come as nuns always taking care of the sick, the elderly, the disempowered, disenfranchised. The most recent St. Theresa is Mother Theresa. Even though the connection and the devotion has often been to the Sacred Heart of Jesus, the connection with the Divine Feminine and the embodiment of those qualities of nurturing, caring, stamina, fortitude and the selflessness and the commitment to the Divine Mother that are integral to the Theresa energy. Purity is the twin of clarity and we witness this time and again in the Theresa energy.

The color of purity is that pearlescent white which means the embedding of shimmering pinks, mauves, violets and pale greens. It is the ray of newborn babies. When babies are birthed into form, they come on this wonderful pearlescent white, which is called luminessa. Picture this ray as the sun shining on the snow with a million sparkling hues. While the energy is strong, the purity is evident, and it gently caresses our hearts.

Clarity is the virtue that allows us to bring the blessing of purity into the here and now of our lives; it is the action piece. The gift of clarity is the ability to see into and through people's hearts, situations and environments to the core issue. It is the laser virtue that not only lets us identify the heart of the matter but to translate that knowing into perfect action to address, resolve, heal and expand the person, situation, group, nation and even planet. Clarity is the translator of purity; where we move into action from a loving position of non-judgment. There are times, like with prudence, when the perfect action is to simply be the observer, to hold the space and do nothing. Never underestimate the power of stillness, it is often the most precious gift we can offer.

"Greetings, I am Theresa, and I welcome you with wide open arms, in humility and joy. I have yearned to speak to you, and yet very often my voice is quiet, so gentle that many do not hear me. But my heartfelt prayer has been to touch your heart, to connect with you infinitely and abundantly, and to remind you not of my purity but of yours.

"Your spirit, your soul, your being is purity and always has been. Some of you have said that you have journeyed many miles and often upon the Earth, and have taken missteps, made mistakes, and harmed others. Yes you have, and you have also opened your heart and loved and tended to those you have loved and cherished, tended to the sacred Mother, the Son, and to Gaia herself. Purity is a twin of clarity, but what does this really mean? It means clear vision and not falling into this trap of minimizing yourself. That trap can become an excuse; an excuse becomes separation, the separation becomes a very solid veil of illusion.

"There is not one of you, whether you finished your life as murderer, thief, or cheat who did not hold the essence of purity, the essence of One. Your divine spark never went out. It has always, always been part and parcel of you. The key is in the acceptance of this divine spark of clarity, purity and love. In that acceptance is also the acceptance of the yearning for unity, of knowing the One. Everybody, saint, sinner, and everything in-between wishes for purity, but it is already there.

"You are in the midst of your ascension process. Most of you have already anchored well within the fifth, sixth, and seventh dimension. You are letting go of the old illusions and you are anchoring, not only in the purity of those dimensions but in the purity of who you are. It is a time of clearing up, that is what the clarity is about. There is a clean-up, a clarity growing on Gaia and within all the kingdoms, particularly the human race of which you, like I, are an integral part.

"Speaking from personal experience, if you never misstep how do you know the right way to go? How do you compare within your heart what is good, and feels like love? Without some missteps, you don't know yourself, humanity, or being alive. Akin to purity is forgiveness, forgiveness of others but also forgiveness of self.

"You are anchoring on this beautiful planet, this Nova Earth the New You. This means when you walk, and look at the flowers, be gentle as you place your feet upon the grass, ground, dirt or rocks. Feel the connection to all sentient beings above and below. Bless them, cherish them. The walk of purity is the acknowledgement that all forms are equal, and that you are part of that vast mosaic of love. You are not simply by choice a piece, you are an integral part. You voted for that yourself; made that choice and decision a long time ago.

"That is why I have returned to the planet time and time and time again. Because like you, I am an integral part of that mosaic, and I have and have had a role to play. That role is regarding purity of heart and intention. The path of purity is now integral to your life and your society. What you are saying is that we are not a group apart, quite the contrary, we are a part and parcel of the mainstream and the mainstream is of love. We choose to exist and to operate in higher realms and dimensions where this is the way it is.

"What else does purity mean? Purity means getting your hands dirty; it does not mean shutting yourself away in seclusion. Purity is action-oriented. Clarity of purpose of action, of movement, of intent is essential; it is essential to the ascension of the collective as well as each of you. If you do not extend yourself into a form of action, and yes, prayer is an action, then you are not participating. Then you are back at the point in your infancy when you had a choice to either stay or go. But that time has passed dear heart, you are part of the collective.

"It is to not only about accepting and embracing yourself, but also embracing the sacred joy of being blessed by the One; to have the opportunity to be in form, to dance, play, sing, and serve. You can only be where you are. That is why we talk about forgiveness and compassion; you can only be where you are in this very moment, what so many of you call the eternal now. The reason I emphasize this is that, if you are not now embracing yourself, then how do you go forward in knowing your divine perfection? When you say, you'll work on that, you are projecting into the future and you are not accepting those qualities right now, particularly this day when I fill you to the brim with magnificent purity and clarity.

"When you do not live in acceptance and in the embrace of you; your totality, body, mind, and soul are not participating. You are not actively being an integral part of the fluid, ongoing, beautiful mosaic of creation. When you move in the now, to the acceptance as the totality of yourself, what you will see is all the lesser functions of the old paradigms fade away. That is why I have focused on prayer, love, and service, because when you are doing that, the rest fades away. The ability comes to let go of those momentary blips of anger, fear or distain, to look at them like a piece of dandelion fluff floating away. You are in the perfection of the Mother's design and plan and, you are in the perfection of your design and plan. It does not need to be altered, but rather recognized, embraced and lived to the fullest. To practice purity does not mean you do not sing and dance with the flowers and the fairies. It means that you do. You do celebrate the beauty that you have been gifted with and chosen for this lifetime.

"Dear heart, make no mistake about it, you are in the midst of chaos. You must stay centered and focused. Other than cement boots, you are to anchor above and below. You are anchor firmly within your own sacred divinity self, into the heart of the planet, Gaia, and into the heart of One, into the 13th Octave. This is how you persevere and get through. This is how you become the totality of who you are. You look at the obstacles, not in denial, not in pretending that everything is rosy when it is not, but in acceptance that you are making a difference. It is a wonderful feeling. When you are in the knowing of 'I am exactly where I need to be' then there are no questions. Situations arise and you deal with them. Of course, you always make room for the divine assistance."

All of us at times have experienced feelings of fear, self-denigration, shame, and underestimating of ourselves. We feel ineffectual while dealing with circumstances all the while yearning to do more, to be more, and to contribute more. St. Theresa shares what worked for her while she was on Earth.

"One of the most effective ways that I have dealt with these emotions is to connect with Gaia; to place my feet, my body, my energy upon this mighty beautiful planet, because she is courageous. She is filled with valor, truth, justice and balance. When you anchor yourself, it helps from the buffeting winds of drama. You are like a little rose with the strong stem. Do not forget the rose also has thorns. So when I say to you to anchor and be the beauty and purity, it also means to protect your sacred self and to stay in the love.

"Each of you has chosen to play in different fields; some very quietly in the background and some on the world stage. It doesn't matter where you have decided to play. The fact is you have decided to play. The heart of the matter is we are not removed from you. When you look to the ascended masters, these holy ones, to the Mother, and to so many who have held the energy, you know us. You have known and traveled with us forever, in and out of form.

"One of the surprising things is how rarely you actually call on us. And I do not mean in moments of desperation. There is nothing I would love more than for you to invite me to take a walk through the pristine snow, through the core of a city, to where the flowers grow so we can pause and admire their beauty; for us to simply be together. All of us, St. Germaine, St. Francis, Yeshua, Maitreya, Kuthumi, we all feel the same way, and the more you invite us the clearer we become. You begin to see us clearly with your third eye. Invite us as you would invite your best friend to go for dinner, to cook, garden, travel, or go for a bicycle ride. Francis loves bicycle riding. We are your best friends, we are the family who has loved you forever, we want to feel your love as well, and we want to feel your invitations to share your life."

A question arose in a conversation whether St. Theresa would be among the ascended masters to help humans leave behind the illusions of the old third dimension and raise up to anchor in the beauty of the fifth dimension. She replied:

"I have not fully made my decision and chosen my assignment. But yes, I will be upon the Earth, upon the planet again. I was the early ground crew in the 1200s and 1850s, and I will be part of the ground crew again. My job, my journey is not over. Right now I am assisting from this side but my intention and part of the Mother's Plan is, I will return yet again and I will walk amongst you. I will be part of this wondrous crew of star beings cleaning up the atmosphere, the air, the water. I am not waiting for the distant future, when everything is bright and clean and shiny.

"I have seen the devastation of Gaia. I have seen the pollution, the pain and suffering of the collective. I am coming back to celebrate the renewal, to walk amongst the flowers and the Cities of Light, to listen to the birds and the sound of children laughing in the inner city. I am coming back to see the change. I am so excited to be on a cleansed Earth where there is no suffering and pain, no poverty, hunger, or disease. So, look for me, when you meet a star sister called Theresa wink at me, acknowledge me. This is one celebration I am not going to miss.

"What I see, and what will come to pass, is that humans will truly be shining from the inside out. There will be smiles and laughter, quiet and consideration, and the look in the eyes that mirror the soul. You see the purity and the joy at being alive. That is what the embodiment of purity and clarity is about. It is about the choice to be fully present; in body, in the now, embracing the perfection of the gift from the Divine Mother."

As we ponder these words from our sister St. Theresa, I leave you with a prayer that has been attributed to her:

"May today there be peace within.
"May you trust you are exactly where you are meant to be.
"May you not forget the infinite possibilities that are born of faith
in yourself and others.
"May you use the gifts that you have received and pass on the love
that has been given to you.
"May you be content with yourself just the way you are.
"Let this knowledge settle into your bones and allow you the
freedom to sing, dance, laugh and love.
"It is there for each and every one of us."

Purity can sometimes feel illusive, particularly within the human realm. The Council tells us that purity is "beyond motivation and prior to intent." In other words, purity is one of those foundational qualities that simply is a part of who we are. Sometimes, we don't recognize that core within ourselves or others.

We search for the outer expressions of purity and clarity but we don't acknowledge that it also is the bedrock of our being.

When I was considering this section I asked the Council for examples so we would know how to recognize purity. Many of the examples are in nature and Gaia because we are more open to accepting and seeing these. Travel with me to a part of the world that has four seasons, and let's discover the very first shoot of a flower deep in the forest in the early spring – snowdrops, wild violets, and trilliums. The flower that will blossom is still surrounded by patches of snow on which the sun shines brilliantly, melting away the old. But the snow does not suffer or bemoan its demise, it sparkles with a million diamonds of white light; luminessa. It refreshes the forest and nourishes the ground. It knows it makes room for the new flower, and all is in balance. The snow and the new shoot are perfectly clear about the harmony and beauty they are co-creating. Come with me to a pristine waterfall, to a glacier fjord, to a rushing river with salmon jumping upstream, and you will find the purity you are yearning for. Gaia will joyously reflect that knowing deep within you.

It is often harder for us to identify purity within. Clarity is easier to grasp, but purity can be illusive. One of the reasons is, we are usually looking for consistency within ourselves. As humans in transition, the outer purity is not always consistently present. We tend to judge ourselves and others harshly. The guidance is to look for the moments and actions of purity, when the light of the soul is so vibrant it shines right through; it becomes undeniable. The Council gave me the example of Whitney Houston whose music I adored. They brought me back to when Whitney first hit the music scene, fresh from the church choir. She not only had the voice of an angel but shined like one. She was the embodiment of purity. Did she forget that sometimes along the way? Perhaps. Did it disappear? Never.

Purity tends to be quiet, not showy. When you are looking for purity in others, look to the quiet ones – the ones who efficiently go about their mission without bravado or fuss. And when you see that light of purity shining in someone, please acknowledge it and reinforce it. Let the person know that you know. In this way we build the paradigm of seeing each other as we truly are, angels in form, playing and being the light.

The key to purity is to always be looking for it; to become aware and heart cognizant of when it is right in front of you. Purity abounds in nature and the spiritual realm. However, it also surrounds us in the human realm – in the sweet cheeks and baby fingers of an infant; in the random acts of kindness that we witness every day, in the wisdom eyes of the elderly, in the first love of a teenager. When you get used to seeing purity all around you what you are doing is allowing the purity within you to come forth. You are anchoring, accepting and surrendering to your core purity, not the perfection but the purity, that lies within.

BEAUTY

"Beauty: Inner and outer. To be in a state of beauty with all that is, in all realms, physical, emotional and spiritual. The ability to create and maintain beauty. To be in a state of beauty is to be in harmony with all. To become a perfect mirror for all of God's creations. It is two separate colors, silver and magenta."

Two phenomenal beings, Quan Yin and Mary Magdalene step forward to speak to us about the blessing and virtue of beauty. Mary Magdalene had been very clear that she was the one who wanted to come forward to address this subject. Then Quan Yin started to make her presence known, reminding me that "there is nothing more beautiful than the goddess riding the dragon."

This blending of east and west is interesting. Both of these wonderful beings who carry the energy of the Divine Feminine are emphatic when talking about beauty that it's not just the state of appearing beautiful, it really is the ability to be in beauty in all realms, all aspects – physically, emotionally, and spiritually. It is also about the ability to create, see and find beauty in everything. Beauty can never be about competition; you don't see the flowers competing to see who's the most beautiful, they both just stand there and allow you to gaze at their beauty.

The colors of beauty and for you to be in that perfect state of beauty are magenta, which is that perfect balance of red and blue, and silver. That's an unusual combination. Silver is also the ray of Archangel Uriel. It's the ray of clarity and the ability to see in darkest places.

Beauty, like all the divine qualities are infinite and eternal. Together we expand our understanding of beauty; our holding of beauty, and of our ability to accept and cherish ourselves as vessels of beauty.

"Greetings, I am Quan Yin, goddess of compassion, but as I say to this channel so often 'Is there anything more beautiful than this goddess riding a dragon?' Well I invite you this day to ride the dragon with me. It is not an imaginary creature, it is the creature of power and fire, of movement, and might I even say destiny. In beauty there is strength, there is power, nobility, sensitivity and the ability to rise above, because you know the dragon flies. However, it is also the ability to transmute and cleanse. Too often beauty has been seen in a very narrow ways, which do not reflect the truth of this divine quality. Beauty is not simply what sits on your face or your skin or upon the rack of your body. Beauty is everything and everywhere. I say to you there is nothing more beautiful than my dragon, for it is strong, brave, courageous and willing to go forth. In order to do that one must have the strength of balance and harmony within and without. It is not simply an outer commodity to be traded. In fact in many ways, particularly with the situation of women, beauty has resulted in lack of power. It is time to eradicate the false illusions of beauty.

"Beauty is in everything you behold on your planet, this wondrous Gaia. It is a failure of some to see that. I am not speaking only of the majestic peaks, gracious valleys and the mighty rivers; I speak of buildings and old men under old garbage cans trying to stay warm. I speak of children, who believe they are young men, flashing their knives. They have forgotten they are the holders of beauty and that they contribute to the beauty of the planet, and to the collective. Who reminds them other than me and the Magdalena? Who reminds these ones who embrace what they believe is the ugliness of their soul, their desperation? Who reminds them that they are of the beauty?

"I am not suggesting that those who are in pain and suffering and committing heinous acts are in harmony; they are not. But until they are reminded that they are a mirror of God's creation, that there is only one Source and it is perfection, they will continue in their way of illusion. How does this translate into the masculine being that has not considered himself to be of beauty?

"Oh, there is nothing more joyous than gazing upon the perfected masculine. They are as beautiful as the mountains of Switzerland, the Nile and the woman, the Divine Feminine. There has been a disconnect between beauty and power; a misunderstanding that beauty is not power and visa-versa because the masculine thinks of action and movement. When you look at the way the universe is structured the divine masculine is still, quiet, infinite and is held in adoration. Most men like to think of themselves as strong, good looking and handsome. They do not always look within because beauty is also sensitive. You cannot be a bestower, a creator, or a holder of beauty and not be aware of beauty around you. What that implies is that you are sensitive. Think of Greece and Rome when it was the male form that was considered the essence of beauty, strength and nobility. So, it is not an either/or, it is both."

Mary Magdalene also brings forth her insight on the meaning of beauty and how we incorporate this virtue into our lives and core.

"I am the Magdalena. I am Mary, I am Maré. Welcome to you my brothers and sisters of the journey. The journey has been long but has it not been beautiful? When I have walked the world I was known as a great beauty in the physical sense. There were times when that troubled me and caused me difficulty, and I wondered why I had chosen to incarnate in such a way because from a very early age I was in training and on a spiritual path. A path men and women might call a path of beauty, but I call a path of service. There were many who liked to criticize me and who thought that I had seduced Yeshua, my beloved husband, with my outer beauty. That simply was not true.

"When Yeshua and I first encountered each other, we instantly recognized the beauty within; the beauty of our soul and the beauty of our eternal connection and the soul agreement we had formulated. We endeavored to create beauty in everything we did, the most precious being the creation of family, and the creation of children. It was very difficult to be in the presence of Yeshua and not to feel a sense of beauty and the wondrous balance of all realms. One of my roles was always as the creator of ritual and ceremony. I was always a channel and so when we engaged and embraced each other it was as natural as breathing that we communicated telepathically, even if he was many miles away. It was in this way that the bond was maintained and is maintained to this very day.

"What you are here for, on this magnificent, beautiful planet Gaia, is to experience a life of beauty. It is simple is it not, straightforward? But if you do not see and embrace the beauty in every moment, then it is not a beautiful life and therefore it is not a life of joy. It is not a life that makes your heart sing. Even in what you think of as the most hard and horrendous moments – such as the death of a loved one – the beauty of your love continues, it does not dissipate it does not disappear. You can see it in the clouds; or in the waving grass of wheat fields; or in the sand or the stones of Galilee. But always return to your own inner beauty. You have been birthed directly from the heart of the Mother, and you carry her essence beauty in every way. More than you can even imagine.

"If you say 'I am not beautiful,' then you are denying your divine essence and that is not truth. It certainly is not acceptance or allowance. Denial freezes you in a false belief system. You know, right now, you have anchored fully and completely into the fifth dimension and into the realm with Gaia where relationships tend to take on new meaning. One of the things our beloved Quan Yin refers to the old third dimension where equality was often not present in relationship. There were elements of control, lust, greed or denial in many male/female relationships.

"What is happening with you as you anchor in the higher realms is freedom. This was exactly what so many people objected to in the relationship between Yeshua and me. We claimed our freedom to engage in true love, in sacred union, and partnership. That is the ability to step forward, and allow someone to truly see you, to see your beauty, to see what you think. I use the word 'think' because what you judge as your shortcomings may be some of the sweetest aspects you carry. That is why there is no room for judgment.

"In a New You relationship, there is not the hesitation that the parnter will be with you until it is no longer convenient, or, until it feels like they are not growing. I am talking about a genuine sacred union, which is the heart, soul, mind, body commitment for two people to go forward in union as one. You both stand equally strong, resilient, and powerful. Each of you brings to the relationship your own sacred attributes, your own qualities, your own history of magic.

"Sacred unions are bonds of light between two hearts and souls that last forever. When you have been in truly sacred union that is why you incarnate with that person in various forms again and again. It is why that person is so familiar, and why you so quickly say 'How do you do? I trust you. I cherish you. I want to be with you.' It is the physical embodiment of beauty. It is precious beyond measure. That occurs not only with partners but also occur with your children.

"Sacred union is the acknowledgement of the beauty of another's soul. That is the heart connection; the acknowledgment heart to heart, person to person, personality to personality, nation to nation, universe to universe, that I acknowledge you, I see you, I honor you. Beauty is a stand-alone truth, whether it is in the humans, your star brothers and sisters, Gaia or love. This is always an eternal topic of conversation. Beauty is not determined by anything other than the willingness to truly embrace love.

"What you are doing in speaking the truth of beauty and love is the vibration for those who are still stuck in the old third, in the 'show me' paradigm. You are saying, 'You will have your signs but in the meantime let us speak, practice and be the embodiment of freedom, because that is what is real and that is what is meaningful.' When Yeshua and I walked the Earth, we used our feet, sometimes a donkey, but mostly we walked so the pace would connect us with Gaia, and those who wanted to speak with us. The pace of beauty is the pace of love; it allows for connection to happen; it is about slowing down. Your societies are moving so rapidly that you are not creating the time and space for beauty and freedom."

The Magdalena speaks to the concept of being able to see the beauty outside of us because it is a reflection of what's inside of us. We know what we focus on grows. The importance of seeing the beauty all around us just keeps it growing and building, and that is the active, co-creative process of anchoring in this realm.

"Beauty is an outer reflection of your inner reality; it is the law, the Universal Law of Within and Without, Above and Below. You cannot say: 'when I arrive in the fifth, sixth, seventh, or eighth, then I will see the beauty.' No. It is seeing it today, it is seeing it in your home, your family, in your community, in everything and in the seeing it just continues to grow and flourish.

"Are there many things that attract (or distract) your attention such as abundance, star technology, visiting with your star brothers and sisters, healing ships and information beyond what you can imagine? Yes. But the foundation of peace is within; love is within. And when you have love there is peace within your heart no matter what is happening externally. That is what harmony truly is. It is the ability to see beauty in everything even in what some may say is horrid, awful and tragic. Out of that comes lasting, eternal peace where people do not kill and maim, emotionally, mentally, spiritually, they do not hurt each other. The Cities of Light follow and come because they are places of peace, creation, music, portals for your star brothers and sisters, healing, art, culture, communication. All of this is fallout from a change of heart, from shifting out of the ego and the old paradigms to the reality of love."

"Surround yourself and go out of your way to find the beauty every day whether it is a picture of nature, of incredible art, or wandering through a museum, staring at a beautiful portrait. This is what I ask of thee: stare at yourself in the mirror and see the bright angel, the beauty that you are, that you have always been. Practice love and beauty.

"Beauty is eternal. Notice it in nature: the oldest, most majestic trees, the mountains, the rivers, and the beauty of the Mother. Your Mother and mine is eternal. There are also seasons of beauty and I want you to think of yourself in this way. What season are you in? No, it is not a matter of the equinox or the moon, where are you, my beloved ones? Are you in the springtime? Many of you who are ascending are. See the beauty of your rebirth just like the buds pushing through the Earth, that gentle green demanding to be reborn.

"Perhaps you are in the cycle of the winter and you think my beauty has gone; age has taken my beauty. There is no such thing you know; it is eternal. Witness the beauty of the barren tree, the beauty of the snow; of the gray water, cold against the rocks; of the winter sky, and embrace the beauty of who you are and where you are each day. Do not hesitate, celebrate and embrace your beauty. In so doing you will embrace the beauty of Gaia and of each other. Go in peace."

While beauty would appear self-evident, to be one of the easier virtues to embrace, I am always surprised how many people go day in and day out without taking the slightest moment to see it. Beauty is one of the most generous gifts of Gaia. The splendor of her beauty surrounds us constantly. The key is to stop, even for a moment and breathe it in, to acknowledge it, and to acknowledge that the beauty we recognize in the outer world is a reflection of each of us. There is a beautiful scarlet cardinal that often perches on top of the Kelly-green road sign at the corner of my street. I am always on the lookout for him when I walk my little dog Eliza in the morning. When he is there singing his song for all he is worth, declaring a new day, both Eliza and I stop and admire this tiny bird that gives us such joy by his bright beauty. The other morning as I put out bread and seed for the birds, there in the underbrush was a gnarly frog perched on a toad stool – how much more perfect can life be? The point is that beauty can be seen in the little things. It doesn't have to be a magnificent sunset over the ocean or the model perfect face. Beauty is everywhere.

There is a special gift in seeing beauty outside what our society has deemed as beautiful. Looking into the eyes of an old person and seeing that the twinkle is still there. Playing with an old arthritic cat who still thinks he's a kitten. It is a particular gift to be able to see beauty in what is also terrible – the eyes of a child starving, with a deep gaze that speaks of such wisdom, compassion and peace; a magnificent blood red sunset that occurs because of a forest fire. Gaia never leaves us bereft of images and examples of beauty.

The key is, when you see that beauty, whether it is energetic ties of love or the stunning power of a raging ocean in a hurricane, is to take it inside of your heart, and accept it as an outer reflection of your beauty, your power, your resilience, your joy and your place in the universe. You are beautiful. When you acknowledge that within your sweet self, you can begin to share it with the world. Heaven knows we need that.

JOY

"Joy: To be fully thankful, grateful and one with the gift of life purpose and spirit. To be a reflection of the perfection of the creation of self and all. To live in and remain with the heart for all time. Joy is the color of gold. This is the core of the essence as defined by the Council of Love. This blessing and virtue is presented by my go-to gal, Archangel Gabrielle. She is one of my favorite beings in the universe."

The first question people always ask when hearing from the Lily of Love is 'is it Gabriel or Gabrielle?' When I first started working with Archangel Gabriel, she very clearly had feminine energy, and wanted to be known in the fullness of her feminine identity. Now it's not that it cancels out or in any way diminishes that energy of the masculine face of Archangel Gabriel, but over the years she has come to be asked to be known as Archangel Gabrielle. In fact, when we talk about the fullness of her name it is Suzanna Michaela Gabrielle. The Suzanna piece of it comes from the derivative of suzerain, an ancient word meaning "the leader" or "the head of" denoting leadership. The Michaela, of course, is just honoring her brother, Michael.

Gabrielle is the Central Administrator for God. She is also known as "the Lily of Love" and "the Trumpet of Truth." Gabrielle brings us her golden essence of joy, and assists us with healing and creation. She's the only archangel that comes forward to me as a feminine energy. When we post the Archangels, Mikhail, Raphael, Uriel, Jophiel, which are the masculine energies around the four corners of a room, Gabrielle is always in the middle bringing into that sealed space that quality of the Divine Feminine.

In my early days of channeling I was doing some past life work with the Apostle Peter, and every day he would show me a past life. I had this recurring vision of a lifetime where I was on a ship; where I was traveling from England to North America. Every day on ship, I walked the deck with this woman who had become my teacher and mentor. She was incredibly beautiful, with striking blue eyes and electric hair of the most beautiful blond I had ever seen. Even though we wore bonnets, the cover did nothing to restrain her gorgeous hair. I was a Quaker, and she was broadening my perspective on spirituality. In hindsight I remember she introduced herself as Elizabeth Goldberg, a Jewish scholar of the sacred teachings of Kabbalah. She would joke with me and tell me that when we reached New York she was going to change her name to Gold because of the prejudice against the Jews. She didn't let this prejudice affect her excitement about her next adventure in a brand new land. As a Quaker and healer, leaving England because of accusations of witchery, I needed this example.

Years later Peter had me review those lives to learn a deeper lesson. I was shocked when I looked down at that young woman walking the deck and realized that she was alone! It was then I understood my beloved teacher wasn't a physical being after all. It was Archangel Gabrielle who walked the decks, and gave me lessons to prepare me for my mission in the United States. She is as present today as she was then.

Sometimes people think joy is going about the day feeling happy all the time. While it can be, it doesn't always mean that everything is going smoothly and we're happy, because happy tends to be reactive. Happy tends to be "we are happy about something." Even when we're having a hard time in the moment, we know if we go a little deeper, joy is there. We tend to think joy is something we have to go out and get, but it isn't. It can be catalyzed by what we do, and we can build on it, but the essential spark is already inside of us.

Joy is this sense of rightness and alignment, divine perfection, and what I call the smile in the tummy. It is in each of us and is our natural state. It's inherent in every being. It's part of our light, and our divine spark. Joy is one of the essential qualities needed to create.

As we bring Gabrielle in to discuss joy, see her in what we call the "Gabrielle Gold", that deep, rich Florentine, burnished gold. Let her come into your heart, and share her understanding of joy.

"Greetings, I am Gabrielle. I bring you a bounty of joy this day for there is always enough to go around and share richly, fully and lavishly. Joy is who you are. You are the substance of love and the matter of joy. You are the embodiment of that essence of laughter and the tinkling of gladness, the song of freedom. All of these are interwoven as one, interwoven uniquely into your tapestry and being. You have shifted, my beloveds, into the fifth dimension, into the new reality of Gaia.

"Why do I choose to speak of this? Because in this reality (of the fifth) there is enormous joy, there is infinite and eternal. Does this mean there are not people or situations or environments where the old debris of the third that crumbles, hurts you, irritates you, and causes you momentary pain? No it doesn't. What it does mean is when that occurs, you are witnessing the destruction of the old. At the same time, you have this wellspring of my golden radiance to drink, and it will nourish you. When you wish to heal, fill yourself with my golden elixir for it will permeate every cell, every pore, every organ, your blood, everything, and it will renew you.

"Joy is the anti-aging agent of the century and it makes you beautiful and radiant because there is nothing more beautiful than joy. I am a little biased, but I also know the truth. I am the Lily of Love, Trumpet of Truth and dear heart, my trumpet is gold. There is nothing meek and mild about gold. There are many who say I am the most outspoken archangel there is. I take that as a complement because joy is outrageous, a clarion, but also gentle.

"You do not need to claim your joy, but it does need to be built upon because you are the wayshowers, pathfinders, teachers, healers, and channels. You cannot do any of those if you are stuck in depression and the doldrums. What is the antidote for depression or clearing or the doldrums? It is a very generous dose of joy.

"Joy is the stillpoint between masculine and feminine. It is all; it does not pick and choose. It is free and abundant to all. I am infusing you with it even as you read this. I want you to call and sing from the treetops to spread your wings and fly, to rise like the phoenix from the ashes of the third, and ascend. I will carry you if that is what it takes and I will do so joyfully. Come with me; let us explore this wondrous mystery called joy.

"I have given the very practical prescription for joy: Fifteen minutes every day in human reality, not in meditation, not in bliss, not out of your body, rather in your body; in physicality doing something that brings you joy. Perhaps it is simply staring at your sleeping child; looking at family photographs; looking at pictures of beautiful places; listening to music, or taking bubble baths. When you these things it reignites your joy and it spreads. It infuses your entire being. Fifteen minutes of this kind of joy is enough to carry you the entire day.

"You did not choose this mission out of a sense of obligation, or because of need to do something better. You chose it because it is the most exciting, fulfilling offer on the table and you jumped at the chance. You said, 'This sounds like a blast; let's go!' Remember this truth because it is the pure joy of you.

"Let go of things that don't serve you. That includes old belief systems, relationships habits, what you do for work, and where you live. Step away from the drama and conflict. Those things compromise our state of joy.

"There is a village in South Africa, a very simple community. At first blush, one could say they don't have anything, they are living in huts and don't wear much clothing. Yet, they were identified as some of the happiest, joyous people on Earth because they had community. There is such great love in their lives. Their simple lives have such richness, connection to their sacred selves, each other, and to Gaia.

"Joy is not only outrageous, but courageous. Let's use this tribe as an example. When one of them loses their joy or missteps, there is acknowledgement that not only does it affect the person, but the tribe is also immediately affected. So the tribe – the community – comes together to heal the person, and to help restore that sense of balance, of rightness, of joy.

"So often in your community you will hear some people say they don't see a person anymore because it just brings them down. I have spoken about the quality of free choice in what brings you daily joy, but practice courage, and say to that person 'Hey, what's going on? Let's fix this.' This is part of the Blessings and Virtues; it is related to compassion, love, and truth. Joy is contagious, it is a strong viral energy, and it moves at lightning speed.

"The community we know as Gaia has anchored in the fifth dimension and her inhabitants are also moving into the fifth. Because of this, Gaia has improved dramatically, she is in joy, she is singing to the planets in her galaxy, and she shines brightly.

"You say, 'I have been clearing, dealing with old issues or debris. I have been doing this for myself and for millions.' But why are you doing it? Because you are claiming your joy; the joy of the kingdoms, devas, mountains, and trees. So go out and dance on the skin of Gaia, touch her, touch your plants, your flowers, your snow, your water, and let that joy be communicated to your very core. Let it act as a catalyst in your life.

"My joy is that the Divine Mother comes forward, and makes her presence known upon the planet. I am the messenger, for the Council of Love, and so often the messages have not been fully received. Now the Mother speaks to you of how to bring forth your new world and your New You.

"You need to make joy a top priority. There is not one person upon the planet that is not being transformed, transmuted, and growing into the fullness of their fifth dimensional being. Go to where your joy is. It may be at a campfire; in front of a Quan Yin statue; playing a game with your children like Snakes and Ladders, or watching The Lion King. There are places that bring greater joy, yet not make the mistake of believing that joy is geographic. It goes with you wherever you are. It is within you. No one can interfere with your joy.

"You are not joyful about poverty, despair or hunger. Angst, despair or disappointment never resolve and raise the vibration of the very thing that you are upset about. When you hold the joy and you bring the light, not Pollyannaish, or in denial, then you are truly in your creative force. The tribe in South Africa does not spend time in angst and despair there may be a drought coming or perhaps the well four villages over is dry. They have learned to cope, to share the joy, to raise the vibration. And when they do, the water comes.

"You are now coming to the realization that joy is a state of being. It is not something that floats in and out. You can maintain a state of joy and still be in that place of recognizing that your situation isn't as good as it could be. We can acknowledge that, and take action in our own ways to address it. Just remember you can bring joy to yourselves and in so doing it raises the vibration of the human collective."

COMPASSION

"Compassion: The ability to love and serve without judgment.
To be able to understand and heart-feel another's situation, without

entering or assuming that cloak. The understanding that another has a chosen path, and that we can only offer assistance and love. Tenderness. Its colors are green and red."

I can't think of a better quality than compassion to make the bridge between the first six Blessings and Virtues and the last six. Compassion is key to real change; we don't often practice compassion on our sweet selves.

To understand compassion the Buddha steps forward and invites you to sit under the Bodhi tree with him. The energy of the Buddha is massive, thick, huge, making me feel like I weigh two thousand pounds. This Buddha energy is a collective energy which comes as one voice. Which is probably why is feels so enormous.

Compassion is a divine quality common to all beings. You witness it in nature, with the Ascended Masters, and our star brothers and sisters. Compassion is a key to our moving forward together, never in judgment, always in support.

"Greetings, I am the Buddha. I come as the Wayfarer and welcome you to come and sit with me before we pack and leave everything behind to wander the countryside, to minister, bring hope and demonstrate compassion. The name I give myself is 'the wayfarer', the one who wanders and not attached to anything. I invite you to be a wayfarer.

"You ask, 'What is the difference between being a wayfarer and being a wayshower?' There is significant difference. The wayshower helps guide and direct in a demonstrable manner. A wayfarer merely says 'Let me walk with you for a while.' Our conversation and my energy will add to your heart and understanding. I am not pretending I will guide you to the end of your journey; I simply will be with you, to walk with you.

"There are some of you who don't know what your journey, purpose, and mission is along the path. Sometimes you are too shy, foolish or you think the dream is too big. You then deny yourself which translates as not practicing compassion. Compassion is not just a feeling but an action. It is not one-sided; it is in perfect balance. Compassion is what is sorely needed on Earth. You are speaking with one who has a tendency to think in terms of thousands of years, so when I say to you compassion is important right now, I mean for the previous thousand and the next thousand years. However, I also mean in this very moment.

"You are guided in all of these journeys by the Universal Laws, and might I say, the Law of Compassion. There is often a tendency to try and heal, fix, recalibrate or redirect the journey of another. Often this is done out of the kindest motivation and love. But balance is key. It's one thing to have a conversation with someone because you believe they are going off track. It's quite another to pull them in a direction they really don't wish to go.

"This practice is commonplace. When you try this type of re-direction, you are denying the soul path and journey of another. You're assuming you know the outcome and the lessons to be learned; the experiences to be had, and their value. You cannot possibly know.

"I have watched my own son go to war, and die. It challenged my faith, my stillness, even my journey. Even though I was aware of the dangers that lay ahead, I thought I knew best. One can provide wisdom and love, insight and sharing, and then one must stand back, detached and attached at the same time. One holds the higher vision for that person and their journey; honoring their choices.

"Now, it is natural, I do not wish for you to think that I speak against the laws of nature, so it is natural, particularly as parents and guardians in form to want to keep your children safe and protect them from heartbreak, sorrow and disillusionment. But then there is also the balancer, which is trust, that while these children are of your loins, they are also ancient wise ones and they know what they are doing. That is particularly so with the children of today, these bright pinks and magentas, crystals and rainbows, being born unto Gaia to lead the way into the new realm of New Earth. These presents an even greater challenge and difficulty, my fellow parents, of standing back as you honor the pathway of your children, and not judge yourself. It is letting go of the strong belief that if your child fails or missteps, then somehow you have as well.

"Compassion is the complete honoring, without understanding, of what someone is going through whether it is winning the lottery or dying of cancer. It is understanding you don't always comprehend the meaning of what appears to be transpiring. It is complete trust, not only in the divine plan but in the plan of the individual. It is, at times, the heart-wrenching, conscious decision to be the observer, to support yet not interfere.

"You ask, 'Do you mean that I do not perform an intervention when I see someone in harm's way?' No, that is not what I mean. What I mean is, you do it in without any judgment of what you think that individual is experiencing or going through. Hold out a helping hand but with compassion.

"So, how do you proceed? Long ago I taught this channel the value of attach-detach-attach. Attach to the person or the situation, to the truth of it as you understand it, not in interference but just to assess and understand. Then you step back and detach from the drama; from the lower vibrations; from what holds someone on a painful journey. You detach because you never wish to contribute to the situation. You become the silent observer. Then attach to the fulfillment of that person's journey, not describing it, or deciding what it should be but to the divine rightness of the journey they determined eons ago. Attach to that vision and rightness with them without judgment, or interference.

"Because of your need-to-know society, you want explanations for everything. What I am saying is to let go of some of this need. Do not judge every day as if it is your last or first. You are in the eternal flow of the Divine Mother, you are not about to enter or exit something that is eternal. Know the difference between what is important to understand in your own journey, and what is unexplainable.

"When you find yourself in a wheel of confusion, come and sit with me under the Bodhi tree. Empty your mind and your heart, and simply sit with me in the All. When the time is right, we will venture forth to share the knowing of nothing with the rest of humanity.

"Compassion on the planet is so necessary. It is growing because you are letting go of the judgments, of the old third prison so many were kept in. But compassion is infinite, and it has the capacity to grow.

"When you have compassion, you practice it constantly, and you give it as a gift. As soon as you practice it, it comes back to you tenfold, one hundredfold, a thousandfold. It sucks judgment right out of the equation. It removes the need for approval. This is a difficulty so many lightworkers struggle with. Sometimes, their journey is lonely, I know. That is the way of the wayfarer, to walk the planet alone. I may walk with you for a while but I am alone, and I am you at the same time. So many lightworkers wish for compassion, yet are dismissed, and there is injury. If you switch in that moment of feeling 'less than' and send compassion to yourself, then you will be rewarded. Compassion starts with you; therefore you cannot judge or deny yourself.

"You are given thousands of opportunities every day to practice compassion with yourself and others. You are practicing compassion by holding the higher vision, taking sensible action and going forward. Don't contribute to the chaos and mayhem. Hold the higher vision. Compassion for the self is where it starts. It is infinite and so is your potential."

As we, the human collective, move toward ascension, the awakening process, all of us feel the need to practice compassion for Gaia, her kingdoms, and one another. When community and family work together the understanding of compassion is more immediate because it is more personal. You see and feel compassion for all those who are starving. But if you have never had an empty belly, or witnessed a child crying in hunger, or seen the beggar on the street, then your compassion is more theoretical, I do not say less genuine. It just shifts depending on what your time and place is.

When I take time out and watch a movie on TV, unfortunately I chose those times and networks when the ads for the ASPCA (Humane Society) are on. Those ads about abused animals make me cry. Usually they are followed by ads for starving children, and those make me cry as well. My point is that our tender hearts are not difficult to reach – we feel compassion by the boat-load. Where we have difficulty practicing compassion is with those who don't fit the mold of who we would normally think of sending compassion to – the dictators, warlords, drug-lords, the abuser. Yet each of those beings needs our compassion and healing as well. They have lost their way and if we do not hold the space and send the love, who does? Please include them in your heart and healing work. Infuse them with compassion for those they harm and victimize, help them remember their spark of divinity within.

Truth

"Truth is clarity. Truth simply is light and love. It is the whole-ness of knowing. It is factual information that can stand and does stand alone, whether people know it or not, truth is. For example, the Divine is a supreme knowing. Whether anyone in this room or on this planet knows this matters not. That truth cannot be altered. Wisdom is the virtue of having the good sense to know and understand that truth. Truth is the color of silver, with tinges of pink and lilac."

I don't know whether you can imagine archangels having a debate about who was really the best choice to speak about Truth. First, Archangel Gabrielle came in said, 'Child, I want to remind you "I am Gabriel, Lily of Love, Trumpet of Truth, Messenger of One." Then Michael said, "But I carry the Blue Flame of Truth." Now I'm thinking this could be the clash of the Titans if those two go at it. Then Archangel Uriel said, "But I am the carrier of the Silver flame, and what do you think the Silver flame is? It is the flame of clarity and what is truth but clarity." So, they all wanted in, and I think why not?

"Greetings, I am Michael and always I would gladly step aside for my beloved sister, Gabrielle, or my brother, Uriel. I am the spokes-being, but know that this day we carry a triangulated energy into your hearts of silver, pink and lilac, and of course, of blue and gold. Do not think that archangels don't know what excitement is, quite the contrary. I am excited to bring you my blue flame of truth, my gift to you. First we also will wrap it in silver and gold, then unwrap it so that it will shine brightly within thee.

"Truth is clarity, but truth also speaks to the other Blessings and Virtues, especially joy and hope. Where there is truth and the simple knowing of 'what if' you cannot help but gaze in wonder and awe and experience the wellspring of hope and confidence that all is in unfoldment and according to plan, yours and the Mothers. Truth simply is; it is a stand-alone. It is the truth of love; the truth of Mother/Father/One/Source; it is eternal and the infinite.

"There are many upon the planet, yes even now, who tend to deny the truth; that does not alter it. When we gaze upon those who deny the truth or the existence of love, of One, it is sad. It is sad because what they are doing is denying one of the greatest sources of their joy, which is the connection to who they are and the connection to All. They are not accessing what is their birthright. You see, it does not alter the truth on this side or throughout the omniverse; it simply alters their life journey and path. So it limits, and of course, limitation is of the old. Limitation is a human invention; an invention of control.

"Truth is liberating, it is the ability to know with clarity simply what is. Often we have spoken in terms of the other Blessings and Virtues, for example joy as being within you; well, truth is within you as well, in your divine spark. We have spoken to you about how you may expand, access and grow joy, but that expansion, that infinite and eternal existence is also within truth. It is very much the pillar upon which so much rests and is constructed; it is foundation, the beginning, and the end. This holds true for each and every lifetime for the entire realm of existence.

"Of all the Blessings and Virtues perhaps truth is the most misunderstood and misappropriated, which is why we are all glad to bring our energies to this topic. Truth does not require proof, it simply is. You may acknowledge it or you may not, you may interpret it to fit whatever your reality is at any given moment; but it does not alter the stand-alone truth.

"Truth is bedrock and it is not alterable. When people say, 'Well let me explain my truth' what are they talking about? Unless they are in alignment with One, their truth is simply their idea, feelings, ego, and expression. There is only one truth and it is much broader than the experience of one person.

"The key for discovering your own truth is the alignment with love. You cannot be in the truth of knowing without being in alignment. That is why I say that there are many misuses of the word truth; much the same as there is much misunderstanding and misuse of the word love.

"Some will say, 'I know myself.' The statement is a limited one. 'I know myself,' really means 'I know my limitations, my faults, my strengths.' When you declare 'I know my truth' you should be connecting with the Divine Mother/Father/One, through the heart of the Mother. Then there can be no shortcomings.

"We talk about these stages of ascension. One of the stages is to completely release denial. We have talked of judgment and how there is no room for it any longer. But so often there is denial of the human potential for perfection, 'I'm not perfect, I'm human.' Do you really, in any reality believe the Divine Mother births anything that is less than her divine perfection?

"The truth of who you are is that you are perfect. What you're doing is coming to a place where you accept your wholeness, the fullness of your infinite potential. That was the miracle and is the miracle of your ascension. It is the closing of the circle of the fullness of your potential which was lost and now is refound. This is the shift; this is the opening to the full heart-consciousness of your being.

"Often we hear 'I think I'm supposed to do this' or 'my guides, or my guidance, or Archangel Michael told me to do this, what do you think?' That's good, because you are engaging with your spiritual family, and building community. However, I suggest you elevate the conversation to 'what is your knowing, what is your understanding of the truth of this behavior, of this situation, of my feeling?' Because what you are really doing is requesting your fellow human beings, or this side, to truly share with you what is known; and the clarity of truth is always, always of love.

"Sometimes someone will speak what they perceive to be the truth, but they do not say it in a loving manner. Let it go. What you are searching for is a sharing of truth and love.

"Every day take my blue flame within your heart and burn away doubt and denial. That is the first piece. Begin your meditation, anchor in your heart, and then burn them away. Allow my blue flame to consume you as if you are the blue flame. Allow your infinite potential, from throughout the universe, the multiverse, the omniverse and the Source to fill you. Allow enough time to feel this sense of expansion. Ask, 'Today, Michael, what is the expression of my infinite potential?' I will tell you. It will be different on each day because you are diverse.

"The truth of your creation is that you are love. It is the divine spark you have carried forever, and will carry home. Everything else is an illusion. When you finally acknowledge that, and realize you have never been anything but love, it explodes. For some it is a raging fire, for others it is the warmth of a cozy campfire. That is how you become your infinite expression, not just the potential but the expression of that potential."

When you release false grids and illusions, there sometimes is a struggle with the remnants of the old third dimension, particularly when it comes to suffering and support. Archangel Michael gives us some practical wisdom relating to this.

"Truth is within your heart, the Truth is within your being. Suffering was never part of the Divine Plan. Put yourself into community that is supportive of the heart and of the truth.

"Many of you chose to be in families not supportive of your path. However, you are with these families as catalysts, to be beacons of love; to teach love and to give them the opportunity to open their hearts. I know, you're saying free choice is making you hurt because they are not choosing to love. Don't judge, just distance yourself.

"Some of you believe there is no support for you if should

you leave the family. Turn to the Mother, turn to me, turn to the company of heaven, turn to your guides; open to the potentials that are there for you. Then be glad to be alive. Let your heart lead you. It will lead you to joy. Trust your heart."

Gabriel speaks:

❙❙I am Gabriel. I am Gabrielle, Lily of Love, Trumpet of Truth, and Messenger of One. It is my joy also to speak about this core issue; this cornerstone called truth. Sometimes, you say, 'Gabriel, how do I know truth?' When I say to you that I am the Trumpet of Truth; truth sounds like my horn, it is the clarion call. I also give you that trumpet, so when you speak, it is with truth.

"How do you know truth? How does it anchor within you? It is that deep sense of knowing and alignment; there is no doubt. If you are not feeling that silver cord to the truth of One and All, then trust what you are doing is drawing upon the truth of your sweet being and that is all you need. It will still take you where you need to go, where you have guided. It also will guide you back to home.

"Many of you avoid this deep knowing. You are afraid like a child of the dark. You're afraid of what you'll find. I bring you glad tidings of joy. You will learn that you are magnificent. You are love. You are worthy of love, and every expression thereof, human, divine, from your star brothers and sisters. You are worthy because love is essence, expression, movement, creation; it is the fuel of everything.

"In truth you will find your divine self. But before that, you need to clear away some of the cobwebs of doubt. Then you will clearly hear my trumpet in your heart. I am glad to awaken you and dear hearts, it is time."

Archangel Uriel shares his thoughts on truth.

"I am Uriel. I am archangel of the silver ray, bringer of the future and the future is now. You are inside and outside of time. Long ago, I have given you my silver flame of clarity and truth so it may light your way on this journey of ascension. I placed this flame, in your heart and in the palm of your hand to light your way as you explore your heart.

"I offer you my arm, my shoulder, my back, my wings, my presence, and my love. I give you my light to guide your way, so you may know that you do not travel alone. You are cherished far beyond measure. This is the truth we wish you to embrace. Not because we say so, but because it is already within you. Don't underestimate yourself; you are in a place of centered awareness and truth. You are doing it for the many. This is my offering to you. Thank you and blessings."

The challenge of the New You warrior is not merely to know truth but to live it, to be that embodiment of the qualities of honesty, forthrightness and valor. It is the ability to balance truth with prudence and to know when to speak and when to hold our tongue; when to name injustice and when to know that speaking will result in violence; it is balancing truth with charity and consideration for others. Truth is not brash but moves, often silently, in big waves – like the waves in the middle of the ocean. Truth moves everything into alignment but does so with the gentleness of grace, hope and beauty.

Each of us has had at least one terrible experience when someone thought we needed to hear the truth. Such statements are always couched in the terms 'it's for your own good; it's because I care about you' and even when the validity of the forthcoming statements have been factually accurate, the spirit of delivery has not been of love and therefore not of truth. Truth is kind, considerate and always acts from a place of higher perspective, is always a reflection of One. So practice discernment when you are speaking, not your truth, but the Truth. Listen for that clarion call of Gabriel's trumpet.

WISDOM

"*Wisdom: Understanding the Divine plan and the unfoldment within that plan. It is the ultimate respect for all because all is a reflec-*

tion of the One. It is the ability to comprehend the difference between believing, thinking and knowing. It is the beauty of the elders; of those who have gone through the planes of twelve existences, those who have arrived at the end of the path, and are ready for a new time. Wisdom is the color of claret."

From my perspective, wisdom is the ability to be in that place of heart wisdom and just stand back, even in the middle of all the turmoil. There's a divine plan being experienced, related to the elimination of the old third dimension. I was pleasantly surprised when the Buddha indicated he wished to address the virtue of wisdom. In all these years of channeling, the Buddha doesn't speak often, which is an indicator of how important this quality is.

We live in an age where we are bombarded with energy and data of all sorts. We also live in a society where we are info-junkies. Often that information being transmitted on the air-waves isn't truth, and certainly not wisdom. It's a terrible thing when you turn on the TV or go to the Internet and hear about the craziness and misinformation. It affects you. When it's up close and personal and it's aimed at our heart center, it takes a lot to stay in the place of being the observer and knowing there's rightness to the plan. What is important about detachment is not getting caught up in the drama, holding a higher perspective. We sometimes forget we are straddling dimensions. As we straddle dimensions we continue to eliminate false grids, false beliefs and old paradigms, and that takes wisdom and discernment.

"Greetings, I am the Buddha, I am the Wayfarer. Please come to sit with me again beneath the Bodhi tree, so we may gaze across the universe, the multiverse, the omniverse, in harmony. As you have seen – as this Council of Love has woven this tapestry of the Blessings and Virtues – they are connected; you do not have one without the other.

"There is a place for everything. Does that mean, everything is in its place? No. It means the grander unfoldment, in the plan of the Divine Mother and the Source of All Being in life, is in the process of putting things where they belong. Where something belongs in this moment we share today does not mean that it is there forever. It is a wise process to move things around, because it keeps the energy moving and circulating, it keeps it fresh and allows for infinite creation and creativity within you.

"Do you hold yourself in the reverence that we hold you? Do you hold yourself with the deepest regard that is possible, or are you dismissive of who you are? Wisdom is the knowing of the divine plan. But you cannot even commence to have this sense of wisdom if you do not have reverence for your sacred being.

"If I cannot give you anything else except this grain of sand to carry away, it would be sufficient and it would make my heart sing. When you are in the wisdom of complete knowing, not only everything in your universe, you know that grain of sand is a reflection of One, and you are an integral part of it. That wisdom alone will sustain you.

"You live in a society, particularly those of you in the Western world, where you think or believe you have a right to know everything. This is supported by the various media. You are a curious bunch and again that is why sitting in the stillness with me is so important, because if you truly wish to know, it is not found externally. It may be reflected, confirmed and celebrated externally; reflected through a thousand external mirrors. But wisdom and true knowing is only found within.

"One of the greatest embarrassments in society is the phrase, 'I don't know.' Such an admission is not only an expression of truth but humility. It is the wisdom that you don't know everything. You have chosen, in a brief period of time to place yourself in a position where all the information, as you think of it, is not available. Many believe they have transcended and anchored in the higher realms, the fifth, sixth, or seventh dimension. They believe they have full knowledge. But until you've return home to the One there is always more to know, and that is the core of wisdom.

"Too often the wisdom of children is dismissed and overlooked. The wisdom of the elders is also dismissed. Don't be too busy, to listen and integrate, the wisdom of the children and sages. Take this granule of knowledge make it part of your wisdom for all ages, all time, and of All."

Buddha gives his perspective on the connection between being in a high, vibrational state and accessing truth and wisdom. He says it's is like climbing a ladder or perhaps crossing a bridge across the canyons, using rickety rope bridge. There are many who are not trusting and are fearful of going across this bridge. But as you cross the interdimensional bridge you gain deeper wisdom. When you are crossing this bridge I want you to know, not think, but know that each step is the entire journey. Don't look back. Don't look up. Don't look down. Be in the moment and keep your eyes, your heart, and your focus on what lies ahead. Place your feet, step by step, with confidence and knowing. Even if the bridge should completely collapse, it does not matter because you have completed the journey.

"Wisdom is a walk of valor. At times you will feel it is as a lonely walk. But know you are not alone. There are many who have crossed this bridge, but you all do it alone. You can see that on both sides of the canyon, there are humans, star beings, sheep, goats and angels cheering you on, creating a force field to assist you in that journey. Wisdom is not only the brother of truth; it is the brother of trust because you do not arrive at the wisdom unless you trust yourself enough to take those steps."

Our beloved Buddha closes with these words of wisdom:

"How do I choose to close? Never. I continue on with you, just as I have before. Come and sit with me under the Bodhi tree, let's explore wisdom. Let's look at the truth and the wisdom of who you are. Let us forget limitation. We will honor its passing, we will bless it for what it has taught, and then we will burn it and send the ashes back to the sea. I am with you. I honor you with the deepest reverence. Farewell."

Wisdom always follows guidance, and guidance always follows wisdom. Although we tend to think of wisdom as spiritual enlightenment is can also be practical. When I was initially pondering the examples of wisdom to share, my thought was where is wisdom evident in our world? Other than the Dalai Lama, who embodies that knowing of the Divine plan, who truly carries that quality? As soon as I posed the question I was flooded with answers, beginning with the kernel of corn that has the wisdom of its plan within to be planted within the rich earth, grow with the nourishment of sunshine and rain, harvested with gratitude, and then feed the world. The Buddha reminded me that wisdom is found in every kingdom and that the knowing of the Divine plan and one's place within that unfoldment is not only spiritual but practical.

One of the funniest situations I have ever witnessed occurred when I was a little girl at our summer cottage. Our family was composed of five kids. My cousins lived next door who also number five kids. During the week, the dads worked in the city, so it was a tribe of ten, plus the two moms. That was until my grandmother came to visit. That was always a special treat – she was wonderful, kind, soft and had a gentle heart and a way with baking bread.

Evenings were spent outside until after dark playing chase, run-sheep-run, kick the can or swimming. Late night called for cards, cribbage or scrabble, but as kids we were usually too tuckered out to do anything but fall into our bunks and fall fast asleep. There was very reassuring to fall asleep to the glow of the gas lamps in the next room and the sound of the fire or my aunt and mother talking quietly. Occasionally, a bat would find its way down our chimney and into the house. It always scared the heck out of my mother and Aunt Alice. The primal scream-ing woke us up that night, as usual when a bat would make its appearance.

We peeked down out of our bunk beds to see our mom and aunt running around the open space ducking and hollering. It was then that my grandmother collected them and put them in my parent's bedroom, closing that door, but luckily leaving our door open to see the show. She deftly wrapped an old dish-towel around her head, opened the door to the outside, grabbed a broom and showed our unwanted guest the way out. She did this quietly, efficiently and with a minimum of fuss. She then opened the door for her two adult children, shushing and reassuring them that everything was taken care of and card playing could resume.

My grandmother had the practical wisdom of women who understand their role within the Mother's plan. She understood fear and how to take care of her family. She did not criticize or laugh at my mother and aunt – she simply took care of perceived danger, let the kids enjoy the show and learn that adults can be vulnerable, and that there are ways to address situations that don't include hysteria and drama. My grandmother taught us so much wisdom through her gentle practical approach to life.

The animal kingdom teaches us wisdom every day. My beloved cat, Nike, who was very ET, came to me about a month before I began channeling the 13th Octave. I am a night writer; I do my best work in the wee small hours. Every night I would be at my computer and Nike would be right next to me, curled up the chair she asked be set up with her favorite blanket. Nike and I had many incredible adventures together. We moved across country several times, and when I would travel to teach, people would vie for the pleasure of cat-sitting the princess. She was a gem, a guide, familiar and my best friend. Last year, at age seventeen, Nike died. She passed gently two hours after I finished *The Great Awakening* book. She knew she had completed her mission. She had seen me through bringing forth the 13th Octave and finally getting it all written down. She understood her unfoldment within the Divine plan; her journey with our family was complete. Do I like it? No. Do I understand it? Yes, but only because she still visits.

AWE

"Awe: The ability to feel and experience always and fully the wonders of creation, the Divine. The knowing there is always more to learn, experience, to understand. It is the innocence of the small child within, the sense of wonder. It is the sense of understanding the magnificence

of the universal plan, the unfoldment. It is the thrill, the expectation and joy at being; enjoying new miracles as they unfold. It is the relation of purity. It is the color of yellow saffron. Yellow saffron is the color of deep mustard, even into a curry color but with the highlights of gold."

Out of all the Blessings and Virtues, awe is one of my favorite qualities because it gives us this wonderful sense of innocence and magic. It's just phenomenal. We live in this information age where we are overfed with too much information from every corner. One of my favorite things about my job is that not a day goes by when I don't have one of those wonderful "aha" moments. Perhaps because I am not deeply entrenched in the mainstream, I get to see or perceive something from a completely different perspective that's new. That daily dose of awe has kept me going all these years, constantly changing and expanding. There's always the sense of "there's something new around the corner; something I never even thought about."

When I do a class called The 13th Octave, part of the class is talking and working through the 13 Blessings and Virtues. People break up into small groups, brainstorm, and then bring something back that is interpretive – a poem, movement, skit or dance. However, I've noticed over the years that when it comes to awe, what groups normally bring back was something from nature, a pine cone, wild flower, acorn or kitten. What gives more awe than puppy breath?

There was a real competition for who would speak about awe. The Divine Mother could certainly address this topic. Archangel Gabriel made the case that awe is the color is golden saffron, so the topic was his. St. Germaine started throwing about purple dust saying he's used to awing people. Finally, Archangel Jophiel started talking about his experience of being on Earth, and his gift of Jophie dust which is sheer energy. But then he started talking about the awe of being married to Mary, and the awe of being Yeshua's father. He wins the topic.

To me, Archangel Jophiel is an unusual archangel. He's an awesome archangel and when he appears, he's huge. Most of the archangels are tall. Archangel Michael is muscular but Jophiel is built like the archetype of a pirate. He's big, muscular; there's nothing meek or mild about him. He's got black eyes and black, curly, long, wild hair, He comes with the ray of magenta and amethyst, and he often says he's our island, our place of safety. When I meditate and post the archangels, Jophiel takes my back. I just feel him standing there with his enormous wings. I am crazy about this big sword-carrying Archangel, Jophiel.

Jophiel also knows what it's like to be human because he came and incarnated as Joseph, the husband and partner of Mother Mary, the mother of Jesus. I've had people say, "I thought that was St. Germaine." No, it's Archangel Jophiel. It's interesting, they both travel on the same ray of that I AM Presence. Jophiel is the anchor of the future, which is what he did in that family; he anchored the future.

He knows what it is to have the everyday life; the challenges and the opportunities. I know Yeshua was a challenging child. Mary has talked often about her relationship with Joseph as physical. She has often declared "I loved Joseph passionately." It was that love and that sense of "oh my gosh, look what we're doing here" that sustained them. They knew the bigger picture.

All the archangels have brought us gifts; tools for us to use when we need help with a situation or just to feel them close by. The gift Archangel Jophiel brings is Jophie dust. That alone demonstrates his sense of magic and humor. Jophie dust is a bag to sprinkle of sparkling dust that can transform anything. It is sheer energy, and has the power to transmute form, matter, emotion – you name it. This magic bag is never empty and those sparkles of sheer energy transmute heavy energy or energy that has been sullied into bright, sparkly, wonderful energy. Take Jophiel's gift and use it everywhere that could use a little sparkle.

"Greetings, I am Jophiel. You are welcomed to call me Jophie, just as you call Yeshua Yeshi. I am in awe of each of you. Much has been said of this process of transition, ascension, shift and becoming. Yes you are in the middle of a big change. But that is not the core reason that I hold you in honor and awe, is my wonder at your magnificence. First of all, I am in awe of your divine perfection in human form. Your human and soul design is perfect. Much is said of your tenacity, valor, courage, and beauty, but it is the core of your being that stops me in my tracks. It is the purity, the innocence, and the sweetness of your hearts.

"I have walked amongst you and many of you have known me and therefore also know of the trials and errors of Joseph, husband of Mary, father of Yeshua and his siblings. It was a very busy household. I would look at Yeshi, the children of the village, my own children, the adults of the village and I would be in awe of who they were, and the promise of what they brought to the planet. I was in awe of them, and you.

"You have chosen to come to this awesome Gaia in the fullness of your being; not living in the shadows but declaring your wholeness, brightness and mastery. Many of you chat about becoming whole, which is ridiculous; you already are whole. Because of that you are here to love in the physical form and remember that you are multidimensional, angelic, hybrid, starseed and Earth-keeper. It is not one or the other; you are all of the above.

"Remember more of your sweet self, and what you are truly capable of doing. You are creating a new planet, creating new societies and cities of light. You are painting the Earth the same way Michael paints the aurora borealis. It's supposed to be fun! So when you need to be reminded of this joyful journey and lighten up, turn to me. I have your back. You're free to play, to do as you desire because your heart is accurate; it does not lie or mislead you. Bring the totality of your being to everything you do and if it looks a little dull, liberally use my Jophie dust. Sparkle up the planet and let the beauty be seen.

"How many times do you hear people ask, 'I am so bored with my job?' How can this be on the heels of what my beloved brother, Michael, says that there are no day laborers on the planet? You are thinking and creating mundane lives, jobs and routines that don't feed you the golden joy. Without awe and joy, you can't create.

"If you did not have the innate capacity of your mastery,

then you would not have the ability to look with innocence, purity, and awe. So often we hear, 'tell us what is going to happen? What is the next event? What day and time will it occur?' That's not how it works. One of the ways, apart from my dust and more laughter is growing your understanding of how things work, and accepting what you innately already know. Accept that things do change. It is one of the constructs, not only of your planet but of the infinite, expanding universe. It is really quite absurd for anyone to think things won't change, and people will not evolve.

"You had gone pretty much to the limit in terms of your creative ability, collectively, to create darkness, hatred, greed, control, lack and self-limitation. You've done that and might I say, 'You did an awesome job!' Now your soul is looking around and saying, 'Okay, we're in a new realm, what can we create?' That is why people are restless and tired. That's good because what's happening is the creative juices are boiling to the surface. Many are already feeling that 'I want to remember what it feels like to be full of piss and vinegar; wanting jump out of bed, excited about the new day'. That is what's changing. It's happening in people's homes, careers, families, and communities. You're already sensing this. When people are in their creative mode, there is no stopping them. That is what you're witnessing, and the true measure of the shift.

"When people are in survival mode it is difficult carry on with life's business. They are so deserving of a break, and it comes first with this inkling in the heart, tummy and sometimes the head. That inkling is your clarion call to the entire universe, and certainly the entire team of the Mighty Ones, the archangels. That 'something has to change' inkling is the best news we can hear because it is the beginning of not of looking outside but within.

"Go and create what makes your heart sing; what gives you a sense of incredible, indescribable awe. There is an element to creation that includes awe, innocence and the knowing that there is always more. It cancels out limitation and lack. When you're dreaming, give yourself the latitude and the credit to know you are mighty. Do what makes your heart sing, not simply what you think is going to bring you money. I know because I have toiled; I have been a day laborer. It has its rewards but it isn't exactly what I would want for you. My toil was done in humility and reverence, creating something. Where you go awry is thinking just in monetary terms rather than what will give you indescribable pleasure. Go work and manifest what makes your heart soar; the money will follow.

"I am inviting you to invite me into your life, to hold your back, to lead the way, to sparkle with dust. You, my beloved ones, are the creation of the Mother. Each of us above and below is the creation of the Mother and does that not give all of us a profound sense of awe? Come play with me, play with the fairies, devas, animals, trees, flowers and mountains, and dream big. Go with my love."

Throughout my life I have been blessed to live in incredibly beautiful natural places. Nature feeds my soul and allows me to do my work in ways that blend solitude and social. Years ago I lived on a spit of land in Niagara-on-the-Lake which faced magnificent Lake Ontario in the front and an undisturbed wilderness of wetlands out back. My tiny, rustic cottage was at the end of a dirt road surrounded by ancient fruit orchards that brought a little piece of heaven every spring.

One Saturday afternoon I fell asleep on my couch underneath the windows that looked out to the melting ice flows of Lake Ontario, one of the first signs of spring. When I awoke I looked straight up into a mountain ash tree that stood outside my window and blinked, then blinked again wondering if I were dreaming. The tree was filled with an entire flock of red robins. They were feasting on the vibrant orange berries of the mountain ash, resting, eating, resting, and not going anywhere. I didn't move a muscle. I just lay there in complete awe. While I had been gifted with many sights in my then thirty-something years, this was a gift of such heart-opening that the sense of wonder and potential flowed right into my soul. It was a hard time for me financially, a transition time from a comfortable corporate salary to very little;

a walk of trust that guidance was correct. Seeing those bright red robins, a family of red against a gray winter's day, reminded me of the promise of spring. If they could fly thousands of miles, if they could be guided in that moment to my house and this mountain ash in the middle of nowhere, if I could wake up at that exact moment from a rare nap, then anything could happen. Anything was possible. That, my friends was one of the most precious gifts of awe I have ever received.

CHARITY

"Charity: The genuine ability to share all things, material, spiritual and emotional. Based in the understanding there is always enough for all to thrive, and we are all richer in the joint expression of sharing. A heart-felt need to be generous. Knowing knowledge and gifts are never intended solely for one person. The vibration is green." This is the green, the ray of St. Francis, the Master who knows what it is to be human, and teaches the knowing of charity.

Charity is a virtue we can all benefit from a deeper understanding of, because somewhere along the way, I think charity got lost, or misunderstood, or minimized. We tend to think of charity in terms of money. We think giving a monetary donation to a deserving group makes us charitable. Yet, it is so much bigger than that.

Some of the stingiest people are those who won't share their feelings, their emotions. That is such a part of who we are, how we progress, open and thrive. We've all experienced where somebody is going through something, either really blissful or really difficult, and we ask, "What's going on?" or "How are you feeling?" When the reply is "nothing or fine" it is such a slap in the face. The irony is often the person believes they are being stoic, but if they opened up a little and shared, allowing the flow and exchange, they would get rid of the issue more quickly. There is nothing better than feeling you're supported, that somebody hears you or really feels what you're communicating.

St. Francis speaks:

"Greetings, I am Francis, but you can call me Frank. Why do I say, you can call me Frank? Because in the time when I lived, Francis was a very common name, and formality prevalent. But as I left my life behind and note that I say 'my life' not my family, but the life of ease, I wished to also let go of the trappings of behaviors, beliefs, customs, and traditions that did not feed my soul. So Frank, it is. I am your buddy and friend.

"Well my beloved friends let us speak of charity. Let us speak of the ability to give and receive, because this is an aspect of charity that is often overlooked. It is one thing to be generous with your mind, heart, emotions, ideas, beliefs, and spiritual path. But if there is not a recipient on the other end, what good is it? So I am also speaking to you about the ability to receive because it is part of the balance of your life, the universe, and certainly of charity.

"Historically individuals are deemed good or charitable if they have given to the arts, sciences, education, poor, or whatever their favorite cause has been. Those actions have often been based not on heart but simply on acceptable societal values, or worse an expression of control and self-aggrandizement. . The quality of charity of giving with the heart, and receiving with the heart, even when it is simply gratitude, has been absent. The key to charity is the sweetness of energy when one extends themself in the fullness of heart and in the fullness of knowledge that they are richer, in every meaning of the word, by giving and by receiving. Charity, in its truest sense, is a courageous act because it is extending yourself.

"The understanding of charity as assistance is wrong. Charity is really the desire to share. In that movement of charity is the movement of the infinity, the movement of the Divine. It flows out to the person and back to you, out and back, and you are meeting in the middle of that figure eight.

"Charity is never an effort or burden, it is quintessential joy. You share because it is joyous, such as saying to a friend, 'look at that bird.' You both gaze and smile. You have shared that unique moment which will never occur again. When you reach out and connect, you are in the personal core of charity. It doesn't matter whether you are giving away a billion dollars or a posy, it is a personal act. It is not about just caring, it is about caring passionately.

"As we delve deeper into this quality, we can add intimacy, the ability to be intimate, as also being of charity; sharing your heart openly and without reservation, be it with an individual, a group, a community, or even animals.

"There is an expression that it takes a village to raise a child. That is exactly the kind of thing that I am speaking of. In the 1960s there were many communes for people to live in like-heartedness. You are going to find the idea of communal living resurfacing in new and interesting ways, particularly in the cities of light.

"Now there are always the naysayers, who say 'Frank, you are being exceptionally naïve.' But what they are really saying is 'you don't understand how things really work. You are an in-nocent.' I choose to be an innocent because in innocence there is awe and wonder of knowing what is possible. I choose to cre-ate what is joyful, generous and supportive rather than simply accepting a paradigm that has obviously demonstrated itself as not working. It is hundreds of years later and still people are in the illusion that somehow these societies based on greed and the collection of riches works. That is absurd.

"But within those creative centers there are many tempta-tions, old grids, old beliefs that need to be eliminated, destroyed, and simply fade away, like a child throwing a tantrum. If a child is throwing a tantrum – kicking and screaming – the par-ent makes sure the child is safe from harm, allows the child to run out of steam, fall asleep, and look like a newborn angel. The enlightened parent ignores the momentary tantrum, but remains vigilant, and aware of what is going on in order to keep the child safe. They honor the child's experience but don't participate.

"Now the form of intervention you do is two-fold depend-ing on your role. If you are one who has volunteered to go to the heart of chaos, then you may be holding and a beacon of light, the anchor of love and simply beaming into that chaos. If you are part of a spiritual or physical healing team, a spiritual S.W.A.T.

team, you may be doing emotional, psychological or mental intervention within that chaos. But, if you have chosen to be one who works on the perimeter externally, in quiet places, then you send energy and healing on a daily basis, in your peace or healing meditations and then ignore the rest.

"Charity is sending healing and love to both victim and perpetrator; both need it. This is a perfect example of compassion, of forgiveness, and of charity. Charity is not latitude, it is balance. You do not have community without charity. Inside charity is an element of forgiveness. It is a vital part of spiritual evolution.

"All the animals are your teachers. You know this innately. They are not just the teachers of love but the givers of love; the teachers of balance, survival, and how to live in community. They have a human capacity as well. This is important to know because it is part of your evolution and part of your movement into the different dimensions and particularly the fifth through seventh dimensions.

"Celebrate charity. It is a celebration, a party, a sharing, a generosity of your very core. Share your hearts, heart knowing and heart being. Share your core, emotions, sadness, gladness, just let it out, share the joy of being alive and know that I am with you. Give the green generously, fully, every day. And yes, my final words to you are, eat green. I would be remiss, and Archangel Raphael would call me to task, if I did not remind you eat green.

"Remember, I plan to walk the Earth again. Many of us are returning, we have talked about this for a long time but the expression that we would have is the time is neigh. I will walk the planet yet again in its verdant green. I will sit on the Earth and kiss Gaia. I can take any form I want. I guess I could come back as a bird. I have a wonderful affinity for our winged friends. They taught me all about angels. My plan, however, is to come back as a human being, crystalline and in my prime. I'll be the one wearing jeans and a T-shirt."

In closing, St. Francis shares a beautiful meditation to open our hearts further to the divine quality of charity:

"See yourself sitting on an enormous time piece. Then, see yourself at the center of the clock. Visit each moment, each hour, each second, and feel the giving and receiving from each point. Some of you will do this in silence. Others will sing or whistle. Some days you will find yourself stuck at one or three o'clock. It matters not, sit in the center, and simply receive. The key is to be in gratitude, be in that place of balance so that you are in the place of charity when it's your turn to be generous. Receive from the animals, trees, Earth, sky, and the people around you. Meet their eyes; allow their warmth to touch you. Allow their smiles to quench you. Allow their beings to intermingle and dance with yours.

Most of us have grown up with the belief system that it is more blessed to give than to receive. St. Francis has been very clear on this point, so open, balance and allow yourself to receive – in joy, gratitude and the knowing that you will pay it forward as well.

HUMILITY

"Humility: Twin to piety. It is the ability to be grateful for the many blessings bestowed upon each of us. It is the knowledge that alone, we are incompetent but united, with One we are All. Humility is necessary for all works and sharing of service. Its color is red." Red, particularly in the Eastern tradition has many different connotations, but it's also vitality that humility brings because it's still an action blessing and virtue.

Lao Tzu steps forward to enrich our understanding of humility. Lao Tzu is the father of Taoism, master of balance and the middle way. He's the one who brought forth, with St. Germaine, the 13th Octave LaHoChi healing modality given to him in Atlantis from our star brothers and sisters from the Pleiades.

I'm crazy about Lao Tzu. The first time I met him, he appeared in front of me as an ancient wizened Chinese man. At first I thought if it was Confucius, but he introduced himself and told me his name. He would stand in front of me with a gnarled branch; one of those old branches with a million twists and turns in it. The branch was balanced on his finger. He wasn't a chatty kind of guy, and at that point he hadn't said anything other than telling me his name.

So here I am, in the early days, going to Vallecito, Colorado. to do a 13th Octave workshop. That was a phenomenal time where we met our galactic star brothers and sisters, but that's another other story. I'm on a little puddle-jumper aircraft, when all of a sudden Lao Tzu is standing there in the aisle, looking down at me, again always wearing his white robe, with his gnarly stick on the tip of his finger, when he said: "You are to teach and to learn balance. All the while that stick didn't budge.

He has these wonderful deep, kind black eyes, and wispy white hair. He's not a big being, well I mean physically. Lao Tzu has appeared or incarnated on Earth several times. When he was on the Earth as Lao Tzu, it was about 400 BC. The he came again as Caspar, one of the three wise men of the Magi who came to give gifts to Jesus. He was the bringer of gold. More recently, he was incarnated as Djwhal Khul, also known as the Tibetan, a teacher and master who works with the Tibetan lamas in spirit. Lao Tzu's theme is still "balance."

About ten years ago, he came to me with St. Germaine and said, "We are going to teach you 13th Octave LaHoChi, it is a healing modality in which the key is the restoration of balance." It's been an exciting journey with this master who is a plain-spoken being. When he has something to say, he just says it flat out. He doesn't mince words. To have him instruct us on humility is a real treat.

Traditionally, our idea of humility is related to modesty and respect, with piety representing deep devotion and reverence. We can't be in service without the balance of humility. Being in service alone is meaningless because it is a group activity. Lao Tzu talks about false humility, and how sometimes when people will give us a compliment we reply, "oh, it's nothing." That is a form of false humility. Or we pretend to be humble, which we see a lot in public life where people will make the statement "I'm a servant of the people." But it's not a true heart declaration, merely a power and control game. That's not humility; that's not even service.

"Greetings, I am Lao Tzu. I speak on this beautiful virtue of humility. It is the ability to serve in whatever capacity and role that is open to you. Humility is to know you are an instrument of love, and in making that heart and body commitment sometimes you are led to service that is not exactly as glamorous or as rich or as fulfilling as you hoped it would be. It matters not because the reward of service is the service itself.

"When I walked the Earth long ago, my name was Li. Eventually they came to call me Lao Tzu. It is a name I cherish because it means old master. I was called to do many things. I was not simply a philosopher; I was a healer, teacher, and at times a tender of rice. I was a father, no I do not mean simply to my own children, but to many. I traveled freely, not always where I would first choose to go. I served the emperor in the sacred city. When he would take ill, he would call for me, and I would tend to him in my very simple way. Each time he would say to me 'Li, I think that it would be best if you simply stayed here in the palace walls.' And very respectfully and humbly I would say, 'No, because my work also is in the villages and fields.'

"Life was not as complicated but there were challenges, often challenges of survival. We would sit by a fire; brew our tea and herbal concoctions of medicines. I would give people the LaHo-Chi which was given to me to re-emerge. It was a gift from the brothers and sisters of the Pleiades. It was important I be able to serve the poorest and the richest; the most powerful and the meek. My joy came from serving those in the villages because they would listen to my heart and receive what I had to offer, which was love. Healing energy is love.

"How can one not fall down in awe, joy and reverence in the presence of love? False humility is nothing but pride. Humility understands that it is a privilege to be able to serve. It is not a duty or responsibility, it is an honor. This sense of humility is a unifying factor, not only for humanity but for all beings. What it does is it brings you into the balance. If you are embracing the virtue of humility you realize there are none above and there are none below. All are brothers and sisters, each on a unique and sometimes, perilous journey. So what is your role? It is to go into these situations, and to diffuse them.

"You cannot have humility without compassion. They are connected, and it is essential you know yourself equal with others, not above or below them. It is not only serving but allowing yourself to be served. When you receive a gift, be it of healing, friendship or support, and you wish to return the favor, but the person refuses, it hurts your heart because you have not been permitted to serve. The balance is broken, my stick is on the ground, and that is humiliating. Humiliation is one of the things you must remove from Nova Earth.

"Now there are many times when somebody will say, 'Oh you do not need to repay me, I just wanted to help you'; it is out of the kindness of their hearts. But they need to be reminded, that you too have kindness in your heart. For example, I would go to the fields, and help tend the rice paddies because there was always need. I would give a healing, or talk to a family in distress. Then they would give me some rice and a cup of tea and I would be so grateful. Now, were these things of equal value? You cannot measure that because the rice and the tea were made with gratitude and healing was given in love.

"When you come from a place of humility, it is a unifying force. It is a force that says I am your brother and sister, and we are on this journey together. I will serve you; otherwise I am not fulfilling my soul purpose and mission. Then you will serve me so you can fulfill your heart's desire. Then we will both go and serve another and another, and so it grows.

"This is how you create the new way; the way of change, and the way of Christ consciousness and of love. Jesus Sananda, the master is very humble and knew what it meant to walk barefoot and dusty, and share whatever food he had. It has been the same for thousands and tens of thousands of years.

"Long ago when I was in Atlantis, we were honored to have the star brothers and sisters come. They brought the LaHoChi, the healing modality of light, movement, sound and symbols. What could we offer in return? We offered, humbly and gratefully, our willingness to learn. This exchange raises the frequency. It brings the vibration of love and inside that love, is acceptance, which is part of humility as well.

"Part of what you yearn for, each of you, and I know this because I have been human, have also yearned for it, is this yearning to be accepted for who we are; to be seen and known; and in that knowing, to be cherished and valued.

"The starting point is acceptance. It is enough to say that 'I accept the reality,' because what is reality anyway? It also is to accept possibility. Can you accept the possibility of love and of your intrinsic value? Not that it is a given but just the possibility.

"When I have walked in form as Lao Tzu, I did not think of myself as a master. To call someone a master in that time of China was a sign of respect. I did not think of myself as having achieved more than anybody else. I had these flashes of enlightenment, but I assumed these insights were given to me so that I could share them. That is humility; it is not the feeling that you are so special something is given only to you. The insights, understanding and energy that are being given to each of you right now on Earth are given to share. To keep it hidden because you think you have a special favor with the master, is arrogance and ego.

"Sometimes it is also fear. When I would have students, both as Djwhal Khul and in Atlantis, I would hear them say, 'Oh, I do not dare tell my parents about this, they will think I am crazy.' You do not need to share all the whys and wherefores, the insights; what you need to share is the love. You are just like them, each of you. I see not only your capacity to love, but that you do love, that you do walk in service.

"As we move along in this process of ascension, you wonder where humanity is in terms of living these beautiful Blessings and Virtues and accepting the truth of our wholeness. You are doing exceptionally well. I am not a master who works in percentages. You see, I already see you as one hundred percent; even those who think they are in the darkness, or who are oblivious. I see you and know you as completely whole.

"You are being given some very strong situations to clear in humility, clearing the old ways of violence and control. These are important steps. It is no different than my going to serve the emperor or working in the field. You do both and you are richly compensated for both; perhaps not in money but in shifting your planet to a place where money is no longer the issue. This is what Gaia teaches. She does not just share her riches with some and not with others. She is generous with all of you. All you need to do is to look, observe, see, accept, receive, and then serve.

"I humbly give my thanks for giving me this opportunity to share with you. Don't forget my gnarled stick; don't forget the middle way; don't forget the balance. Balance is not what you are aiming to achieve, it is who you are. Go in peace."

Too often, particularly in the West, "attitude" is a trait that has come to be both accepted and admired. Humility has no attitude. When I go somewhere I am being served, be it a restaurant, supermarket, healer or drive-through, I am always exceedingly grateful for the person who willingly helps with a smile and courtesy. That quality is becoming far too rare in our society, and that's sad. When I have the opportunity to channel for someone I consider it a privilege, a sacred trust. I am the lucky one. When I cook for someone I love it – it's a chance to infuse some tender love and nurturing into the food. When I do a little favor for a friend or neighbor it makes me feel so good, it's my chance to give because I receive so much every day. Humility and gratitude are twins. So practices being humble, whether you are the president or the janitor – both are equally important.

GRACE

"Grace: the quality of being a true and exact expression of divine spirit and will. This is a state of beauty, of wholeness, of oneness. It is the final blessing and virtue, encompassing service and action. It is the color of pink."

It's phenomenal what we are doing with computers and the phone. I think sometimes we forget how lucky we are that we get to speak with these incredible beings, archangels and members of the Council of Love. But my personal sense of amazement at being able to channel and speak with the Divine Mother, with Universal Mother Mary never dims.

When I talk about Mother Mary, what people often do is go to either a biblical reference or the Catholic reference. When I refer to Universal Mother Mary, I'm talking about a wondrous being who is one of the unique faces or aspects of the Divine Mother. When we talk to Universal Mother Mary it is the Divine Mother giving us a voice we can connect with. Mary isn't bound by any religious connotations because she is the Mother of all of us. We've all been birthed from her heart. The added bonus of talking to Universal Mother Mary is she has had this experience of being on the planet and human. As mother, woman and human she can really understand and guide us in what this journey is all about.

Mary is one on the few beings who didn't die, she ascended; took her body and left. I think we tend to forget that. She was already this incredible interdimensional, multidimensional being, and when her time came, she just zipped away with her legions of angels.

There are approximately seven billion people on planet Earth at this time, and yet there isn't another you. You are unique; even your aspects and parallel lives are uniquely you. Think about the grace you are, and move into your true creator self. As we work with this final Blessing and Virtue of grace, celebrate the uniqueness of your grace. Celebrate that this is the time of the rebirth of the Divine Feminine upon Gaia. Breathe pink, the color of grace, and allow it to balance your spirit, heart, will, physical, emotional, and mental bodies. Welcome the angels of the pink ray, defenders of the throne of God. They are the strongest, and the most beautiful. Feel your own pink diamond, part of the triflame within your heart.

"Greetings, I am Mary, I am Maré, Universal Mother, Mother

of love, Mother of hope, Mother of change, Mother of constancy, and Mother of each of you, my beloved angels, of every hue and color, of every ray. I embrace all of you. I embrace the totality of your being. As Mother, I marvel at your design and magnificence and how you have come to demonstrate this in this reality, and in this time of the unfoldment of the divine plan.

"It is not that there is a plan in some distant future and I will let you know when it is time to activate it. The time is now. I come not simply to bless you and to give you grace, but to reawaken within you that state of knowingness of being in the state of grace. Grace is being in alignment with who you are, not just with one, two, or three aspects of your beautiful self, but with your totality. Whether you acknowledge it or not you it has brought the totality and wholeness of your sacred self into form on Gaia at this time. Grace is not something you need to retrieve; it is integral to who you are. It was activated years ago when I gave you the gift of the Pink Diamond. I give it to you again this day; I amplify it, I ignite it. I blow on the embers of your soul and desire so it will burn brightly in your expression of who you are.

"You are the child of creation. You're the child of my heart and being. But, I did not clone myself; I birthed you and in that birthing was the birth of the expression you chose to reflect my glory and beauty, and your love for me. That is what service and action is about. It is about the expression of your love for me and within that, is the love that you carry for your sacred self. Tucked within that is also my love which I have embedded within you.

"There are many upon the planet who choose not to know me. I do not take offence at this. Even the most stratified being yearns for connection and for love, particularly for a Mother's love. This desire for love and nurturing to both give and receive is part of your spiritual and physical DNA.

"There are people you may lean on who stand clearly in the state of grace; who do not require reciprocity or payment but who simply support, love and nurture you because of who you are. Similarly, there are those you will chose to cherish regardless of what they do because you know that actions not of love are simply situations requiring healing, tenderness and more love.

"When we speak of grace it is heart acceptance, translated into heart consciousness, of your alignment with Divine Spirit and Will. It is accepting that you are a creator and co-creator, and particularly during this time of ascension, you are co-creator of your New You and Terra Gaia. Your physical form is shifting and you are incorporating not only the Blessings and Virtues, but a deeper and better understanding of Universal Law.

"Being in the state of grace is not being solemn and thinking one is holy, it is being playful, joyful and full creative inspiration, ideas, and taking action. Do not confuse grace with innocence. Grace is the blessing of being in your wholeness, and in alignment with God, with One, with Source, with me. That is why so many babies and infants cry blue murder. They arrive and say 'Oh no, I had no idea.' It is a very hard adjustment even for the happiest of babies who incarnate and realize they are with the soul family of their choosing. There is a feeling of discomfort as the vastness of who they are is trying to be expressed in a very small physical form.

"Your divine spark, which comes into form, contains grace. Grace tends to be in a category of its own. There is a desire and instinctual drive to obtain and maintain more and more grace because innately you know being in a state of grace is being connected with All.

"Most of you have forgotten you already have this grace within you, which is why I gave you my blue diamond to heal; the pink diamond to awaken; and finally the gold diamond to move you into action. But you have short memories. You forget, feel bereft and go into a state of yearning and pain. You pray, ask, request, beg and scream for the blessing of grace that you already have. Innately you know that infusion of grace will reignite within you. Grace is like watering a flower; your soul thirsts for grace the same way your body thirsts for water. It is important for reconnection, and alignment.

"To receive more grace you must be active. Your actions

need to be loving, kind, generous, charitable, humble and pure; expressions of fortitude, patience and piety. These are the ways you build your reserves. Grace is not simply dormant. You have examples of who embodies grace, such as Mother Teresa and St. Francis. Grace poured from them because they were divinely active. Activity catapults you to higher realms where grace becomes a fountainhead. As you build these reserves, it overflows, and you share it with everyone you encounter. You share it with the collective. All acts of love and kindness open your perceptions enough to allow you to recognize grace is already present. It builds and builds, just like joy.

"There is a Universal Law called Instantaneous Transmission and Transmutation, and if there is a correlation to this Law, it is grace. It is a blessing of dispensation; we are talking over and above the gift of karmic dispensation. If you ask for the dispensation of grace for removal of what you ego thoughts and behaviors they will release quickly and come into alignment with who you really are."

The Divine Mother gives us an action-oriented meditation to bring grace more and more into your life.

"Feel yourself invoke the infinite grace within and without, above and below. Open your crown, your heart, and allow yourself to be filled with the gentlest pink imaginable, because grace is soft; it is powerful yet soft and gentle. Think of it this way; there are blessings and qualities that feel like the ocean and its powerful waves. Grace is the dappled sunlight through a deep forest; it is the quiet stream running over a bed of rocks in the quiet of that forest. It is the stillness that comes upon you when you see a deer and you remain perfectly still seeing the beauty, the grace. So take these qualities, visuals and feelings and allow them to fill every corridor of your being, every fiber, every cell. Allow yourself to become pink, not to the exclusion of your beautiful ray, but to simply merge and marry with the state of grace.

"Remember, you cannot be in a state of grace if you have not embraced and incorporated humility because to be in the state of grace is to be in a state of union with me. I have said it is being in unity but it is also being in union with my heart. Humility is the ability to know you have need for connection, and the expression of connection is service. It is not a coincidence the ray of humility is red and then it fades with the light into the pink. So they are intricately connected. Know of my eternal love. I am not a distant Mother, I am with you. Go with my love."

Practice this wonderful meditation given to us directly from the heart of the Mother. For most of us, while we know and cherish moments of grace we find it hard to accept and believe that we live in a constant state of grace. When I watch the ballet "Swan Lake", or see a row of apple trees in blossom swaying as gracefully as those swans, then I know and recognize grace. It isn't as easy in the daily world.

Yet this is not only the invitation but the truth that the Mother shares with us – we are born of grace. It is integral to who we are. Look around you, look into the mirror, acknowledge the richness that surrounds us; accept, allow and then gaze in wonder. You are grace.

Universal Law

Each of us has heard reference to Universal Law our entire lives. Chances are those references have been ambiguous and hard to pin down. Rarely did we ever hear reference to a book or other material that we could go to and understand this code. Religions are great at saying they have the corner on Universal Law – from the ten Commandments to the Quran. We have all heard the vague references to laws of karma "what goes around, comes around", but what really are we talking about when we refer to Universal Law? Prior to working with Sanat Kumara on this very subject the only Universal Law I believed in is the over-riding Law of Love. Love your neighbor and yourself has always felt to me like pretty good and sensible guidance.

Years ago when the Council started talking to me about creation and co-creation, it was a little unsettling. While I am fully aware that we create our reality and our lives, the discussion about dimensions, creation, co-creation, stillpoint, creation formula, Universal Law, creation codes and the inter-relationship of all these elements was frankly overwhelming. If the purpose of our existence to know love, be love and live a life of love, then that seemed more than adequate guidance for me. But you know the Council – they always have a way of convincing you that the next step is essential and something you not only need to know but then share and teach. Resistance is meaningless.

Over the years I have channeled and worked with incredible beings, archangels, ascended masters, enlightened beings – even Source. I have embraced the sweetness of Universal Mother Mary, the no-nonsense guidance of Archangel Gabrielle, the strength and flamboyance of St. Germaine, the tenderness and love of Yeshua. None of these encounters prepared me for the full flat-out working with Sanat Kumara, or Raj, as he likes to be called.

Who is Sanat Kumara, Planetary Logos and Keeper of Universal Law? There are reams of material written about Master Sanat Kumara from Venus. He has an incredible history and following. But I want to share is my experience of working with this wondrous ascended master. There is nothing meek or mild about Sanat Kumara. He is a vibrant radiant gold, bright and shiny, completely different from Archangel Gabrielle's deep Florentine gold or Yahweh's platinum gold. While he is not overbearing or aggressive, there is no denying his strength and power. His position in the universe as overseer of the evolution of the plan of Earth is self-evident. Holding this energy for any prolonged period of time is a challenge that is exhausting. We're talking big boy here – and yes, his physical appearance is also huge; extremely tall, muscular, golden white hair and eyes of blazing blue. If you want a visual, think ascended master on spiritual steroids.

Yet, it has been under the sweet tutelage of Sanat Kumara that I have channeled most of the following information on Universal Law. His patience and willingness to make things humanly understandable and applicable is remarkable. His calm assurance and delivery of incredibly complex understandings has been not only phenomenally user friendly but heartwarming as well. Never has there been any sense of trying to catch up. Throughout the channelings you will note Sanat Kumara's offer of assistance and guidance. This is not a pro-forma offer, my friends I can attest that this offer of practical help is as real as the air you breathe. So although the energy is powerful, breathe and accept the gentle guidance of our beloved master of Universal Law.

THE INVITATION FROM SANAT KUMARA

"Greetings, I am Sanat Kumara, Planetary Logos, Keeper of Universal Law, best friend, fellow Venusian, call me Raj, or SK, but call me. I welcome you, my sisters and brothers, to the closing of this circle, to the return of your sacred self, to the place of creation and co-creation with the Council of Love. You've been gone a long time. I am not suggesting that you do not create infinitely, each and every moment of your day. But it is time for this expansion of humanity, of Gaia to take place and for the fullness of your ability to create what your heart desires and sings to come forth. I have spoken to you of the Law of Unity, of the interconnectedness of all, so when there is a tear, a gap, or desire that you are working on how we gather to help you. For a very long time many of you and most of humanity, has said. don't bother, you would rather do it yourself. That really means it hasn't worked out all that well.

"Now we change the playing field, the game, because you, my beloved ones, are truly willing to engage with us. We do not in any sense of the word minimize your ability to create independently, freely, and through your free choice. That is your birthright and the core of who you are. But co-creation is also a great deal of fun. So we will act as your 'gofers', we will act as your sewers and menders, we will act to help you and then we will say 'Now, will you join with us? Can we join with you in the completion of the dream?'

"You are already anchored, not only in the fifth but in the twelve realms and so are we, and then some. But let us play, explore, expand. Now is the time. We have been waiting and we are ready, but dear hearts, so are you; and for this we are grateful. Go with our love and go in peace."

THE NEW GRID OF HUMANITY

"Greetings, I am Sanat Kumara, Keeper of the Universal Law, keeper in many ways my friends of this planet of Earth, our beloved Gaia, and of her place within the universe. My dear friends, I come this day with Archangel Gabrielle to speak to you of the new grid of humanity, the new grid of the human collective.

"As the channel has indicated, many of you have been doing the final removal of the old paradigms of Earth, the old paradigms of false beliefs and illusions, and you are doing tremendously well. My advice and request to you from this entire Council is keep going. We need this cleaned up. We are helping you. We are energizing you. But you, my friends, are the plowmen; you are the workers. You are the ones that have offered your life in beloved service to the Mother and to Gaia. You are here to witness this miracle of unfoldment, the reinstitution of love.

"Many of you have asked me how will this happen, how is the tide going to turn, the tables tip? Well the answer, my beloved friends, is with the overlay and over-lighting of each of you and this beautiful new grid of humanity. It is platinum gold. It is as gentle and as strong as silk. It is as powerful as the essential element of love, which is the fuel of the universe. My beloved ones, it right here, right now. This is the time of love. It is born out of the hope, the blue flame that the Mother has given you and which is instilled within each of you. The hope is allowing you to go forward and open your hearts to receive. When there is lack of self-worth and self-love, you are not truly open to receive all the gifts we give you. This, like all of the blessings we bestow are done with you, not for you – those days are over – with your consciousness, physicality, essence and being.

"Now what does this mean to have a new grid? You have spent years anchoring and bringing forth the beauty of your unique soul design, all the talents and abilities that you have brought forward for this time. You have called home all aspects and anchored them within. You have acknowledged past and future lifetimes. All of this hangs upon your grid. Many of you are war torn and weary, feeling depleted; your strength, endurance and physical body diminished and compromised – and it is. You have been magnificent, peaceful warriors. You are the bravest of the brave, and you are cherished to infinity.

"However, you need a new grid. Humanity needs this golden fresh start. We are honored and blessed to bring it to you, to place it upon you that we may all go forward. All grids are united as one. There is no separation or isolation, we are all connected. Allow us to now take this fragmented, frayed grid that you have carried and replace it. We overlay it and reinforce it with the gold platinum.

"Take time as you read this or over the next few days to simply lie upon your bed, marvel and receive. Notice how bright and shiny you are. I am proud of you. I am proud to walk with you, to serve with you. I am proud to be the one to bestow this gift. Go with my Love."

THE NATURE OF UNIVERSAL LAW

"I am Sanat Kumara, and I come to speak of the Law. I come, that you will understand the meaning of what you create for each of you are masters and creators of your own universe.

"As I have watched this world and this universe change, evolve and transmute, I have been pleased. It is as it will be. My children, you are creating your planet. You have always known this, since the moment of inception, inception of this being, Gaia, planet of green and blue. You have created below what is above. You have followed the dictums of balance. Do not think that you are not creating your own life as well. For eons you have practiced this art (of creation), and now you are practicing the art of anchoring. Each of you has been an anchor in many regimes, dimensions, lives, planets, existences and experiments.

"You will change what is beyond, for it is truly an evolutionary process, not static, not fixed. It is fixed in time or space, and it does grow and change, as improbable as that seems. You did not return to this undertaking with a fixed plan, a set agenda. Never could we or would we try to control you. It would be impossible and not desirable. You have said, 'Let us go play, and let us create this planet of beauty and love.' You have asked the guardian angels who surround you to help and make suggestions; but it is you who are creating this planet of joy.

"It is the Law that which you give, you will receive – to infinity. What you love is what you will to come to you, that is the Law. Where you focus your energies is what will magnify and grow. That is why it is time, for your sake, to let go. The time of preparation and completion is over. Do not live in the past; live in present and future where all is at your fingertips. If you wish to live a spiritual life, then do so. Do not focus on wanting, for that places you in a place of need. If you wish to be perfection, you are. It is soul recognition. If you wish to be a magnet for abundance in all forms, then do so. When you alter your thought and heart patterns you alter your existence. It is very simple. These Laws have not changed, they are immutable. I suggest you follow them.

THE FRAMEWORK OF UNIVERSAL LAW

"Greetings, I am Sanat Kumara, Keeper of Universal Law, planetary logos.

"Universal Law is the framework that explains how things work. It is part of the universal grid, and the understandings of how things do or don't happen. The Law provides the explanation for the alignment necessary in terms of your own process of ascension, and your eventual return to Source. Universal Law is a reflection of Divine thought and existence. It is a construct of creation. These Laws are laid down, given, and shared directly from One.

"Universal Law is the framework upon which creation and the 13 Blessings and Virtues, or Divine Qualities hang. It is the grid upon which you come to understand how things work. Isn't it peculiar that you, as a human collective, have such an obsession with this word law? You have judicial law, laws of mathematics, quantum physics, natural law, but you do not have, and you have not aligned fully or completely with Universal Law, even though it is the starting and finishing point. When you are in alignment with Universal Law, you understand how to position yourself, particularly within time and space; how your actions or inactions can be measured and reflected.

"If you think of it in terms of structure, the Law are the steel girders, the two-by-fours, the foundation, and the qualities are the covering and the innards of the building. When you are in the purity of adherence to the Law then you are embodying the 13 Blessings and Virtues. You cannot separate these out; if you have one, you have the other.

"Universal Law is the guideline laid down by the Mother/ Father/One for adherence to the Divine Qualities. When you are seeking how to eliminate or clear issues or blockages, reflect upon the Universal Law and determine what is not in alignment. So often when you are in a clearing process you say to me, 'Raj, I have been working on this false grid or issue but it does not seem to click for me, it does not produce the results.' How I guide thee is to go back to this codification, this grid, this framework upon which everything hangs.

"All of the Universal Laws are interconnected. It is not a matter of simply working or understanding one individual Law, that is insufficient. Each of you, in tandem with the kingdoms and with Gaia, have reached the point in your ascension that you are ready to fully embrace, understand and build societies and a planet that is in adherence and alignment with the Law.

"Why does Universal Law exist? Why do we speak of the Law? Because it is the rules of how things work, and these rules do not change. You are at a juncture in your spiritual journey where you have need and desire to understand the immutable nature and function of the Law. You are at a point where you are yearning to be in alignment. One of the issues of being human is that you are in an environment of constant change, whether you acknowledge or realize it or not. That is not only challenging but difficult. When you can understand and refer to the Law, you have the framework within which to work with that phenomenon of constant change, and to reach a place of balance.

"The purpose and foundation of the Law is balance. It is to assist and guide all beings to the place of balance. In the very beginning we said to the Mother 'How will the beings, not only on Earth, not only upon this beloved jewel, Gaia, understand how to construct, how to proceed?' And so the codex of the Law was shared. Now, you do not go about every day thinking if you are in alignment with the Law. Rather, it is a way of being and of being in balance.

"When you are breathing, acting, feeling, processing, praying and creating, you are operating within that framework, on that tapestry, on that grid of Universal Law. You cannot absent your-self from this framework. It is not possible. The Universal Laws that I speak to you of is not simply Universal Law that is applicable to the humans. It is the Universal Law that we all adhere to. It is the guideline for where each of you is headed, the crux of interdimensional shift; it is that heart knowing, love alignment with the Law.

"Many human laws are not in alignment with Universal Law. That is where things have gone awry and where false grids and paradigms have grown up and assumed the illusion of solidity. But such laws do not have a reference point in the heart of One and are contrary to the Law of Above and Below. When misalignment occurs people become disenchanted, disillusioned, disappointed, because they believe they are adhering to law, but it is not having the results of creation they desire. The reason is because they have not taken the time to understand and align with Universal Law, which is actually very simple.

"If you think in terms of human laws and behaviors, you are not necessarily thinking in each of your actions, 'Am I behaving within the confines or the prescriptive definitions of behavior that are acceptable in this country that has laid down these laws?' You don't really think about it, unless you are breaking the law. Now, the difference is, is that human law is based on punishment and control. So they have no genuine divine essence, do they? One can argue, and many do, that the underpinning of human law is order and love and not taking advantage of some people. But that is not the nature of Universal Law, it goes far beyond expediency.

"How do you come to know Universal Law? You do so by going into your heart consciousness. This is the compass all have been given and it has recently been reset within you. You know Universal Law by asking yourself one very simple question: Does this situation, this action, this feeling, this behavior feel that it is in alignment with love and with One?

"You may ask yourself further: does it feel within me, in my heart knowingness, that this is in the balance? Is this an action, behavior or situation that moves me along my chosen path?

Does this jettison me forward in this time of rapid change? Does this align with the love that I know within me, that is my divine essence? Does it align with the love of the Mother? Does it feel like love? And make no mistake my beloved friends, there is not one human being who does not know, when they are completely honest with themselves, what love feels like.

"Often you make excuses to and for yourself for not aligning with love, which is to say you have not aligned with the Law. Now excuses are fine, because in many ways they cause you to be very honest with yourself. So understand when you are making an excuse what you are really doing is addressing an issue that is not in alignment with the truth of your universal self.

"The practice is simple and straightforward when working with Universal Law. Go to your stillpoint, and simply call me. Practice your Divine Qualities. Notice that when you are practicing certain qualities, they more naturally align with different Laws, with different thoughts, with different expressions, shall we say, of God, of One. But also note and acknowledge the wisdom which is already within you.

"Working with the Law is being in your heart consciousness and discerning, considering. You live in a world, and I distinguish this from the Gaia, that has become very busy. Now, it is not that you need to judge busy as good or bad; it is indifferent. However, understand that busy is a very good place for ego to live. Part of that busyness is an emotion of self-imposed struggle. Being busy does not engender a sense of smoothness. It is a self-imposed condition where you do not take time to discern what you are doing to yourself or to the I Am Presence.

"When you stop and ask that question, the guidance is already there because your beauty, your heart, your soul or however you conceive of that knowingness, is divinely intelligent. It knows, and you know. In the knowing, you can shift from busy to being, and being does not mean that you are not taking action and building Nova Earth. You are, and it is well under way, I am happy to say.

"We look forward to the human collective decision to adhere to the higher Laws of Love, which is another name for Universal

Law. We guide you to adhere to the meaningful existence and the truth of who you are. Know my sweet friends that this is already being expressed by many of you. Trust me that gives me incredible joy. Never underestimate how well you are doing."

1. THE UNIVERSAL LAW OF SACRED PURPOSE

"Greetings, I am Sanat Kumara, Master and Keeper of the Universal Laws, and I return this day, my friends, to speak to you of the Law of Sacred Purpose. The Law of Purpose is very important in your very life and in your sacred form of human being who walks the Earth. The Law of Purpose is the freedom to be in alignment with your sacred self and the embodiment of your sacred self. It is the Universal Law that all adhere to and that all are assisted with throughout all universes and all places and times. Hear what I say; it is applicable to all.

"When I have spoken of the Universal Laws, the Laws of attraction, of movement, I do not simply speak of the Universal Laws applicable to Earth. I speak of the Laws for all. I explain to thee how things work. There is a similar principle upon the Earth that is valued, that is in keeping with the Law of Purpose. It is called your principle of self-determination. It is the right of all beings to choose. This is how the Law of Purpose works for me, for Gabrielle, for Sananda, for the Mother, for She has invented this Law.

"When you are undertaking something whether it is combing your hair or bringing peace to the planet you need to examine whether it is in alignment, in keeping with your purpose. In order to do this, dear hearts, it is essential, critical, that you understand and anchor, know, embrace and celebrate the sacred purpose of why you exist, why you have chosen this form and a million others time and time again. What is it that you do? What is it that your essence, the ray that you travel upon in your uniqueness? What is it that you choose to do? What is your expression? All creation, all action, all co-creation, all thought, all feeling, all emotion, everything, every speck, subatomic particle of your being has need to be in alignment with this Law of Sacred Purpose.

"Many of you have often wondered why you try to do certain things which never work, because there is an automatic override by your sacred over-soul (your Stranger) to not allow things that are not in alignment with your sacred being.

"It is true that sometimes it is a matter of Divine timing and each of you has certainly experienced that. But sometimes, dear ones, it is simply not in alignment with your purpose, your expression of the unfoldment. This is important for you to grasp. Just as important is for you to connect within every fiber of your being and align with that purpose each and every moment of your day. We have given you the litmus test – does it feel like joy? If it does not, we advise you not to undertake it. Joy is present when it is in alignment with who you are, with what you have chosen as your expression of divinity. Do not deny the wholeness and the huge expanse of your purpose. Sometimes there is a tendency, dear friends, to think small, to underestimate what you are truly capable of. Do not be blind to your potential, see what you are doing, look at what you are trying to create, and check if it is in alignment with your purpose.

"Think of this Law as operating as red light, green light. When it is in alignment with the plan and your purpose it is green light the whole way, All will come to assist you. When it is not, that is when you experience sluggishness, not being clear, feeling like there are obstacles, wondering if you are on track.

"If you do not know your purpose, do not spend one millisecond in judgment or chastisement. Simply sit, open and allow, because all it means is you have not fully explored the corridors of your heart. You have not gone to the places where your own being lives. Go deep within your heart. Go through that pin-prick of light to the inside of your heart, to the still point, and read what is written upon the walls there. See what is indelibly etched, not ever to be erased. That is your purpose. And then choose how you express it. If you still do not know, turn to me, for I am ever-present, and will gladly help you. We all will for you are loved.

"Some of you ask, 'Sanat Kumara, why do you bring this to

the forefront now?' Because it is a time of stepping forward, the Light is upon you. We have told you time and again the changes upon Gaia work with you. They come through the people. You are the unfoldment, but only in alignment with who you are. That is what has gone awry with the planet, people have not aligned. As you align, you align for many. Do not step back in fear. Many maladies, many illness, many lethargies, many feelings of depression are because you are not in alignment. Let them go and dream big and know that I am with you in love and gold and radiance always. Go with my blessings. Go with my sacred purpose, which is to keep and to teach Universal Law."

In a separate channeling Sanat Kumara continues his explanation of the Law of Sacred Purpose:

"As you are in a process of embracing your Divine Qualities and eliminating your false grids, it is important to know, and to connect with and understand, the Universal Law of Sacred Purpose.

"All energy that emerges from the heart of One, regardless of form, has sacred purpose, expression, direction. That energy is also connected to your unique journey of completion and continuity.

"The Law of Sacred Purpose is the understanding, in the universal sense, that the purpose of all existence is to love, to be of joy, and to find your way back home. However it is also a key element in your sacred path to understand your sacred purpose within the greater design of the Divine Mother. How does your purpose, your expression, in this lifetime, as a fragment of your broader journey align with the Law of Love?

"In many ways, this is the starting point of understanding your journey back to One. The starting point of divine union is understanding your sacred purpose? The Law of Purpose is intrinsically aligned with the Law of Intent and the Law of Completion and Continuity. It is aligning your entire being, all realms, all dimensions, all realities, all experience, all thought, all emotion, with your intent. It is the power of intent married to sacred purpose. It is the alignment of the Mother's intent that you know and experience love, and return home in fulfillment of your promise and Her promise."

2: UNIVERSAL LAW OF INTENT

"Greetings, I am Sanat Kumara, Keeper of the Law, Plenetary Logos, Servant of One, brother to all.

"The Law of Intent is how do you fulfill your sacred purpose with intention that is clearly aligned with your sacred purpose? It is the alignment of every thought, action, association, behavior, and relationship with the intention of the sacred fulfillment of your soul design, contract, and mission and purpose of your life and soul journey."

The Law of Intent is tied to our earlier discussion on the interdimensional self as well as the understanding of your soul mission and purpose. It is doing the work to not only understand but know what your foundation is, then work to align your intentions with the fulfillment of that sacred purpose. It is consciously working with the intentional element of the creation formula and process. It is being mindful, directed and focused. Does that mean you do not take time to relax, play, act silly? Absolutely not. The purpose of Law of Intent, like all Universal Laws, is balance. That means balance in all parts of your life, and, balance with action, stillpoint and creation.

Sanat Kumara continues:

"If your intention is not in alignment with your sacred purpose, then you are not in alignment with the Law. Every intention, big, small, and in between is an intention to live a life of purity, of grace, but that is reflected into action. It is reflected into the qualities of kindness and truth-speaking and sharing and tenderness and mercy, cooperation and compassion. Each particular intention as well as the overall intention of your life needs to translate into the practicality not only of your actions, but your feelings and thoughts as well.

"There are currently many on Earth who will do what appears to be 'the right thing,' because they want to appear to be kind or generous or thoughtful or sincere, but the intent is not there. What they are doing is working from an ego place, or they are taking an action because they think they have to, but in fact they are angry — what is your expression, 'mad as hell?' So, that intention just went awry, it is not genuine.

"There are also many who take action from a place of fear. Ask yourself I am doing it because I am afraid if I don't do it I am going to get in trouble, either in trouble with the law, with my wife, with my husband, with my children, with my neighbor or with God. Because if that is your motivation, that is not good enough. That is not the alignment with the Law. Pay attention to your emotional and mental processes in forming intent. You cannot think, 'Well, I will do this so I will be in alignment, but I really think this is a bunch of hogwash.' That is not sufficient. But also remember to keep your beloved sense of humor dear heart. Laugh if you see false intent, go into your heart and reframe, and then proceed bravely.

"Bring all parts of you to the stillpoint of your heart and your knowing, and allow the purity of your intent to flow. Never will you be coerced into such an alignment. Intention is a sacred act of free will. There are times when you drop into concern or even fear of punitive ramifications if you do not adhere to the law, but that is not so. The punitive ramifications you experience are self-created and result in the feeling that life doesn't work. It is not joyful or loving feeling, it is not sustainable, it is not rewarding, and it simply doesn't feel good. And you see this every day on the streets of every country. You see this in the quiet of homes where people isolate in desperation. The ramifications do not come from on high. The concept of punishment, of judgment, is a human construct, not a divine one. But are there ramifications? Yes, because what you are doing individually and collectively is hurting yourself, making yourself miserable.

"As your tutor, there are some of you who reading this and thinking 'Well, that's terrible. He's putting it all on us!' No, my beloved friends, I am not putting it all on you. What I am saying is there is a body of understanding that if you adhere to it, you will fly free. And I will fly with you, support you, and catch you dear heart if you ever falter. I am with you always."

Sanat Kumara speaks to us further about the formulation of intent in the process of creation and co-creation. He enlightens us on the balance of partnership of above and below with regard to intent – how our actions and unfoldment are part of the intent of the Masters, and how they are part of our intent. Powerful insight. Raj also addresses the issue of integration and the up-heaval that is currently being experienced by so many of us.

"Greetings, I am Sanat Kumara, Keeper of the Law, the Law of Love, the Law of the Universe, the laws of your heart. I am pleased to speak to you again as we began with the formulation of intent.

"What I ask of you is to not make and create these Laws into universal mysteries. It is why I have distilled it, with the help of many, to a formula that is fully understandable, comprehensible to your minds, body and heart. For it our dearest wish, my friends of Earth, that you join in this co-creation of your new planet. It is an interesting undertaking, for not only are you the co-creators of this new reality, you are also part of it. It is the intent of this Universe of the Mother and the Council of Love that you participate, fully and completely in this creation. Each one of you has come from very different corners of the Universe and planet to do this. Each one of you carries a unique expression of your personal miracle. Never have I looked into a heart, and it does not matter whether it is your heart of the heart of All, that I do not see a smile or adventure, a desire and wish, for that is part of the unfoldment, the evolution, the ongoing creation of All.

"Your expression of divinity has never been limited but the false grids of humanity have been heavy. The illusions have been thick, but my brothers and sisters you have shed them, and your heart is open. I ask you to join with me, first in the creation of your heart's desire. Do not worry about the Universe or the planet. I am asking you to start with yourself, because this is transmitted throughout time and space, the wavelengths of the grid, and it penetrates the hearts of your brothers and sisters, throughout all time and all space.

"Some of you have experienced great difficulty as you have integrated all aspects, all markers deep within your heart and deep within yourself. You have seen parts of yourself that you have not recognized, and you have not witnessed for a long time, and you say, what is that and what is going on?

"It is your soul intent to bring all parts of your being, your essence, your soul design and the aspects that have fulfilled parts of this design home to be reintegrated. There are parts of you that have been in service to the Mother/Father/One, for eons. Now, I wish you consider for a moment, if you were sent to the wilds of Afghanistan to hold the light of peace, and you were left there for centuries. You might be a little disheveled, why, you might even be irritable. You might wish to cross your arms and say, it's about time. So, welcome your essence back, and understand the grumpier parts are often your markers, and your markers are simply parts of you, not the wholeness of your being that you sent off on brief mission to do very specific things, and then forgot about it. You are growing. All of this reintegration is part of your intent to create, to bring back the wholeness of who you are, and it is from this place of solidarity of unification that you will go forward.

"Now, let us speak of that intent. We have spoken about how you are part of our intent. Understand that we are also part of yours. A long time ago you said to me, 'Sanat Kumara, I will go to Earth, but I do not intend to go alone. So, I will go, but when the time comes, give me a gentle reminder. Do not leave me like my markers out there, wondering what the heck is going on.' We are in sacred union, sweet angel, in partnership. I am Master and Keeper of the Law, and I am your dearest friend. I do not wish to be separated from you. I will walk within you, I walk with you, I will walk behind you. We will fly. Do not shut me out.

"It is my sacred mission on behalf of All to help you remember. You are my golden flame. You are my beloved one. You are the courageous one. You have said, I will go again, and some of you have done so because you love this planet, and some of you have done so because you have been asked, but all of you have done so because of your love for the Mother. You have come because of your belief and intent that love will rein on this planet, that peace will survive and thrive on this planet. Your lifetime, here and now, is your action. You will refine it, you will direct it, and, you are already half way there.

"Intent is the feeling of your heart, it may be a prayer and it may be a whoop, it may be a cry of joy or a cry for help. It is all the same, and it is all heard. Now when I have asked you to start with yourself, I did not mean to start out small. Dream big, you are magnificent. The wholeness of your being shines and attracts your brothers and sisters from galaxies near and far. Ascended Masters line up at your beck and call. It is because you are loved and honored, and even if you do not know, we know who you are. We invite you; we implore you to play with us. Remember your heritage, the stars, and come with us, and when our traveling is done, you will gently land upon this planet. Bearing not only flowers, but fruit. Thank you."

3. THE UNIVERSAL LAW OF WITHIN AND WITHOUT/ABOVE AND BELOW

"I am Sanat Kumara, Keeper of the Golden Flame and Keeper of The Law. I come to speak with you of the Universal Law of Balance and the Law Within and Without. You are all familiar with the Law of Above and Below; as above, so below. But it is also so as within and so without. I come to remind you of this. My friends, it is not a matter of deciding who you are, for you have been the essence of who you are forever. It has been entrenched and etched throughout the heavens, Earth and throughout the stars of many galaxies for a very long time. Understand this.

"What does this have to do with within and without? What we are speaking of is the decision that you have made and are making to step forward and accept the mantle and joy of responsibility, the fullness of your mission on Gaia. You are the teachers, messengers, healers and pathfinders. You would not be here had you not decided to do this. Yes, even kicking and screaming. Understand, there are many who stayed away, which is also as it needs to be.

"Balance means not carrying your brilliance simply within, but also allowing for its outward expression, in the without. It is the way of balance and it is the way of wholeness. Do not ever worry about what it is exactly you are going to do or how that will look. Simply remain within the stillness of your being, then project and move into action. It will be in divine accordance with mind, will and heart, above and below. That is the Law. When you are truly in the stillness of your heart, and a decision within is made, the projection of action externally will take place.

"When you do not know whether what you are about to do is right or wrong, turn to me and ask 'What do you think?' We will answer. Do not think we do not have interest in your individual life, soul and mission. You are the expressions of God through the expressions of Love. What transpires upon this planet has impact throughout many universes. It depends upon you.

"We guide, direct, teach and counsel, but the actions, dear one, are yours. Simply know you have decided; you are prepared. You have been given many tools. Even when you knew all you have need of is your heart and hands, we gave you tools, not to depend upon, but to play with; not because you need them to be healer or teacher, but because the humans you interact with also love of gadgets. It does not matter whether they are sophisticated Internet tools or a simple crystal, humans love toys, and that is particularly true of the United States of America. You may thank St. Germaine for that.

"Know, my friends that I am with you, as Keeper of the Law. I am not judge and jury, for there is no place in the Law for judgment, not of self and not of others. I am your assistant. Go and play."

We finish this section with a beautiful message of hope from Archangel Michael on the Law of Above and Below:

"What has taken thousands of eons can be healed in one

moment. That is the truth of the Universal Law of As Above, So Below. What has been healed in heaven will be healed on Earth. That is why so many have returned to Gaia, and you will return home victorious. For many of you, the illusion of power has meant separation. It was a false belief. Be strong enough and courageous enough to come home. I will be your honor guard. I will let no one harm you. I will hold my shield high that no injury or barbs will hit you. There is no need to live in your personal hell. You know this, so let it be. You are already powerful, worthy and whole. Look into the mirror of my shield and see your own glory and behind you see the ten thousand fold that you lead back home, all smiling and thanking you, gratitude in their hearts. When you are all home then I will return to my music. But not until then. Farewell."

4. THE UNIVERSAL LAW OF CHANGE

"Greetings, I am Sanat Kumara. Welcome my children of the rainbow race; my beloved circle; agents of change; catalysts. I come to speak about the Universal Law of Change. It is not only one of the fundamental laws of creation; it is one of the fundamental laws of the universe. We do not simply mean your planet, for movement is a constant throughout all places, all states of being, all dimensions and realities. Change is the fuel of love. Within movement there is change.

"The wise words that have been spoken about change are accurate. It is the one thing that you know will occur with each breath, each moment of your existence. Now many of you are working on creations and doing brilliantly. However, there is a tendency of the human race to be impatient. This impatience has been inherited from Archangel Gabrielle, and that is a good thing. Nevertheless, there is a time and place for patience. Right now upon your planet with the rebirth of love, and the unfoldment of the planet and the Mother, there is need for movement and action that is far more rapid than you have ever witnessed. That is why you have received such amplification. You are the agents of change. You may anticipate that things will move rapidly, but I digress.

"Many of you feel the unfoldment does not move rapidly enough, while others are feeling overwhelmed the amount of change being presented. I speak to both issues for they are the same, simply different ends of the spectrum. Change is constant. Never is there a lack of movement in the universe. The only time where the stillness occurs is at the instant, a millisecond, far beyond the measurement that you know, of creation. It is when the joining takes place and the implosion into form occurs. Other than that there is always motion.

"I am asking each of you to take time each and every day to be the observer, and look at what has occurred in the span of twenty-four hours of your day. I ask you to undertake this practice consistently, at the time of your meditation. Note all the changes that have occurred during that span of time. What are the actions that have taken place; the interactions with others? Were they and you of love? Were you holding the environment of love, the energy of creation? Or did you fall into frustration, anger and bitterness? Be honest and understand that it is not an issue for judgment but discernment. If you find the answer is yes to anger and bitterness, judgment, then release and surrender it unto me, unto the Mother, unto Gabrielle, unto your gods. We do not care who receives it. But give it away! That is movement and action in accordance with the Law of Change.

"Pay attention, make a journal note so you can see what has changed and the progression of your mighty self, and the unfoldment of your plan. Call on me. Now many of you have been very busy working with the Law of Elimination, and you are doing well on this as well. But, dear children, remember not everything is to be eliminated. Yes, we are watching over you and making sure you do not destroy the Empire State Building. So do not worry, but also remember at the time of elimination you are also working on your creation. Go forth on this.

"I wish to address those of you who are feeling a little overwhelmed with the enormous opportunities and possibilities that are being presented to you. Maria, the Lady of Guadalupe, has said unto you, accept all invitations. Accept all opportunities, all offers of help and assistance both in the physical and from this side. Yet still you are feeling a little overwhelmed. Again, do the same exercise and recognize that there is a sequence to unfolding; there is a patterning throughout your universe. Don't think the pattern is simply chaos, it is not. There is a plan unfolding for you but it is sequenced and sequential; that is the key. Open your heart, because the reason you are feeling overwhelmed is that you are still living in the false grid of limitation. Go back to the meditation on Eliminating False Grids and let go of any limitation and lack. Open your heart and receive.

"This is a time of action and change, but it also a time when the construct, the belief, that Earth and those who sit upon her can only receive so much at a time is being broken. My children, that old belief is incorrect. When you are in the flow you are literally in the endless potential of reality. Flow upon the infinity sign, and from time to time visit the still point in the center of this symbol, this energy. Stay in the flow. Note your progress, note the change. Note the movement and open; open not only to the possibility of what we can give you but also to your own unlimited ability to receive, to create.

"Many of you are working with the Elimination Law, and are being given rapid demonstrations of how well you create. For you no sooner eliminate then instantly recreate what you have just eliminated. That is ludicrous, and a waste of energy. It is a cosmic joke. So have another look and make sure you aren't doing this. All in all, my children, you are doing well. Understand we work in eons; you work in frameworks of months and years, days, and sometimes even hours. When in doubt, turn to me. For I am not only your teacher, I am your guardian and friend."

5. UNIVERSAL LAW OF GIVE AND RECEIVE

"I am Sanat Kumara, old friend, Keeper of the Law on Earth and beyond. The Law of the Universe is balanced, and you cannot enter into partnership with your intergalactic friend or each other without balance.

"Many of you have skirted the Law during this life. You are

prepared to give and give but turn away from receiving. Now I ask you, what shall I do? Shall I arrest you? I think not. I am here to remind you of the two sides of your being; you cannot live in one area. You cannot live in spirit and be in a physical body. You must do both. You cannot live in only a part of yourself. You cannot love another without cherishing yourself. What you create within will be what is.

"That is why you have worked with Archangels Michael and Gabrielle to relinquish your lack of worthiness, so you are prepared to go forward. My request of you lawbreakers is simple. I wish for you to eliminate the phrase, 'but' from your very soul and essence. It was not our invention, it was yours. Relinquish it. I will remind you daily with my golden flame to let go of this limitation. This sense of limitation causes upheaval throughout the universe. Please do it for yourselves but many.

"Allow creation to take place. In the spirit of partnership, I ask you to receive. You have accomplished much my friends from any perspective, from Venus, from Mars, from the ships, and from the center of your Earth. You have done well, but it is not enough. You need to expand more. You need to experience the wholeness of your own potential. Know this. It is the time of the transformation and the return of many to this dimension and planet. I suggest you stay and enjoy the party.

"Join with us, with this Council of Love, daily. The Law does not require you to spend every minute of every day thinking and working on balance. You can take time out and simply live it, to catch up on news on board ship, to enjoy the peace of quiet conversation with your friends. Make no mistake your star brothers and sisters are broadcasting clearly to each of you. Do not worry if you think your transmitter is out of order. It will be adjusted and it is activated now.

6. UNIVERSAL LAW OF ATTACHMENT AND DETACHMENT

While most of the information pertaining to Universal Law has come directly from Sanat Kumara, there are insights and guidance from other members of the Council of Love who also contribute to this body of knowledge. Here, the Buddha speaks of creation and co-creation, and the Law of Attachment and Detachment.

"I am the Wayfarer. I am the Buddha. You did not expect to hear so much from me during this discussion of creation and co-creation, did you? My beloved friends, I have things I wish to speak to your heart and to your mind about. So come and sit with me. Let us sit under this bodhi tree together and watch the world go by.

"I wish to speak to you as mothers, fathers and teachers. For even though some of you are not parents, you have been mothers and fathers so many times and teachers always that you will understand what I say to you this day, and why I use this example. I wish to remind you of this Law of Attachment and Detachment.

"I wish you to think as mothers, and how you feel as your small child goes off to school or to war that first day. Fathers know what this feels like as well. Even if you walk with them or run after them, there is still that time when you have to let go and hand them over to the teacher. You have to allow them to go in the classroom and the classroom of life or the war where you know there are all kinds of perils and dangers. Even before your child was born and throughout all those formative years, you have attached to the vision of what you wish and dream for this child, for all the things that you wish them to accomplish, experience, do, so that they will know themselves; that they will know their truth and strength. Even when you let go, when you step back and detach, sometimes because you have no choice, still you hold that vision for them. You hold the vision in your heart and in your mind.

"If you are lucky enough that your child comes home every day, or even occasionally, you will inquire and prod, and inject where you can to influence, to help them with the fulfillment of their vision. So as you are detaching, you are keeping your vision, but you are also allowing their vision to unfold. Normally, there is a meeting of the ways when you re-attach. And so it is with us, my friend.

"You have your vision, dream and creation, and it is real. It is as real as your skin, hair and eyes. You hold that within you. Then as you move into action, as you release from stillpoint (which is where you need me) you are also detaching. That is necessary and the proscribed process. It is in the release that there is a gathering of energy, allowing it to flow and move as it has need to. Yet, while that is occurring, we are also adding our elements, ingredients, energies, and sometimes magic, to your creation.

"Understand that in this mixed release and add-on, your vision gains greater substance, it is bigger. It is still essentially yours, but it is thicker, a combination. Sometimes there are elements that need to be added to your desires and creations that you don't know of, nor do you need to. You may think that our adding to your creation is a diversion but it is not. It is an essential element, even when it does not appear so.

"Then you continue on in action, in stillness, joy and trust. You may watch for your child, pace outside the school or even the classroom. You will do the same thing when you are forty-five years old. It never changes. The child or the grownup will return to you but they will be essentially changed, for the experience and the energy has gone outside of you. The process is fluid and continual. So even while your child or creation is returned to you, the building, the add-on continues. It does not end. It does not even end with what you think of as death.

"When you feel discouraged, sidetracked or dismayed, or when you have need simply to be my friend in the stillness, come and sit with me. I will not interfere. I will sit with you and that will help. Farewell."

The Buddha has taught us over the years this lesson of attach, detach, re-attach. It is a powerful method of creation. This is how it works:

As always anchor in your heart, surround yourself with the Archangels and call forth the Buddha. For purposes of illustration let's use a perfect harmonious marriage or partnership. Visualize your current situation. Be honest with yourself about why you are choosing this particular area to begin your creation work. Be vigilant on what's not good, what's awful, what needs changing. Similarly examine what's right with your current situation; what you wouldn't want to change in the slightest, what you treasure, what feeds your body, mind, heart and soul.

Now turn your energies and attention to what it is you desire to create. Take the time to visualize and feel deeply what this looks, feels, tastes, and sounds like – you get the idea. Take the time to really feel it, or in the language of the Buddha to attach to it. Attach not only to the 3-D qualities of the creation but to what it brings you in the spiritual and other realms as well. To continue the example of a partnership, feel the sense of being loved, cherished, valued, of being in sacred union, co-creation, safety, security, longevity, the deep harmony of loving communication, sexual intimacy, soul intimacy. Spell it out.

It's important to not limit yourself with this exercise. You are not simply seeking, for example, relief from a fractious relationship, no fighting or arguing, no feelings of less than. You are attaching to the ideal; to what you would create that would support you and bring forth the best part of you, in fulfillment and alignment with your plan.

The second step of this exercise is then to completely detach from everything – from your current situation and from your vision. Often you will have a physical sensation of stepping backwards. You are letting go. This is an important piece of the process of aligning with the Universal Law of Attachment and Detachment, because this is also where your guides, the Buddha and the entire legions of light add their magic elements. So let it go; do not hold on. This is a walk of trust.

Step three is to be still in your heart and in the stillness, to re-attach to the highest vibration and frequency of that creation. The sensation is that you are holding essence, moon dust, and starlight. And trust it to come to pass. Turn it over to the Buddha and allow.

I have been doing this exercise for years and I am grateful

that the Buddha reminded me to share it here because it's my personal reminder to start again. We have the gifts of so many tools, sometimes we forget. Track your progress with this process; you will be amazed.

7. UNIVERSAL LAW OF UNIFICATION

Sanat Kumara speaks on the Law of Unification, the Law of Unity:

"So often upon the planet there has been a misunderstanding, shall I say, about the use of the word Law. In each of your societies, you have a codification. Originally, it was to be based upon Universal Law, the Law of Love, of friendship, trust and fairness. However, very often in your society and upon your planet, law has come to mean control. I want to be very clear with you, my beloved ones, that when I speak of the Law, I do not speak of control, for I, nor any of us, have any desire to control you. Would that not be ridiculous: to create a planet of Love, give the gift of free will and then try and control you? Why that would be very human, would it not?

"When I speak of Universal Law, I am speaking of the explanation of how things work. That is why I wish to talk to you about this. It is simply an understanding, a wisdom that has been born from the heart of One about how things work.

"I wish to speak to you particularly this day during this time of shift, of change, of growth, of expansion, of co-convergence, of the Law of Unification, the Law of Unity. It is very simple. It is one of the Laws upon this planet and throughout the time of darkness that has been forgotten.

"Each of you in your own way is awakening to the understanding of this Law of Unity, of Unification. Your understanding of this Law is important because your participation, your buy-in as it were, is a critical element. It does not do any good to have a Law and have it simply sit there as ancient or future wisdom. This Law needs to be an inherent part of your behaviors, practices and understanding of how things work not only upon your planet but throughout the universe. It is the understanding that all things, all energy is a unified force field. You are one force field. This planet is one force field. There is no separation. There is no division.

"Are you unique in your place, in your qualities, what you have assumed as matter, and even time in terms of this force field? Yes, you are beautifully unique. But you are also fundamentally and irrevocably connected, and that is a gift. That is the miracle of this creation. Nowhere, and I have traveled far and wide, throughout the multiverse is there a planet or a star that expresses such joyous diversity. I do not simply mean the human collective, although I must tell you that is where most of my energy and attention is focused these days. When you begin to conceive of yourself as a force field, then you also begin to understand that you are interconnected heart to heart to heart, soul to soul to soul, skin to skin to skin, to the dogs, birds, kittens, trees, grass and the very floor you walk on. You are unique, and yet bound by this Law of Unity. It is not something that you may opt in or out of. It is part of the infinite grace of creation.

"That is why the dark time upon this planet, the illusion or shall I say disillusion that you are isolated or alone was so erroneous. This is why I so urgently wish to speak to you of this matter, because even now, my beloved friends, you have those moments – even when you are in your heart – when you go to that place of darkness and isolation, and feel unloved and unlovable. You experience moments, sometimes years, when you feel disconnected and you think 'Well, thank God, I am not connected because what would happen if they really saw me? They would know all about me. They would know my secrets, the good, the bad, the ugly.' And so you step back in fear. The fear is that you won't be loved. I tell you dear hearts, this is not possible. Let me be very clear with you: it is impossible. All fabric, energy, subatomic particles of this universe come from love, and that is what you are made of.

"Let me also explain that when there is a disruption in your expanded force field, whether it is a kidney, a past life, an emotion, a thought, a tear in your Seal of Solomon, it disrupts and is felt throughout the entire grid. So what do we do? Do we stand back and say 'Well, they're ruining everything. We will punish them. We will exclude them.' Absolutely not. What we do is we send our energy, we add our energy; we give you our energy to heal that disruption. I want you to understand this because this is the tipping point of humanity. No one, no being, no energy can be excluded. The greater the disruption, the greater the need for love.

"Transmission through the force field does not mean condoning or agreement with the existing situation. Why would any being, human or otherwise, wish to buy in or judge what has gone awry? That would only fuel it. In these situations we guide you to assume the role of observer, healer, channel, human, angel, and/or star being. Be the bright energy force field of who you are.

"Understand that when you wish to create you are doing so because as soon as intention is formed you have already begun. When you are creating, if there is a gap in your force field, then the energy flows to you from us, and allows the completion. It is assistance on a seen and unseen level. That is why creating in a group is so powerful, because you have reinforced and chosen to come together as one unified field. Never is there a need to feel that you may be a little short in one area. That, my beloved ones, is the reason why there is no room or cause for doubt. Doubt is the old paradigm. It is what has kept you for millions of years in the darkness, and now is the time all of you are emerging into the light. Thank goodness.

"Soon my job will be done, for each of you will assume that role as steward and keeper of Gaia, of the Cities of Light, the planet of love. And of course, I will come and visit as I will still be the Keeper of the Law.

"Acknowledge this Law of Unity. It takes a soul of wisdom to embrace it, and you are there. I will gladly help you. If there is anything about the Laws that seems unclear or that you do not understand or if you are uncertain which to use, just call me. And let it be known you can't go wrong.

"Although many of you have not known me until this moment, I have known and loved each of you forever. You are my fellow travelers; you are the courageous ones, the adventurers who come to Gaia at this time to complete the evolution and to begin anew. That does not mean that your planet comes to an end, quite the contrary. You enter a new cycle, a cycle of enlightenment. We can't wait. Go with my love and blessings. I attend to thee."

Again, in a different transmission, Sanat Kumara continues his teaching on the Law of Unification:

"The Law of Unification is part of what you are working with in building Nova Earth. The Law of Unification is the deep understanding that all things, everywhere, throughout the universe, are unified as One. As you go forward on your journey and travelling throughout the multiverse you are doing so not only through the interconnectedness to the heart and essence of One but to everything. That is why this decision by the human collective to go forward as one in many ways, in my role as planetary logos, makes sense because it adheres to that Law of Unification. The application of this Law isn't a passive but rather the active understanding that you are united and connected to all things, all beings and all energy. It is the recognition that you do not travel alone.

"It is the knowing that while you think, feel or believe that you are on this journey back to the heart of One but that you are also on this journey with everyone and everything. It is the alignment with the truth that there is only one grid; that is the Law. How else would you travel? You cannot be jumping from grid to grid to grid. Now, does the grid stretch? Are there times when you access a different portion of the grid by changing dimensions or going through wormholes, black holes or white holes? Yes. But it is still one unified grid, and in the final analysis that grid is the framework of Source/God/One of which you are an integral part."

8. UNIVERSAL LAW OF TRANSMUTATION

"Greetings, I am Sanat Kumara, Keeper of the Law. The Law of Dissipation is also known as the Law of Transmutation."

"You utilize the Law of Transmutation when you are working on anything that needs to be removed but not eliminated, because the core element is grist for creation. In this situation, your role is to clear. Release and destroy in the most positive of ways that which is not of wholeness. That issue or situation is brought down to the finest kernel, to that grain of sand that began as purity. From that place, you allow that cleaned up essence to transmute or recreate into something of beauty.

"I offer you an example. There are many people on Gaia who have great issues of abandonment and self-worth. It did not start that way. It started as knowing in angelic form, that assuming a human body was an act of absolute love. When they arrived on Earth and looked around, and were not acknowledged; the sense of separation and the illusion of abandonment grew. But, the kernel, the core knowing, was a thing of beauty. So, you clear away the debris and you bring the person back to the essence, to the knowing of love. You restore within them the longing and expectation for a physical experience of love on Gaia. Then, you allow the person to begin to recreate, to begin to receive mirrors and affirmations, situations and people into their life that are genuine. What you have done is transmute; dissipated what is not useful down to the purity that is already within them. It can be done with a smile or gesture, it matters not. That is the Law of Transmutation and Dissipation.

"The Law of Transmutation needs to be applied to many institutions and environments upon Earth. It is cleansing what does not serve and restoring it to original intent. A good example is education.

"The core of education was love. The core is still good. It is desirable and helpful, so what you are doing is you are transmuting you are bringing back and eliminating all the debris, not by the poof but by the cleansing. Bringing it back to the core which was founded on Love and joy and then rebuilding. It is

Lao Tzu's grain of sand that becomes the luminous pearl. That is the way you may think of it."

9. UNIVERSAL LAW OF INSTANTANEOUS TRANSMISSION

Sanat Kumara, Keeper of Universal Law continues:

"The Law of Instantaneous Transmission is the Law which creates immediate transformation. It is the Law that is enforced when old paradigms are shifted throughout the universe. A good example of this is the shift in the human experience from the old illusion of the third dimension to the fifth. On an individual level, it relates to transformation and activation of the ever presence of what is within you, including your thirteen strands of DNA. Although you have anchored the fullness of your soul design, as well as integrated all of your aspects, there is still a great deal within thee that you have never accessed and that you are not even aware of.

"Every now and then, you have asked, 'Why can I not be thinner? Why can I not be taller? Why can I not have brown, blonde or red hair? Why can I not be artist and poet, a physician or scientist?' We say to you, that you already are. This is the situation in which you may invoke the Law of Instantaneous Transmission.

"As always, anchor within your heart and stillpoint. You have already surrounded yourself with the Council of Love, the archangels and your precious guides. From this place of stillpoint pull up your soul design, that which has always been present. What you are undertaking is full activation. You do this by simply turning a switch. That is the image we wish you to save – turn the car key, turn on a light switch, and allow, bringing forward the soul design that you are already witnessing, that is already deep within.

"If the desire to create a certain representation of yourself it is because it is already within you. You are imprinted from the heart, mind and essence of the Divine. There are parts of your being that you will never bring in, but that you have witnessed on your planet, such as people growing tails. There is much present within your being, your DNA, that you choose not to activate at this time. Be careful what you are doing; be prudent in what you experiment with. We give you this tool because we trust you.

"We have always trusted you, just as we have always loved you. Somewhere in the corner of our being, even as you have shouted at Heaven, we have known that you love us, and we are one in heart. We share this teaching of the Laws to help you understand how things work because we truly wish you to know, to be in the full partnership of love. Go, my brothers and sisters, in joy and laughter. We add create, create, create. Farewell."

10. UNIVERSAL LAW OF DISPENSATION

Most of us are not familiar with the Law of Dispensation. The Divine Mother describes this Law as an expression of compassion, mercy and forgiveness. In it is in working with this Law that we really see the inter-connection between the Laws and the 13 Blessings and Virtues, the Divine Qualities. The primary aspect of the Law of Dispensation that humanity is working with at this time is the rare and beautiful gift of Karmic Dispensation. Before outlining the specifics of this process please open your hearts to the Divine Mother and allow this channeling to anchor deep within you.

"Greetings, I am Mary, Universal Mother, Mother of hope, Mother of change, and Mother of constancy, for the spirit is eternal and you have changed forms, my beloved ones, so many times that not only have you lost track, you have lost memory. It matters not, for what I wish you to remember is the constancy of my love. What I wish you to remember are the cherished memories of yesterday and tomorrow, and the continuity of all existence.

"I wish to speak to you this day about Universal Law. What does Universal Law mean, except the truth that I have shared with thee that has been laid down in the very beginning that you might understand how to journey home.

"There is much discussion about Universal Law, but there is not enough written about dispensation. And what does dispensation mean? It is simply allowance, and in your terminology, it is a divine quality of forgiveness, compassion and mercy.

"Many of you carry the burden of what you believe you have or have not done, promises that you have or have not kept, missions fulfilled or not. There is underlying feeling of judgment, of 'Did I measure up? Did I fulfill my promise?' We are not sitting here idly measuring your progress or the fulfillment of your mission. Beloved child, never do we point to an action, thought or behavior, and say, 'Well, that is a shortcoming; that didn't measure up; that's not what I asked for.' What I asked for, dear hearts, was for you to practice free will. What I asked for was for you to be of love. What I asked for was for you to love yourselves and each other as much as I love you.

"How does this relate to dispensation? There are times, and this is one of them in your collective reality, when dispensation for what you feel has gone awry is requested and granted. The purpose behind the dispensation is always to make you feel free to continue on, because so many of you are concerned that you will not make it. Such an outcome is not part of my plan or yours.

"When you feel such distress, turn to me. I am not distant; I am infinitely and eternally present. Ask for help, and it will always be granted. Ask for compassion and forgiveness, not that it needs to be granted, but the reassurance does.

"When I ask you to request dispensation, which you tend to think of as forgiveness, compassion or assistance, I have done so in order to help you move forward in the recognition of who you are. There has been and still is, a granting of karmic dispensation for the human collective during this period of transition.

"Archangel Michael has spoken to thee, as have many, of containment which is a very restrictive form of dispensation. Because, what is it? Someone is put in a light box surrounded by love until they regenerate. I also say to thee, my children of Gaia, all of you have been in a period of dispensation, of containment, in the mildest way to assist you in the recognition of your divinity and the choice for love. Each of you has been touched in the heart; the heart consciousness has been activated and awakened.

"Now, do some continue to ignore that? Well, that is the choice that is granted. But the awakening, so that the choice can be made from a place of love, has been completed. Each of you feels a growing sense of love and power, and connecting or reconnecting to a new and different realm. Yet in some way it feels familiar, because it is who you have always been. It does not matter. No matter how terrible or awful you may believe yourself to be, it is an illusion. It is not who you are. Allow the heart awakening to fill you. Allow my grace, love and the gift of dispensation fill you. Because now is the time.

"I do not ask you to do this in your time, next year, or when you get to it. I am asking each of you, right now, in this moment, to not only accept my love but the truth of who you are. Stop the hesitation and confusion. It is not of truth, and it is not you.

"Do not cling to the old, it will not support you. Let me be very clear. In the unfoldment of my plan, the old third cannot and will not support you. It is time to allow yourselves freedom. It is not conceit, boastful or false pride; it is the mere acceptance that you are mine and I am yours.

"This is a reminder, dear hearts, of what you have promised to do. I am helping you fulfill that promise, so that you will not fall into that illusion of disappointment. Can you imagine, in any dimension or reality, that I would ever turn to you as your mother, the One, the movement or the silence, that I ever express disappointment in you? That would be to express disappointment in myself, in the Father, and that is not possible.

"Let go of the old way of creating. Bring forth the truth of what you are capable of birthing within yourself, community, families and upon Gaia. Birth the new reality and relationship with your star brothers and sisters, as they do with you. Allow your vibration to rise.

"Can you be amazed, surprised, delighted? Yes. Come with me. But come with me now. Farewell."

Mythology and belief systems often give us important clues to the truth of a situation. One such example is the Christian belief that Jesus died for our sins. That always bothered me – how come Jesus had to die for my sins when I wasn't even born yet? How did He know what I would or would not do – I thought this was a free will zone. What could I possibly do that would require someone else to give up their life for me? These were questions that plagued me from childhood, and contributed to that guilt, blame, shame grid that was so strong a part of the old third dimension.

It was not until the Council, and specifically Jesus Sananda, came forward and explained the truth behind this myth. That is when I began to have glimmers of how the Law of Dispensation operates. When Jesus Yeshua died, part of the legacy of his life and passing was the gift of Karmic Dispensation. What that means in very practical terms is, at that time, everyone on Earth was released from karmic debt. I am aware that there is a great deal of discussion within the lightworker community about whether or not Jesus actually died. That is not part of this discussion, but I can relate from personal memories and understandings that this most certainly did occur. The point is not about historical fact – the point is about the gift He gave to all of us in passing.

Karmic debt is like the balance scales referred to when talking about Universal Law. On one side, there is a debt which is owed to you and, on the other, is the debt you owe; the one you incurred through various, thoughts, actions and behaviors throughout numerous lifetimes. Karmic debt can be overwhelming and heavy, and may account for many of the circumstances you have chosen to incarnate into, including with whom.

Is it not phenomenal to consider that Jesus made it part of his soul contract to release us all from that burden of debt? Christian, Jew, Roman, or Egyptian – everybody was set free. This action was taken because He conceived that if we were free from that burden of debt that we would chose to follow His teachings of love. That given freedom, the logical choice for humanity would be a return to love. As we know, this did not happen.

In fact in many ways the delusions of the third dimension, the false grids of lack of self-worth and self-love, became more pronounced than ever. I would suspect, that over the past couple of thousand years, the karmic debt of the human collective has grown enormously. Hence Archangel Michael's continued role as warrior of peace.

Did this collective refusal by humanity to accept the generous act of Jesus and remain stuck in the old third result in the company of heaven turning away from us? No, quite the contrary.

Right now we are in a renewed period of Karmic Dispensation – a gift to assist us in our progression home and our ascension. Unlike the dispensation granted by the Mother at the time of Yeshua, this dispensation must be requested and claimed. It is not automatically given. However, I have never witnessed one person's request denied over the course of the past several years that I have been privileged to know of this gift.

The process of invoking and working with the Law of Karmic Dispensation is straightforward, and involves seeking dispensation from the Karmic Board. I describe and share this sacred ritual the way it was described and shared with me by Yeshua.

Like all sacred endeavors, anchor in your heart, the 13th Octave and the heart of Gaia. Call in your guides and the archangels. Determine which of your guides or the Council you wish to have accompany you to the Karmic Board. It helps to have support in such an incredible and critical task, so the recommendation is to not travel alone.

Visualize, or if you are able, simply travel to the location where the Karmic Board convenes. For myself, it is always a judicial looking building. Travel down a long corridor until you reach the doorway signed Karmic Board. Knock and enter – bring your friends. Remain modest and respectful. The room, again to me, always appears like a rather sterile board room. The board table takes up much of the space and on the opposite side of the table there are five beings seated. You will feel like you are being closely scrutinized and you are.

The key to receiving the karmic dispensation is asking, requesting from your heart core. The words that have been channeled to many are always the same. "I request that all karmic debt that is owed to me, and that I owe and have incurred be forgiven, erased." Short, to the point, but incredibly heart and soul generated. The Karmic Board will indicate their decision clearly to you. As I have indicated I have never known the request to be refused. Express your profound gratitude and leave.

Because you are still a work in progress, you may feel the need from time to time to return to Karmic Board and seek dispensation. Once you are firmly anchored and living in the higher dimensions this will no longer be necessary. Karmic debt is primarily the result of the false grids we have adhered to in the old third dimension.

While this process seems straightforward and perhaps even simple, remember that this is a gift beyond measure. It is the clean slate – it is the blackboard wiped clean – it is the fresh start that humanity yearns for. This dispensation allows you to fly free and to complete your mission and purpose unimpeded. It frees you to work with all of the other Universal Laws with grace and gratitude, purpose and clear intent. It is a miracle.

As always, Sanat Kumara has wonderful words of encouragement as we accept this gift, in recognition of the Mother's and the Council's love for us:

"You believe that you are bound by the Laws of the Universe, by the Laws of Karma, by the Laws of Limitation. I am Keeper of the Laws, and I come this day to extend greater light within and upon your life. Know that part of what you do with the entry into the flame of St. Germaine is the burning away of all karma, all history past and present and future. This is what you do when you invoke the Law of Karmic Dispensation as well. You have been purified and cleansed and so my question to you, my friends, is how do you intend to proceed?

"Know that the balance of karma is also the balance of give and receive. For every good deed, every healing, every smile, every whisper of joy is extended throughout the universe and heard, replenished and returned to you. No, not tenfold, but far beyond what you imagine as mathematics. Many of you persist in your false belief systems, in your refusal to heal and believe you are a reflection of One. I wonder why this is so.

"What barriers do you possess that you do not believe yourselves capable of instantaneous transmutation? We are fully able and, therefore, so are you, that is the Law. You cling to your systems of belief, your aches, pains and illnesses; are these your gifts to us? I think not. Allow yourselves, dear ones, to be the reflection not only of all beings but of who you are. You do not need to cry, stifle pain or worry about the future and whether you will be supported or not. Such fears are unfounded and they are your creation, not ours. Invoke the Law dear hearts and create – the time is neigh. Go with my love, support and stamina. Farewell."

A final thought on the Law of Dispensation are the questions that arise from the Divine Mother's words to us. She invites us to seek dispensation in many areas of our lives; in any area of our lives that we feel we may have erred The question is, do we genuinely seek or invoke the Law of Dispensation often enough?

11. UNIVERSAL LAW OF ATTRACTION AND REPULSION

"Greetings, I am Sanat Kumara, Keeper of Universal Law, keeper of each of you, Planetary Logos, overseer and like you my beloved friends, servant and child of the One. Do not put me on a pedestal, let me sit with you in the core foundation of your heart and let me share my love and my golden ray. I cherish you and the evolution of this beautiful planet and everything upon it. Never think my sweet angels that ascension is a race to completion because it is not. Are we anxious for fulfillment of the promise? Yes, as anxious as you are, as excited as you are. But this has always been intended to be a journey of joy, an undertaking of joy, love, beauty, with the sweetness of Venus; for are we not partners, family and friends?

"Let us discuss this Law of Attraction and Repulsion. It is both sides of the scales and it is the balance scales of justice, worth and the universe. The scales are not represented in duality because in duality balance is rarely present. So when I speak to you of this balance of attraction and repulsion, what am I truly speaking of? Well, first and foremost, I am sharing with you a deeper understanding of Universal Law, which is an explanation of how things work, not just on Earth but directly from the heart of One. Universal Law explains the functionality of the universe. It is important to know and work with all of the Universal Laws. But at this time let us speak of Attraction and Repulsion.

"Many of you feel that if you simply declare intention, if you desire something, that you are invoking the Law of Attraction; but that declaration of intent is the starting not the finishing point. Never will I try to dissuade you from working with what you desire and calling forth across the universal grid. That is what you are also doing when you are invoking the Law of Attraction and Repulsion; you are calling across the universe what you wish to claim and bring into your life. And it does not matter whether it is a gold coin, perfect partner, spectacular health, harmonious family, or harmonious planet. You distinguish in magnitude, but the process of what you do and how you work with this Law of Attraction is the same for all these things.

"When you work with the Law of Attraction you are calling from the core of your heart, the foundation and every part of your being and magnetizing towards you that which you desire to experience. There are times when you will casually say, 'I would like, I wish that something or other' and it comes to you. In such circumstances you think 'well that was easy, I do not need to go through all this process.' The reason it is easy is that you were already in acceptance and allowance that such creation was possible. In fact what you have done in the ease is simply know that you are capable of calling across the universe for what you desire. You ordered out and called for delivery.

"We review this in order that you understand that creation and alignment with Universal Law does not need to be a strenuous act; it is not like running twenty miles. It is more a case of becoming aware that when you call throughout the universe you are calling all beings, all energy, and all delivery mechanisms. You do not need to decide how you receive, only that you do receive, in perfect, loving, ideal ways of ease. Stop trying to control it. Control is a third dimensional human obsession and it is time to let it go.

"The key to the Law of Attraction is to call your hearts' desire with the fullness of your expanded field and your foundation. It is not a casual undertaking, even though it may be expressed casually and joyfully. Does that mean that we do not hear your desperate cries in the night? Of course not; we do and we respond. But so often what occurs in the desperate cry in the night is the feeling that 'I am asking for help but I don't really believe I am going to get it.' So be aware of this as well.

"How do you eliminate that sense of desperation when you are practicing with the Law of Attraction? You bring it to the stillpoint and in the stillpoint everything disappears into sheer energy, into nothingness. From there you move into action, and we do not mean that you go scurrying around trying to make something happen. In many ways, when you do this frantic scurrying about, it eliminates the trust factor and hinders delivery. Ensure that your actions are in keeping with your hope, trust, faith, joy, and the love that you know is your birthright and your core.

"Let us review again what the process is for working with this Law. You are sitting in the love of your heart, in the divine essence of your being, and in the knowing of everything, and allowing your heart's desire to well up within. Whether it is a love partner, sacred union, perfect family, or a gold coin, it is made of the essence of love. With your love you call that thing across the universe, across the golden grid; you let it fly, skate, and travel to you in divine timing, which as you are advancing, as you are becoming anchored in the wisdom, is your timing as well. And if there is a timing factor involved in this, then declare it dear heart, for time is love as well; it is not a stand-alone entity.

"What about the other side of the scale which holds the Law of Repulsion? There are things, particularly as you are moving through this collective and individual period of transition and ascension, that you do not want on your sacred doorstep or on any doorstep. These are the things that you repulse back. Now what do I mean by that? Certainly you do not wish to repulse conflict, hatred or greed and then have it land in somebody else's home. What you are doing in aligning with the Law of Repulsion, my powerful, beautiful angels, is speeding that discordant energy on the return journey back to the heart of One. You are returning it from whence it came. But you ask, 'SK, Raj, does it not have to go through spiritual evolution?' The answer is no. It is sheer energy that emerged originally as love. You are returning it, for a tune-up as it were, back to the heart of One so that love can be restored, renewed, and recycled. This is also in alignment with the Law of Transmutation.

"The sensation is of pulling what you desire into the sacred portal of your heart, then pushing back and sending out to the One, the energies that you do not wish to engage with. We are not talking about sending people or nations. It is very important in the Law of Repulsion to identify the energies that are abhorrent. Think energies, not people, objects or any form of being. Identify and then proceed. How you know is very simply to ask yourself, your heart, 'Does it feel like love? Does this feel divine? Does this feel like Oneness? Does this feel like I want to welcome it into my field?' If the answer is no then repulse the energy and hang a Do Not Trespass sign. We are suggesting that this No Trespassing sign be posted a million miles away from you! We ask you to do this immediately because there is nothing that will transform the energy of the old third and the struggles that many are having more rapidly than simply sending the energy of lack, lack of love and lack of worth, back to the Source.

"Are you capable of this mission? You always have been. Are you aware now that you are capable? Yes you are. So I ask you to practice not only the Law of Attraction but it's partner Repulsion, and send back, not to any planet, not to any universe, not to any sacred home, that which is not of love. Let it go back to Source, across the grid, sheer energy to be restored. That is your seventh dimensional birthright and it is what you may do right now. Thank you and go with my love. Farewell."

If for some reason you do not remember how to access your foundation – the same foundation we have discussed in depth in the earlier chapters, try this meditation. First read these brief instructions and then give yourself the time and quiet space to complete the process and anchor in the foundation of your sweet self.

Begin by taking a nice deep breath of pink-gold, that wonderful gold shaded with pink, the angel of purity, the vibration of the City of Light, Hana in Hawaii and breathe in gold. Open your crown wide, and just allow yourself to be, to let go of the day, the week and your to-do list. Feel that gold, that pinky-gold coming down through your pituitary, your pineal, your hypothalamus, your occipitals, and down into your heart. From your heart let it radiate out into every fiber, atom, and subatomic particle of your being.

Take another deep breath of gold; bring it in and let it emanate slowly out of your body, out into your field, into your causal, mental, emotional, etheric and astral bodies. Then bring it back into your heart and go to the bottom of your heart, go to the seat of your soul, to the place where stillpoint lives. Feel the alignment with your beautiful tri-flame. Your tri-flame is constant; this is the core of who you are. Feel your beautiful blue diamond flame from the Universal Divine Mother; your beautiful pink diamond flame – the incredible uniqueness of your being, the totality and wholeness of your being; and then over to the wonderful golden flame, the Divine Masculine of the Father, that deep rich gold. Let it burn brightly and balance, making sure that all three are equal and that all parts of you, all aspects are integrated and balanced. Go deeper.

Go to the core that these flames arise from, the foundation of your being, of who you are and how you are interconnected, unified with everything and how you are part of the One. Take a minute and feel the love that's the foundation, the core of who you are. Just sink into it, remember it, and allow it.

Remember as you do this work with the Law of Attraction

and Repulsion that you are essentially an electro-magnetic being. The sensation you experience or want to focus on when you are practicing the Attraction is that you are magnetic; that you are pulling, with your magnetic self and soul, across the universe that which you are calling forth. The sensation with Repulsion is that you are in an anti-gravity chamber; that you are utilizing your electric power to push and send out across the universe that which is not desirable. The sensation is similar to the pushing out and releasing back to the One.

12. Universal Law of Elimination

"I am Sanat Kumara, Keeper of the Laws, of the Universal Laws of which creation is a subset. But we do not get technical with you. In fact if anything we wish you not to be technical, this is not a course in physics but a course in miracles. You say to me Sanat Kumara how can you talk to me about the Law of Elimination and in the same breath as creation and co-creation? I tell you there are times, dear ones, when the debris is so dense and destructive that it needs to be eliminated. It needs to be gone because it does not serve One. You ask how do I know this? Well, for this planet and at this time, let me suggest to you that usually the Law of Elimination will be used on creations of man.

"Neither God, the Universe or Love creates ways to harm, destroy, or exist in pain. There are patterns, belief systems, illusions, diseases, toxic environments that do nothing but poison, create devastation and pain. We have talked about the value of pain in learning compassion and love, and we have also talked about that method of learning being ancient history.

"We wish to discuss how to create and utilize the Laws that are applicable to your planet, galaxy, and universe. Part of the Law includes the understanding and occasional usage by a select few of the Law of Elimination, which is the truest form of letting go. It is a very interesting concept that human beings have developed that the One Source of All is capable of creating everything, but not capable of getting rid of it. There's a problem here. So, we come to speak to you of the ability to eliminate.

"One of the fundamental precepts of creation is that all creation takes place at the stillpoint of nothingness. How you eliminate is by entering in, by spiraling in to the place of stillness. It is a counter-clockwise motion, and if you wish to think of it as a place within your physical form, it is deep within the center of your heart. It is the place where you stop and simply remain still. Energy is always in motion if it is not at stillpoint. There is always the ebb and flow which is what the infinity symbol reminds you of. At the center of the infinity is the stillpoint, a span of time not measurable in your dimension. Regardless, let us reassure you of its existence.

"For human beings at this point of evolution, reaching the stillpoint is the most difficult task of all. Nevertheless, understand that you are sufficient to the task. How do you do this? Go to the place of stillness and then through an act of alignment join in union with Divine Will. Feel this in your heart and solar plexus, feel the two energies coming together in perfect stillness. You will experience a sense of simultaneous implosion and explosion, at which point the energy being eliminated disappears. This method of creating elimination, or dis-creation, is seldom used because often at the kernel, the seed of the energy, there is something worth preserving.

"However, it is an essential tool for Nova Being because there are many patterns upon this planet that simply need to disappear. When one is plagued time after time by the same issue, it is an act of mercy to help the individual eliminate it. That work is advanced healing, but first you learn to do this for yourself. That is the law of elimination.

"Do not start out large, we do not want The White House disappearing. Start with yourselves. Think about what has haunted you. Not the fear that you have need to confront and transmute into your best friend, but an issue you truly have worked upon. Diligent honesty is required for this exercise. When you have worked on something not only in this lifetime but many lifetimes and it still haunts you, it bars your progress. Through genuine heart analysis discern what is neither serving you, your family, friends, circle, community, or planet. Then proceed, if guided, to invoke the Law of Elimination. You cannot go wrong with this invocation, because your starting point is the proviso that it must be for your highest good and the highest good of all. Additionally, I am with you and will not allow elimination that is not in accordance with the Mother's plan. There is no room for ego in this undertaking.

"Then from the anchored place within your heart and still-point you allow the destruction, the elimination to take place. Again, you will feel the nuclear implosion, the shock wave. That is how you will know in physicality and in your being that it is actually taking place. You are not dropping down and expelling or pushing it out. It is gone in that moment. No there are no ashes, there is no phoenix rising. It is not like the Law of Attraction and Repulsion where you send back the energy to Source. Nor is it like the Law of Transmutation where you transform and cleanse, restore. With the Law of Elimination the energy is simply gone. I will guide your hand in this exercise because never before has it been permitted on Gaia.

"We are entrusting this to you because we wish you, individually and collectively, to go forward. We are helping you not just in the doing but in the saying to you that you have come of age. You are old enough, mature enough, strong enough and you wise enough to know – not to think and not to feel – but to know when this radical choice is required. It is extremely rare, some of you may never use it in this lifetime, but you will carry the information and the knowledge forward henceforth. You will use it in your healing and the rebirthing of the planet. That is the primary use of this Law. It is to eliminate from the planet the toxins, disease, chemicals and poisons that foul your land, animals, air and oceans. Most of this has been caused by either conscious or inadvertent actions of mankind, and therefore it is right and fitting that you will be the ones to eliminate it. That is my undertaking to you. I give you this gift, and I explain this Law in trust.

"I would suggest to you before you practice this elimination procedure that you integrate all aspects. Call everybody home. Anchor firmly within yourself, as it is a powerful tool and it requires integration and all energies to be present. If you undertake this elimination process through bilocation, make sure you bring all aspects of your being with you. For example, if you are in Africa attending to the many animals dying from drought, and you wish to eliminate the drought, and you know that that is the core issue, ensure you send all of your aspects to Africa. Do not send only part of you; you're not strong enough.

"Hatred did not start from a place of Love. Therefore it need not be preserved or even transmuted, now in some cases you will find where someone will say oh I hate that, I hate them, I hate Israelis, I hate Pakistanis, I hate blacks, I hate whites, I hate yellows. You will bring them back because truly what they are saying is they hate themselves. You do not wish them to be eliminated, because what they are really saying is I am so lonely and feel that nobody can or does love me in any race, society, country or galaxy. In that case you utilize the Law of Transmutation, and bring them back to that place of longing that started it all. That is why wisdom and knowing is essential in the practice of the Law. You must truly sit and listen, and be.

"It is part of the formulation of your intent to decide which method or Law to use. Having said that, we are not going to permit you to go astray. So you can take that fear and poof it right now. I will give you another way to make this judgment and it is the golden scales I have given you before to use as balance. When you place something on the scale, and it is all on one side and there is nothing that you can discern or fathom to balance it out on the other then go forward and let it go, eliminate it, and start again.

"When you are using the Law of Elimination in conjunction with an individual or a group you will know to use it because the individual soul is crying out for help. It is in persistent, impenetrable problems, where the cry for mercy has been heard throughout the entire universe. You are interfering in the nicest way possible, with compassion and love. Are you changing the course of that individual's life? Yes. Are you allowing them to move forward into the wholeness of their being? Yes. Do you truly think this is that different than the miracle flower essences that have been gifted? It is not.

"Understand you are not to act as judge. You are to act from your heart, from a place of knowing, compassion and wisdom. If the full knowing is not present then you do not proceed, you leave it to other realms. Let us be clear, not everyone who is in difficulty, in misery, in disease, in pain is asking for relief. Some have chosen this pathway to teach compassion. You do not rob another of their journey. But if there is something that you can do to help, you sweet child of all people, always do so. Do not think that you do this alone. Do not think that you do it external to Creator Force. That is why you always only come from knowing, and from a place of love, and a place of highest good. And, as we have said, many of you will never use this in your entire life; and some of you will.

"When I tell you I am the Keeper of the Laws, I am the universal policeman. I am the one that travels around and explains the Law, and then makes sure it is adhered to correctly, which is why I assure thee you cannot go awry. I do so in the name of one of the Creative Source of the Universe. That is why this Law of Elimination is used so rarely. When you use the Law of Elimination, you come from a place of knowledge, and of Love. As soon as the void is eliminated, as soon as that obstacle is gone, there is a rush of God energy within that place."

13. UNIVERSAL LAW OF COMPLETION AND CONTINUITY

"Greetings I am Sanat Kumara, Keeper of Universal Law. Allow me to continue with you my dear friends on this discussion of Universal Law. Allow me to share with you the framework of the Divine Mother, particularly regarding not only completion and continuity but constancy as well.

"So that there is no misunderstanding, allow us to explain this Law in very simple terms, because we do not wish these Laws to be complex or misunderstood. The Law of Completion and Continuity, in your language, would mean that everything has a beginning and an end, and at the end there is always another beginning. That is the Law.

"Prior to incarnation, regardless of the circumstances that you have chosen to be born into, you are fully cognizant that you have beginning a new journey. The true journey is always the same, my beloved friends; it is the journey back to One, it is the journey back to the love. That ultimate journey is always in cooperation with all Universal Law.

"The Law of Completion and Continuity very specifically addresses the issue of your eternal journey and your specific journey of this lifetime. It is the guidebook about the return to the heart. This guidebook and direction that we offer you is the same for those upon Gaia as it is on other planets throughout the universe, and that is the glue factor in terms of unity and love.

"Is the Law imprinted within that heart consciousness and love? Yes. So when I speak of a specific Law, you will have, immediately, that heart knowing: "Oh, yes, I know that. That makes sense."

"One of your primary drives, as spiritual, human, emotional, mental beings, is to find out how things work and how to I get home. Think of this: you have a spiritual GPS system which manifests as the inner voice; listen to the directions being communicated to thee.

"Actually, for the grid of humanity at this time, there are specifically about thirteen Universal Laws that you are working with. All Laws are inter-connected, forming a grid upon which you travel. As you work with one Law, your heart opens more fully in terms of divine alignment and knowing, and that leads you to the next Law and so on. By that practice your actions become reference points to the Law, rather than some constructed reality, some false grid, or *vasana*.

"What happens when you truly engage with the Universal Law is that it removes the illusion upon which so much of human experience has been based. You become aligned not only the Law but the spirit of continuity and completion. You realize that each action, feeling, movement is complete in and of itself, while at the same time being part of the greater whole of your continuity and the universal continuity."

The final word and considerations as we move forward in the fullness of working with Universal Law and creating Nova Earth again comes from Sanat Kumara:

"I step forward this day because I wish you to understand yet again the nature of Universal Law and how it operates. You are very familiar with the Law of Attraction, and you are very familiar with the Law of Above and Below, Within and Without. Some of you skirt and dance around the Law of Elimination although it could be very useful to you. As you are growing and changing in this daily expansion, it is important that you think, feel and activate this gift, this power to eliminate that which does not serve, does not serve either you or the collective.

"Many of you are afraid to throw things out. What is that about? We have spoken to you, all of us, how this is a time of letting go, of letting go of patterns, behaviors, people and circumstances. We do not differentiate between internal and external; what does not serve you and what does not feel like love, joy or the truth of your life must be addressed. This also includes letting go of pollution, war, hatred, and radiation. In the letting go what you are also doing is cleaning up. You are creating that bright, shiny space for the new, of the New You. You ask, 'SK, how do I do that? How do I let go of something like pollution? How do I put it in the trash and take it to the curb as you have suggested? I've already cleaned up my house so it is not polluted, but I wish to clean for the collective. I wish to clean for Gaia.'

"Many years ago your beloved St. Germaine has said, 'Do not take on what does not belong to you.' Well, that does not apply when you are thinking of helping your beloved Gaia. I encourage you to see yourself, on behalf of the whole and on behalf of Gaia, as taking what doesn't serve her. Wrap it up, put it in the trash and take it to the etheric curb. We will take it and transform that energy back to pure light and pure love because that is the only real energy in the universe.

"I think you do not fully comprehend what I say to you along with Einstein, Raphael, Serapis Bey, El Morya, St. Germaine, Mother Mary and Yahweh. You are not hearing fully in your hearts what we are saying to thee. The fabric, energy, substance, essence and subatomic matter of this and every universe is love. However, there have been times when the love energy has been transmuted and transformed by the lower vibrations of the powerful human collective into false grids, beliefs and paradigms.

"The good news is that you have already demonstrated what powerful, mighty creators you are. It is understood that there are energies that you no longer want to touch or engage with, and that that is alright. Which is why we say toss it in the garbage, give it to us and we will give it back to you as bright and shiny love. If you are fearful in the slightest of being contaminated don't worry, give it to us. We will dust it off, shine it up, and give it back to you. This is our sacred partnership.

"When we ask you to help us, to write Love in the air, Love in the water, Love in your heart, you are doing your part. So let us do ours; let us help you and Gaia. Let us help every human and hybrid soul upon the planet. Let us fortify you because when we talk 'as above, so below' it also means if we are mighty then you are also mighty. If we are humble and meek, then you are humble and meek. When we are loving, you are loving.

"Look in the mirror, look in the mirror of our eyes, look in the mirror of your friends, your family and your partner; see that beautiful truth of who you are. Declare yourself and step forward in love because every fiber, every strand of hair, your eyes, your face, your skin, your body is love. It is love that has taken a form, a form that you decided upon, and a form that is absolutely perfect; just as Gaia's form is absolutely perfect. So during this time of changes and shift, remember you are perfect. Allow that perfection to shine through and if you decide, if you choose that there is something you wish to let go of, then give it to me, give it to any of us. We will be overjoyed to take it. We will not grab it from you; we honor you too much for that. We see your sacredness, we do not interfere, but we wish to be in partnership. Come join with us. Come join with us, my beloved ones. Farewell."

The New You

We begin and end this chapter with heart expanding, awe-inspiring messages of hope and joy from the Universal Mother.

"Greetings, I am Mary, Universal Mother and Divine Mother Maré and I come to you as both on this day of reckoning, resolution, expansion and love, in this time of wonder.

"I reach out to you this day as family, not as servants, not even in service to you. As Mother, I have beckoned you across the universe, multiverse and omniverse. I have beckoned you many times—eons ago; thousands of years, hundreds of years, twenty years, and in the past several months. I have said to each of you, it is time to awaken for I have need of you. You have answered with your hearts, minds, spirits and physical forms, despite some of the physical difficulties of incorporating your totality into the physical reality that you occupy. This is the core of the New You; anchoring the expansion and wholeness of your being and recognizing that it works through your physical body and form so that you may remain upon this glorious Archangel, Gaia, and continue.

"I approach you and I call you, male and female, as mothers because you are the caretakers, nurturers, teachers and showers of the way. You are the pillars and anchors, and you do not hesitate to express your love, to express the totality of your being. Being mothers does not in any way diminish the fact that you are warriors of pink, gold, blue, magenta, and siroun; quite the contrary. It means that there are mother, in this circle anchored and ready to take care of all the rays.

"Most of you are star beings, many of you from the Pleiadian sector. That is why you have been able to adapt to your interdimensional self so easily. It's the hardest thing you've have ever done. Yes, you have done extraordinarily, exceptionally well; and that interdimensionality will continue to grow, shift and thrive because it is key to who you are. You were never created, birthed, or intended to be uni-dimensional; you are far too adventurous, curious and competent to be restricted in one realm. You are assisting the human collective in coming to understand their trans-dimensional, multidimensional, interdimensional self. You are helping them understand that they exist within and without and in accordance with Universal Law. You are demonstrating and showing them how to live in alignment and in the joy of the Divine Qualities, the 13 Blessings and Virtues. You are the living examples of my energy, embodying my gifts upon the planet; that has been my gift to you in your ascent and agreement to encompass the New You.

"Share your victories as you have move through this process. We encourage you to because it catapults and catalyzes the energy for the collective. You have done magnificent work, each and every one of you, and what I say to thee is that this transformation is truly a new beginning; and you have just begun. Dear heart, what you have always loved about me is that there is always more; that I am an infinite and eternal creation. You are part and parcel of that infinite never-ceasing creation. You always have been, but now you truly know it. It is anchored in your heart, in the brilliance of your tri-flame, your actions, the stillness of your being and your discernment. It is anchored in every part and aspect of your sacred self. Hence, as you look, glance, smile, walk, and speak, you are sharing this energy of the New You, your re-patterning. The re-patterning is already integrated, laid down, and active within each of thee.

"I am excited to see what you do with this as your part of our Divine Plan. I do not disappear on you, quite the contrary; gaze into my eyes, my face, my blue diamond, and see me with you. Never do any of us leave your side; that is our promise and our vow. Go in peace. Farewell."

Working with the New You and allowing these expanded energies and new understandings to come forward is the entire purpose of this book. One of the most challenging pieces of the New You is the piece where you are integrated, knowing your wholeness of your mission and purpose, and your interdimensional self, and are stepping into the creation process. You are the re-patterner of Gaia and humanity, and how that demonstrates and fulfills is through the bringing forth of the new normal of creating.

One of my requests is that you be completely conscious about how you are creating. Pause, breathe in and make sure you are always coming from your heart, from the truth of who you really are. Each of us, either consciously or unconsciously, is continually creating. We are creating life with each breath we take, by allowing our cells to regenerate, through the actions of what we do and don't do, how we behave, what we think – the list is almost endless. But the key to the New You is to consciously bring front and center the awareness of not only how to create, but what you choose to create – and then do it!

We are in the home stretch – but I warned you there would be more! We have moved and come so far together – from the understanding of our foundation to the removal of false grids to travelling interdimensionally and on into creation. Of course the ultimate ongoing creation is with your sacred self and your life, the life you choose to experience. Reflect, think and celebrate how you have changed over the course of embracing your New You. Know that that process of expansion is going to continue to grow, morph and delight you. What you have and are you bringing into your life? What personal formula of creation are you embarking on – what is your dream, and how do you, as Nova Being choose to share this with the world?

What more is there? The transformation of your life and of Gaia. I encourage you to come back to this book time and time again – it's intended to be used that way. The meditations will build the energy of your New You grid so return to them and take it deeper, higher. But the key component in all of this is what you do with the energy, where you take it. I have been honored and blessed to be your guide in this adventure. But now the real work beings as you take this transformation and share it with the planet through the truth, sweetness, strength and beauty of who you are. I have no doubts or qualms about your ability to do this in majestic ways. You are the re-patterner of the tapestry of humanity. You are repairing the warp and weave of humanity and Gaia's grid. I have absolute, faith, trust and knowing that that is exactly what you will do. After all, you are my sisters and brothers of the New You. I love you.

"Greetings, I am Mary, Universal Mother, Mother of One, Mother of All, and yes, sweet angels, Mother of thee and I have asked this channel to be the one to come forth to give to you from my heart to yours the love that I carry for you; that I have carried and will carry for you for eternity. My love for you is not fixed, it is not stagnant, it is eternal and infinite, but what does this really mean? It means, my beloved ones, that it grows, it expands continually and forever. So the love that you have known from my heart to yours yesterday is not what you received today; it is more, and it will be more again tomorrow as you move through what you think of as time and space.

"My reason for mentioning this is the expression of my love, presence in your field and life continues to grow as well. Long ago I have given you the gift of my blue diamond, of my very essence, as has the Father with His golden diamond. Then I have called you to the fulfillment, not only of my plan but of your plan within that plan. I have beckoned to you across the multiverse to come and to join with me, not only in the shift, *The Great Awakening*, the movement through the ascension portal, but to the fullness and the totality of who you are bright angels, starseed and earth-keepers. This is what I have meant when I have sent out my clarion call for you to join me in this process of anchoring the New You, the old you, the totality of you.

"It is my desire, creation and co-creation with thee that you come to know, cherish and love your sacred self the way that I love you. It is to know the depth of my love and how it expresses in creation and co-creation. This process of anchoring, becoming, allowing and accepting the totality of the New You is not simply a mental or emotional process, dear hearts. This is an expansion of creation, and it is an anchoring of you in your role as bright angels of change. It is the transformation of you as bright angels of One and of Nova Earth, anchoring, creating, and laying down the paradigm for all your brothers and sisters, not only on Earth, but far beyond.

"You have answered my call; you have listened to the whispers of your heart. Are there moments of uncertainty, confusion, as the old fades away? Of course there are. It is what my son, Michael, is referring to when he speaks of this time of intensity.

"You are already anchored in the fifth, sixth, and seventh dimension. You are already there. It is from there we are proceeding with our work, play and the anchoring, infinitely, not only of my joy, but of yours. It is time, not only in terms of my unfoldment of my plan, of our plan, but of yours as well. Join with me. I am here as I always have been. I am more present than ever. Turn to me, there is nothing, nothing, not above, below or beyond that I will not assist thee with. That is my promise.

"Go with my love. Farewell, farewell my sweet ones, I step aside never away. Farewell."

(LISTEN TO THE "NEW YOU" AUDIO MEDITATION)

Appendix A:
What is The 13th Octave?

The 13th Octave is a state of being in Divine Union, wholly and completely anchored, and aware of being anchored, in the heart of One. It is being in alignment with the heart, mind and will of God. The gift of the 13th Octave is enormous. It changed not only my world but the lives of thousands of people who have said "yes" and stepped forward to join in this state of Union.

In addition to the initiation and re-connection, the gifts of the 13th Octave are plentiful. Each time the 13th Octave sacred ceremony has taken place the Council has bestowed a gift, ability or tool to assist us in our spiritual journey here on Earth. We have been armed with an array of gifts and tools such as Universal Mother Mary's gift of removal, Mary's cloak of invisibility, Gabriel's golden infinity, Archangel Uriel's silver flame, Archangel Michael's sword and shield, Yahweh's keys to the warehouse of heaven. The list is enormous, in keeping with our human desire for tricks and tools, diversity and choice. But each gift is designed to assist us in completing our missions here on Earth with grace, Love, and joy.

One of the best explanations of the 13th Octave comes from Archangel Gabrielle: "The 13th Octave is a something far beyond what has been previously known on Earth. Previously, one would have left physical form – die, to have this experience. The referenced 13th Octave is sound, for it is the point at which vibration and sound is the sound of God, beyond hearing, beyond human ears, but clearly felt throughout the Universe."

Our curious selves have always pursued the question of what

will it be like, what does it feel like, afterward we will be really creative beings for having been through the 13th Octave initiation? One participant put it this way, "Not much has been said about what we will really be like, what we will be able to do, what we are supposed to do, how long it's going to take for us to adjust and to actually begin utilizing the benefits, the gifts that are being given to us. I think all of us would like to know a little bit more about that if you would be so kind."

Archangel Gabrielle's said the first and ever-present gift of the 13th Octave is the ability to heal people's hearts.

"You are given the gift of remembering how to heal the hearts of others beginning with yourself. The rate at which this occurs will be different depending on the acceptance and personality factors of each. So for some it will be instantaneous combustion, others it will be weeks, for they edge slowly into the center of the flower. When you edge back out, or when you walk back out, you have the ability to access universal information, intelligence, wisdom, knowledge, Love, truth, beauty.

"It is not that we cram your heart and soul and mind with facts, figures and experience. Rather, we give you connection for full access to all that is required, desired, needed, wished for, and available. It always has been thus, but humans, as a race, have never actively sought this union. When you finish this initiation and return to your world, you have a choice whether or not to share the gifts you have received here. To not share would render the gifts meaningless. Understand that the touching (connecting) another's heart is a practice, a meditation, that must be done consciously every day. So as you walk within your corridors of your life remember your conscious agreement, and, extend your hand and touch the hearts of those whom you encounter."

Entry into the 13th Octave changes everything. It alters how you think, feel, process and behave. It has been an amazing adventure over the years to share and observe how initiates have transformed. Repeatedly I would hear "well nothing happened during the meditation – well except when Jesus came in, or Archangel Michael, or Universal Mother." And then we laugh, realizing the enormity of the experience.

Some people have incredible experiences, and some none at all, but in the ensuing weeks they report their way of being has subtly but remarkably shifted. Things that used to be triggers, old issues, old hurts, are simply gone. New abilities or the realization of dearly held dreams begin to take shape.

A significant change is that in the early years the changes would be slow and very subtle, gentle. Now the shift occurs instantaneously. There's no waiting to see if you made it, because we all do. The knowing is beyond question, undeniable.

It seems unfathomable that any being would not take full advantage of this precious gift, of the transmutation and transformation it offers. Share this process and gift with everyone you meet, share it with your loved ones, strangers, and the guys down the street. Because, this is part of our collective Ascension process. This is our jumping off point. This is why we came.

About the Author

Linda Dillon had been the channel for the Council of Love (COL, or the Council) since 1984 after a near-death experience from a car accident opened her heart to her true purpose.

As the channel for the Council, Linda brings out the vibration of pure Love into the hearts of those who come to her. These people are always recognizable by the dramatic personal changes and transformation they are going through. Linda channels Jesus Sananda, Mother Mary and Yahweh, as well as the ascended masters such as St. Germaine, Sanat Kumara, and Maitreya, the Apostles and the Archangels, abriel, Michael, Raphael, Uriel and Jophiel. While the energies and personalities of each being are unique, the vibration of pure Love remains consistent.

Having had a successful career as a health care executive, Linda understand the need to make spiritual matters hands-on and practical. She teaches workshops and webinars throughout the year and has a worldwide client base who request individual channelings. She is the CEO of the Council of Love, Inc., and the Nova School of Healing Arts and Sciences, an approved Florida Continuing Education provider in energy healing. She also is the co-host of the weekly In Light Radio programs "Hour with an Angel", and "Hour with an Angel" on BlogTalkRadio.com.

Linda resides on the Treasure Coast of Florida and can be reached through her website, www.counciloflove.com.

Made in the USA
San Bernardino, CA
18 October 2013